Crime, shame and reintegration

Crime, shame and reintegration

JOHN BRAITHWAITE

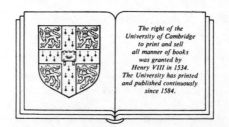

The right of the
University of Cambridge
to print and sell
all manner of books
was granted by
Henry VIII in 1534.
The University has printed
and published continuously
since 1584.

CAMBRIDGE UNIVERSITY PRESS

Cambridge

New York   New Rochelle

Melbourne   Sydney

Published by the Press Syndicate of the University of Cambridge
The Pitt Building, Trumpington Street, Cambridge CB2 1RP
32 East 57th Street, New York, NY 10022, U.S.A.
10 Stamford Road, Oakleigh, Melbourne 3166, Australia

First published 1989

Printed in Great Britain by Redwood Burn Ltd, Trowbridge, Wiltshire

British Library cataloguing in publication data

Braithwaite, John, 1951–
Crime, shame and reintegration.
1. Crime & punishment
I. Title
364

Library of Congress cataloguing in publication data

Braithwaite, John
Crime, shame and reintegration / John Braithwaite.
p   cm.
Bibliography.
Includes index.
ISBN 0 521 35567 2.   ISBN 0 521 35668 7 (pbk.)
1. Crime and criminals. 2. Shame. I. Title.
HV8025.B686 1988
364.6 8–dc 1988-7294 CIP

National Library of Australia cataloguing in publication data

Braithwaite, John 1951–
Crime, shame and reintegration.

Bibliography.
ISBN 0 521 35567 2 hard covers
ISBN 0 521 35668 7 paperback

1. Correctional psychology. 2. Behavior
modification. 3. Shame 4. Rehabilitation
of criminals I. Title.
364.6'01

ISBN 0 521 35567 2 hard covers
ISBN 0 521 35668 7 paperback

LU

Contents

v

Preface

A general theory of crime is an ambitious undertaking. While the theory in this book purports to be general, it is at the same time modestly partial. It is partial firstly because I am conscious of the need for theories of particular types of crime to complement the general theory.

The book does not proceed by systematically demolishing competing theories in order to show the superiority of the theory of reintegrative shaming. For example, the theory provides an account of why women engage in less crime than men. There are some who are persuaded that the explanation for this association is genetic. I have not seen it as my task to attack this competing explanation, but only to argue for the plausibility and consistency with such evidence as exists of the explanation provided by the theory. Prior to a theory having been systematically tested, it is not the time for contentions that earlier theories which have been more satisfactorily evaluated should be jettisoned in favor of the new theory. That may well be appropriate when the evidence is in to show that any variance explained by an older theory, and more, can be explained by the new one. More likely, we would hope ultimately to be in a position to argue that the new partial theory explains a substantial amount of variance not accounted for by pre-existing partial theories.

Happily, I do not need to lay waste existing theories in order to make way for an alternative because the existing theories explain fairly low proportions of variance in crime. Indeed, my strategy is in part to integrate the modest explanatory successes of existing sociological theories of crime into a theory which aspires to be both more general and of greater explanatory power.

Peter Grabosky, Donald Cressey, David Bayley, Marshall Clinard, Gilbert Geis, Dan Glaser, Henry Pontell, Sat Mukherjee, Carl Klock-

Preface

ars, Dave Ermann, Grant Wardlaw, Philip Pettit, Jacek Kurczewski, Ivan Potas, Stephen Mugford, Anita Mak, Frank Jones and other participants at seminars at the University of Delaware, the University of California, Irvine and The Australian National University gave extremely helpful advice on improving the manuscript. Robin Derricourt of Cambridge University Press assisted in countless other ways as well as in improving the manuscript. I am also indebted to my subeditor, Shirley Purchase, in this regard.

My thanks go to Michele Robertson for endless trips to the library to retrieve works cited in the book and Beverley Bullpitt for dedicated assistance with typing. Most importantly, I want to thank Brent Fisse for inspiring my interest in shame as a crime control mechanism through many discussions we had during the years we worked on *The Impact of Publicity on Corporate Offenders*.

The present book is about a concept which was at the height of its popularity in the Victorian era – shame. Lynd (1958) directs us to Victorian novels like Tolstoy's *Anna Karenina* to remind us of how the concept of shame, which plays a more limited role in contemporary literature and conversation, was once a commanding concept. Since Freud, guilt has been a more popular construct than shame. Yet in the New Testament the word *guilt* does not appear, while *shame* is repeatedly referred to; Shakespeare uses shame about nine times as often as guilt (Lynd, 1958: 25). An old-fashioned concept like shame is perhaps uncomfortable for contemporary scholars to use in thinking about crime, though when we discuss white collar crime, terms which connote moral indignation are not quite so passé. In a sense it is the white collar crime literature which leads us into a decidedly Victorian analysis of crime in this book.

I

Whither criminological theory?

The theory in this book suggests that the key to crime control is cultural commitments to shaming in ways that I call reintegrative. Societies with low crime rates are those that shame potently and judiciously; individuals who resort to crime are those insulated from shame over their wrongdoing. However, shame can be applied injudiciously and counterproductively; the theory seeks to specify the types of shaming which cause rather than prevent crime.

Toward a General Theory

Crime is not a unidimensional construct. For this reason one should not be overly optimistic about a general theory which sets out to explain all types of crime. In fact, until fairly recently, I was so pessimistic about such an endeavor as to regard it as misguided. Clearly, the kinds of variables required to explain a phenomenon like rape are very different from those necessary to an explanation of embezzlement.

Equally clearly, there is a long tradition of purportedly general theorizing in criminology which in fact offers explanations of male criminality to the exclusion of female crime by focusing totally on male socialization experiences as explanatory variables. Other theories focus on big city crime to the exclusion of small town and rural crime by alighting upon urban environment as an explanation; others explain juvenile but not adult crime, or neglect the need to explain white collar crime.

Notwithstanding the diversity of behavior subsumed under the crime rubric, the contention of this book is that there is sufficient in common between different types of crime to render a general explanation possible. This commonality is not inherent in the nature of the disparate acts concerned. It arises from the fact that crime, whatever its form, is a kind of behavior which is poorly regarded in the community compared to most other acts, and behavior where this poor regard is institutionalized. Perpetrators of crime cannot continue to offend oblivious to the institutionalized disapproval directed at what they do. Unlike labeling theorists, I therefore adopt the view that most criminality is a *quality of the act*; the distinction between *behavior* and *action* is that behavior is no more than physical while action has a meaning that is socially given. 'The awareness that an action is deviant fundamentally alters the nature of the choices being made' (Taylor *et al*, 1973: 147).

It has been said that there is nothing inherently deviant about using a syringe to inject opiate into one's arm because doctors do it all the time in hospitals – deviant behavior is no more than behavior people so label. However arbitrary the labeling process, it is the fact that the criminal chooses to engage in the behavior knowing that it can be so labeled that distinguishes criminal choices from other choices. It is the defiant nature of the choice that distinguishes it from other social action.

Jimmy and Johnny are confronted with an opportunity to commit crime: an unlocked car. Johnny feels pangs of conscience overwhelm him as he approaches the criminal opportunity; he also thinks of how ashamed his mother would be if he were caught; he backs off. Jimmy, in contrast, goes ahead, steals the car, is unlucky enough to be caught, appears before a judge, admits that he has committed a crime and is convicted, a fact announced in the local newspaper. In all of this, Jimmy and Johnny, Johnny's mother, the judge, and those who read the newspaper all shared a view of what crime was and what the courts have the authority to do when criminals are caught. There is no other way for the participants to make sense of such interactions without some shared view of the institutional orders involved – in this case those of the criminal law and the criminal justice system. The critical point is that by all of them invoking the institutional order they help to reproduce it. Jimmy and Johnny, their families, the police who catch them, their lawyers, the judge, all treat the criminal law and the criminal justice system as 'real' concepts which define what Jimmy did. They are institutional relationships within which the encounters with the police and courts are situated, and institutional relationships that are indeed constituted by interactions such as those experienced by Jimmy.

The criminal law and the criminal justice system are 'real' precisely because countless people like these accept them as real and reproduce them through such social action.

It is not that, as W. I. Thomas (1951:81) said, if actors 'define situations as real they are real in their consequences', because this famous dictum implies that something like crime might not be real: it only has consequences because people believe in it. Rather, crime is reproduced as something real by repeated sequences of interactions akin to those of Jimmy and Johnny. Similarly, shame, conscience, the power and authority of the police and the judge – the things that constrained Johnny but not Jimmy – are structural and psychological constraints upon crime which are themselves reproduced as real by the very encounters in which the crime construct is reproduced. Social structures like the criminal justice system are therefore both a resource for actors to make sense of their action and a product of that action; social structure is reproduced as an objective reality that partially constrains the very kinds of actions which constitute it (Giddens, 1984).

A theory of any topic X will be an implausible idea unless there is a prior assumption that X is of what Philip Pettit (pers. comm., 1986) calls an explanandary kind. To be an explanandary kind, X need not be fully homogeneous, only sufficiently homogeneous for it to be likely that every type or most types of X will come under the same causal influences. There is no way of knowing that a class of actions is of an explanandary kind short of a plausible theory of the class being developed. In advance, giraffes, clover and newts might seem a heterogenous class, yet the theory of evolution shows how the proof of the pudding is in the eating. A general theory is not required to explain all of the variance for all types of cases, but some of the variance for all types of cases.

The homogeneity presumed between disparate behaviors such as rape and embezzlement in this theory is that they are choices made by the criminal actor in the knowledge that he is defying a criminal proscription which is mutually intelligible to actors in the society as criminal. At the end of Chapter 2 we will show that most criminal laws in most societies are the subject of overwhelming consensus. However, when dealing with the small minority of criminal laws that are not consensually regarded as justified, as with laws against marijuana use in liberal democracies or laws that create political crimes against the state in communist societies, the theory of reintegrative shaming will not explain the incidence of their violation. In liberal democracies the crimes that involve doubtful consensus are victimless crimes. Thus, the way to eliminate this problem is by measuring crime rates based only on predatory offenses against persons and property (Braithwaite, 1979: 10-16).

If the awareness that an act is criminal fundamentally changes the choices being made, then the key to a general explanation of crime lies in identifying variables that explain the capacity of some individuals and collectivities to resist, ignore, or succumb to the institutionalized disapproval that goes with crime. Indeed, the theory in this book construes as the critical variable one type of informal social support for the institutionalized disapproval of the criminal law. This variable is shaming.

Contrary to the claims of some labeling theorists, potent shaming directed at offenders is the essential necessary condition for low crime rates. Yet shaming can be counterproductive if it is disintegrative rather than reintegrative. Shaming is counterproductive when it pushes offenders into the clutches of criminal subcultures; shaming controls crime when it is at the same time powerful and bounded by ceremonies to reintegrate the offender back into the community of responsible citizens. The labeling perspective has failed to distinguish the crime-producing consequences of stigma that is open-ended, outcasting, and person- rather than offense-centered from the crime-reducing consequences of shaming that is reintegrative. This is why there is such limited empirical support for the key predictions of labeling theory.

Astute scholars of criminological theory will already be concerned about my formulation. Braithwaite, they will say, is setting out to build upon two mutually inconsistent theoretical traditions. One is control theory, which, like my theory, begins from the proposition that there is fundamental consensus about, and rejection of, criminal behavior in the society. The second is subcultural theory, which is a theory of dissensus, of some groups having different values from others in relation to criminal behavior. In Chapter 2, I will argue that this opposition has been greatly overdrawn in theoretical debate within criminology. In fact, only very extreme forms of subcultural theory are irreconcilable with control and other consensus-based theories.

This is not a book which puts a torch to existing general theories to build a new theory upon their ashes. Rather it sees enormous scope for integrating some of the major theoretical traditions which have come to us largely from American sociological criminology – control theory, subcultural theory, differential association, strain theories, and indeed labeling theory. The key to synthesizing these potentially incompatible formulations is to inject a vital element missing in criminological theory – reintegrative shaming.

These theories came under concerted attack through the 1970s from the 'new criminologists'. Today they are under attack from prophets of a new classicism in criminology. My contention is that the middle range theories of the fifties and sixties have survived the assault of the critical criminologists of the seventies and the neo-classical criminologists of the eighties rather more admirably than we are inclined to concede when we teach undergraduate criminology. Yet this is not to deny how profoundly important the missing elements in middle range criminological theory have been. The path to integrating these theories into mutually reinforcing partial explanations is not as difficult as has typically been suggested. If we fail to take this path we are left with a criminology which is the worst of all possible worlds. The next section is devoted to showing how criminology increasingly runs a risk of making the worst possible contribution to modern societies.

Once we put this pessimistic analysis of the contemporary scene behind us, however, and go back to the positive theoretical legacy of the fifties and sixties left by great American criminologists such as Sutherland, Cressey, Hirschi, Cloward and Ohlin, Albert Cohen, and Wolfgang, there is something quite substantial and empirically sustainable to build upon.

Criminology as a Cause of Crime?

At least half of the most influential criminologists in the world are Americans. It is not the purpose of this chapter to suggest that the United States has crime problems so much worse than other industrialized societies because it has more criminologists. The United States undoubtedly has spent so lavishly on criminology because it believes this is a necessary part of a national response to reduce crime. Yet I am inclined to wonder whether the professionalization of the study of crime is part of a wider societal movement which has tended further to debilitate the social response to crime, rather than strengthen it.

Criminology has become an export service industry for the United States in recent decades. Third World criminal justice professionals are accustomed to discreet jokes about American criminologists being funded as UN consultants, or by some other form of foreign aid, to communicate words of wisdom to countries that manage their crime problems much more effectively than the United States. There are reasons for fearing that such foreign aid exports not only American criminology, but may risk also the export of American crime rates.

Professional criminology, in all its major variants, can be unhelpful in maintaining a social climate appropriate to crime control because in different ways its thrust is to professionalize, systematize, scientize, and de-communitize justice. To the extent that the community genuinely comes to believe that the 'experts' can scientifically prescribe solutions to the crime problem, there is a risk that citizens cease to look to the preventive obligations which are fundamentally in their own hands. Thus, if I observe an offense, or if I come to know that my next-door neighbor is breaking the law, I should mind my own business, because there are professionals called police officers to deal with this problem. If a child toward whom I bear some responsible relationship by virtue of kinship or community has problems of delinquency, I might assume that it is best to leave it to the school counselor, who, unlike me, is an expert.

But exactly how is criminology implicated in this process of emasculating community crime control? To answer this question, we must look separately at the three major traditions of policy advice that have flowed from criminology: the utilitarian, the neoclassical, and the liberal-permissive.

The utilitarian tradition is underpinned by criminological scholarship concerned with the design of deterrent, rehabilitative and incapacitative strategies to reduce crime. Criminologists following this tradition of policy advice tell the community that scientific control of crime is possible if criminal justice professionals impose the right penalties on the right people for the right crimes, or if therapeutic professionals apply appropriate rehabilitative techniques, or if criminal justice professionals select the right people to be incapacitated by other criminal justice professionals. Under all utilitarian variants, the thrust of criminological advice is toward professionals taking over in different ways to make judgments for the community, informed by science, to prevent crime.

The neo-classical tradition of policy advice denies the capacity of criminology to deliver sound professional guidance on how to reduce crime. However, it promises another kind of professionalization of justice. It proffers a systematizing of punishments by jurisprudential professionals so that they reflect the desert of defendants. The neo-classical model takes special affront at communities informally resolving crime problems outside the justice system. Police officers should not be allowed the discretion to 'kick kids in the pants'. Serious criminal offenses should not be dealt with by school principals sitting down with parents to try to sort out the problems of a youthful offender: if a serious crime has been committed, that is a matter for the courts, and the courts should administer the deserved punishment. For the neo-classicists, informal community involvement in crime control risks both excessive oppression and excessive leniency by do-gooders. Community justice is unpredictable, inconsistent, and unjust. The ideal is a professionalized justice that is measured to deliver systematically neither more nor less than offenders deserve.

The liberal-permissive tradition of policy advice is grounded in the labeling perspective. Becker (1963:9) told us that

deviance is not a quality of the act a person commits but rather a consequence of the application by others of rules and sanctions to an offender. The deviant is one to whom that label has successfully been applied; deviant behavior is behavior that people so label.

Or, as another labelist, Kitsuse (1962: 253), put it:

Forms of behavior per se do not differentiate deviants from non-deviants; it is the responses of the conventional and conforming members of society who identify and interpret behavior as deviant which sociologically transform persons into deviants.

The labeling perspective was important to the development of criminology as an empirical science because it fostered an appreciative stance toward offenders. While positivist criminology up to that point had seen offenders very much as determined creatures, the labeling perspective opened many eyes to the way offenders were choosing beings, involved in shaping their own destiny. They had an interpretation of what the world was doing to them, and what they were doing to it, which was frequently at odds with the official version that positivist criminology had taken for granted. The policy prescription that grew from this appreciative stance toward the deviant was a call for tolerance and understanding, a plea to the community to see the deviant as more sinned against than sinning, to leave the delinquent alone, to see delinquency as 'just part of growing up'. While it was a good thing for the community to come to understand the many ways in which the deviant was sinned against, the labeling perspective was also telling the community to mind its own business. Certainly, it was at the same time telling the criminal justice professionals to keep their noses out of the affairs of deviants. Thus, while the utilitarians and neo-classicists were giving the community the message that community involvement in crime control could be dropped down their agenda because the professionals would take care of it, the liberal-permissive tradition of criminology was telling everybody, professionals and the community, to try 'radical non-intervention' (Schur, 1973).

If the theory in this book is correct, the tendency of each of these major traditions of criminological policy advice to imply a neutralization of community activism in crime control positively encourages crime. Crime is best controlled when members of the community are the primary controllers through active participation in shaming offenders, and, having shamed them, through concerted participation in ways of reintegrating the offender back into the community of law abiding citizens. Low crime societies are societies where people do not mind their own business, where tolerance of deviance has definite limits, where communities prefer to handle their own crime problems rather than hand them over to professionals. In this, I am not suggesting the replacement of 'the rule of law' with 'the rule of man'. However, I am saying that the rule of law will amount to a meaningless set of formal sanctioning proceedings which will be perceived as arbitrary unless there is community involvement in moralizing about and helping with the crime problem.

There is a fourth prominent tradition of policy advice which, unlike the other three, does not recommend changes to the criminal justice system. This fourth tradition is populated by Marxists who see the overthrow of capitalism as a route to a crime-free society, or at least to a society with much less crime, and opportunity theorists such as those discussed in the next chapter, who see other fundamental structural changes, mainly in class inequalities, as policies for crime reduction. Sadly, however, the policy advice of criminologists is only ever taken seriously when it is directed at the criminal justice system, so this fourth major tradition of criminological policy advice is of no consequence in influencing events. The world is yet to see a socialist revolution inspired by the desire to eliminate crime; and in my own capacity as a member of Australia's Economic Planning Advisory Council, I waited four years without witnessing a suggestion that a consideration against one policy choice rather than another was the impact on crime.

None of this is to deny that there have not been some tremendously valuable pockets of policy advice supplied by criminology. In Chapters 9 and 10 a number of them will be discussed. Perhaps such contributions have meant that criminology has made more positive than negative contributions to crime control. We will never know the answer to a question like this. The contention here has been simply that the three major traditions of policy advice run a real risk of counterproductivity if the theory in this book is correct.

Human Agency and Criminological Theory

Criminological theory has tended to adopt a rather passive conception of the criminal. Criminal behavior is determined by biological, psychological and social structural variables over which the criminal has little control. The theory of reintegrative shaming, in contrast, adopts an active conception of the criminal. The criminal is seen as making choices – to commit crime, to join a subculture, to adopt a deviant self-concept, to reintegrate herself, to respond to others' gestures of reintegration – against a background of societal pressures mediated by shaming.

The latter pressures might mean that the choices are somewhat constrained choices, but they are choices. This is especially so because the theory of reintegrative shaming explains compliance with the law by the moralizing qualities of social control rather than by its repressive qualities. Shaming is conceived as a tool to allure and inveigle the citizen to attend to the moral claims of the criminal law, to coax and caress compliance, to reason and remonstrate with him over the harmfulness of his conduct. The citizen is ultimately free to reject these attempts to persuade through social disapproval.

An irony of the theory is the contention that moralizing social control is more likely to secure compliance with the law than repressive social control. Because criminal behavior is mostly harmful by any moral yardstick, and agreed to be so by most citizens, moralizing appeals which treat the citizen as someone with the responsibility to make the right choice are generally, though not invariably, responded to more positively than repressive controls which deny human dignity by treating persons as amoral calculators. A culture impregnated with high moral expectations of its citizens, publicly expressed, will deliver superior crime control compared with a culture which sees control as achievable by inflicting pain on its bad apples.

In addition to the epistemological rationale for conceiving people as choosing in light of societal pressures rather than being determined by them, there is thus also suggested an empirical rationale: moralizing which then leaves agency in the hands of the citizen is more likely to work in the long run than a policy of attempting to remove agency from the citizen by repressive control. The epistemological claim and the empirical claim are linked to a normative claim: a shift of the balance of social control away from repression and toward social control by moralizing is a good thing. The tradition of linking the empirical claim that repressive control does not work with the normative claim that it is wrong dates at least from Durkheim:

> Ideas and feelings need not be expressed through…untoward manifestations of force, in order to be communicated. As a matter of fact such punishments constitute today quite a serious moral handicap. They affront a feeling that is at the bottom of all our morality, the religious respect in which the human person is held. By virtue of this respect, all violence exercised on a person seems to us, in principle, like sacrilege. In beating, in brutality of all kinds, there is something we find repugnant, something that revolts our conscience – in a word, something immoral. Now, defending morality by means repudiated by it, is a remarkable way of protecting morality. It weakens on the one hand the sentiments that one wishes to strengthen on the other.
>
> (Durkheim, 1961: 182–3)

Hence, shaming is conceived in this theory as a means of making citizens actively responsible, of informing them of how justifiably resentful their fellow citizens are toward criminal behavior which harms them. In practice, shaming surely limits autonomy, more surely than repression, but it does so by communicating moral claims over which other citizens can reasonably be expected to express disgust should we choose to ignore them. In other words, shaming is a route to freely chosen compliance, while repressive social control is a route to coerced compliance. Repressive social control, as by imprisonment, restricts our autonomy by forced limitation of our choices; moralizing social control restricts our autonomy by inviting us to see that we cannot be whole moral persons through considering only our own interests in the choices we make. We are shamed if we exercise our own autonomy in a way that tramples on the autonomy of others.

A moral educative normative theory of social control aspires to put the accused in a position where she must either argue for her innocence, admit guilt and express remorse, or contest the legitimacy of the norms she is accused of infringing. It seeks to foreclose the alternative of terminating moral reasoning over alleged wrongdoing by 'exclusion' of the accused. Such a theory therefore accommodates civil disobedience better than traditional theories of punishment. A moral education theory forges a vital role for questioning by the person who challenges the justice of the normative order: she forces the state 'to commit itself, in full view of the rest of society, to the idea that her actions show she needs moral education' (Hampton, 1984: 221). A deterrence theory, in contrast, raises no problems with the silencing of critics, the suffocation of moralizing on both sides, by locking the offender away from community contact.

For some readers the theory of reintegrative shaming will undoubtedly raise the spectre of a society of informers and busybodies, of thought control, a society wherein diversity cannot be tolerated. Shaming can foster such a society. As Andrei Siniavsky said in his trial before the People's Tribunal in Moscow, 1966:

> Think of it please, I am different from others, yes different, but I am not an enemy. I am a soviet person and my art is not subversive – it is only different. In this tense atmosphere anything which is different would seem subversive – but why do you have to look for enemies, to create monsters where there are none?   (Quoted in Shoham, 1970: 98)

Siniavsky makes two pleas here. He asks not to be treated as a 'monster'. (In the language of my theory, he asks not to be stigmatized.) Second, he is claiming that his art does no harm and therefore should be tolerated. These are reasonable pleas. Behavior should never be punished or publicly shamed as criminal if it risks no harm to other citizens; and even when it does harm, the offender should be shamed or punished with dignity rather than stigmatized as a monster or outcast.

Shaming which complies with these two requirements will not be oppressive. Shaming which eschews stigmatization, which shames within a continuum of human respect, maximizes prospects that behavior which is not harmful to others will be tolerated. In a liberal society, shaming is needed to sanction those who do harm by restricting the freedom of others to engage in non-criminal deviance.

A society which neglects the need to shame harmful criminal behavior will be a society which encourages its citizens to amoral encroachments upon the freedom of others. In Chapter 9, it will be argued that societies which fail to exercise informal social control within local communities, families, schools and other proximate groups find themselves with no political choice but to resort to repressive control by the state. Communitarian societies, it will be argued, are more free to choose their mix between formal state control and informal community control. Effective communitarian shaming therefore expands the scope for pursuing less repressive criminal justice policies. As Feinberg put it: 'Today we prefer not to become involved in the control of crime, with the result that those who are charged with the control of crime become more and more involved with us' (Feinberg, 1970:240).

Shaming is a dangerous game. Done oppressively, it can be used for thought control and stultification of human diversity. Not done much at all, it unleashes a war of all against all, the maximally repressive state, and tolerance of a situation where some citizens trample on the rights of others. Whichever way we play it, it is a game that matters. Happily, the way the shaming game unfolds is not inexorably determined. There is scope for political choice; this scope for human agency makes it worth our while developing an understanding of the power of shaming.

A Preliminary Sketch of the Theory

The first step to productive theorizing about crime is to think about the contention that labeling offenders makes things worse. The contention is both right and wrong. The theory of reintegrative shaming is an attempt to specify when it is right and when wrong. The distinction is between shaming that leads to stigmatization – to outcasting, to confirmation of a deviant master status – versus shaming that is reintegrative, that shames while maintaining bonds of respect or love, that sharply terminates disapproval with forgiveness, instead of amplifying deviance by progressively casting the deviant out. Reintegrative shaming controls crime; stigmatization pushes offenders toward criminal subcultures.

The second step to more productive theorizing about crime is to realize what scholars like Sutherland, Cressey and Glaser grasped long ago – that criminality is a function of the ratio of associations favorable to crime to those unfavorable to crime. If this is a banal point, it is one that criminological theorists systematically forget. As Daniel Glaser commented on an earlier draft of this book:

What we need to develop and operationalize in various social contexts is a theory of tipping points, of the persons and circumstances in which particular types of labeling and punishment shift the predominant stake of the subjects from conformity to nonconformity with the legal norms, and vice versa. Much of the difference between delinquency theorists reflects the fact that the samples they studied were on different sides of this tipping point. Hirshi focussed on the 75 percent of a cross-section of secondary school students who completed his questionnaires, and were predominantly not very delinquent, while Shaw and McKay as well as Murray and Cox studied repeatedly arrested youths in delinquent and criminal gangs from high crime-rate slums. Like the blind Hindus in the legend, each generalized from the different parts of the elephant that they encountered.

The theory of reintegrative shaming contends that we can sensibly talk about criminal subcultures. We require a theory which comes to grips with the multiple moralities which exist in contemporary societies. A severe limitation of theories that deny this, like Hirschi's control theory, is that they give no account of why some uncontrolled individuals become heroin users, some become hit men, and others price fixing conspirators. At the same time, we must recognize that the criminal law is a powerfully dominant majoritarian morality compared with the minority subculture of the heroin user or the industry association's price fixing circle. There is a powerful consensus in modern industrial societies over the rightness of criminal laws which protect our persons and property, if not over victimless crimes. Even most criminal subcultures do not transmit an outright rejection of the criminal law, rather they transmit means of rationalizing temporary suspension of one's commitment to the law, symbolic resources for insulating the offender from shame.

The theory is one of predatory crime – whether perpetrated by juvenile delinquents, street offenders or business executives – of violations of criminal laws which prohibit one person from preying on others. Societies that shame effectively will be more successful in controlling predatory crime because there will be more shaming directed at noncompliance with the law than shaming (within subcultures) for complying with the law. It is important to understand that for domains where the criminal law does not represent a clearly majoritarian morality, the theory of reintegrative shaming will fail to explain variation in behavior. It provides a thoroughly inadequate account of nonpredatory criminal behavior like homosexuality because, even in a society with great capacities to shame effectively, if half the population does not believe the behavior should be criminalized, there may be as much shaming directed at gays who refuse to come out of the closet, and at those who oppress homosexuals, as there is shaming directed at the offending itself. The theory of reintegrative shaming is not a satisfactory general theory of deviance because its explanatory power declines as dissensus increases over whether the conduct should be viewed as deviant. It is best reserved for that domain where there is strong consensus, that of predatory crimes (crimes involving victimization of one party by another).

While it is true with respect to this domain that criminal subcultures are always minority phenomena, some types of societies will have more virulent criminal subcultures than others. For example, societies which segregate oppressed racial minorities into stigmatized neighborhoods create the conditions for criminal subculture formation.

The theory of reintegrative shaming posits that the consequence of stigmatization is attraction to criminal subcultures. Subcultures supply the outcast offender with the opportunity to reject her rejectors, thereby maintaining a form of self-respect. In contrast, the consequence of reintegrative shaming is that criminal subcultures appear less attractive to the offender. Shaming is the most potent weapon of social control unless it shades into stigmatization. Formal criminal punishment is an ineffective weapon of social control partly because it is a degradation ceremony with maximum prospects for stigmatization.

The nub of the theory of reintegrative shaming is therefore about the effectiveness of reintegrative shaming and the counterproductivity of stigmatization in controlling crime. In addition, the theory posits a number of conditions that make for effective shaming. Individuals are more susceptible to shaming when they are enmeshed in multiple relationships of interdependency; societies shame more effectively when they are communitarian. Variables like urbanization and residential mobility predict communitarianism, while variables like age and gender predict individual interdependency. A schematic summary of these aspects of the theory is presented in Figure 1 (page 94).

Some of the ways that the theory of reintegrative shaming builds on earlier theories should now be clear. Interdependency is the stuff of control theory; stigmatization comes from labeling theory; subculture formation is accounted for in opportunity theory terms; subcultural influences are naturally in the realm of subcultural theory; and the whole theory can be understood in integrative cognitive social learning theory terms such as are provided by differential association.

into one theoretical framework, we cannot escape the labor of summarizing the things they have to say that are relevant. This we do in the next chapter, along with a justification of the premise that substantial consensus over the evil of predatory crime exists in modern societies. Readers who are not particularly interested in an account of these theories, of their strengths and of the limitations requiring redress by a more encompassing theory, need only read just the first section on labeling and the conclusion to the next chapter. Chapter 3 then runs through the facts a theory of crime must fit to be credible – the well established correlates of crime – and argues that the dominant theoretical traditions, read in isolation from each other, do not supply a compelling account of these facts. Less than diligent readers might skim this chapter also. In Chapter 4 we get down to the theory itself.

2

The dominant theoretical traditions: labeling, subcultural, control, opportunity and learning theories

In this chapter, a number of criminological theories will be briefly discussed which later become important to our analysis: labeling, subcultural, control, opportunity and learning theories. These are the major theoretical traditions that have guided twentieth century criminological research. It will be contended that the theories are not as mutually inconsistent as their proponents would have us believe.

Let us simplify the relevance of this chapter by imagining Fagin's lair as something of a caricature of a criminal subculture. We need control theory to bring young offenders to the doorstep of the criminal subculture (primary deviance); stigmatization (labeling theory) to open the door; subcultural and learning theory to maintain the lair as a rewarding place for secondary deviants to stay in; and opportunity theory to explain how such criminal subcultures come to exist in the first place. This is the scheme supplied by the theory of reintegrative shaming for synthesizing the dominant theoretical traditions. Figure 1 (page 99) summarizes how reintegrative shaming is the central linkage among these explanatory frameworks.

Labeling Theory

older sociology...tended to rest heavily on the idea that deviance leads to social control. I have come to believe that the reverse idea, i.e., social control leads to deviance, is equally tenable and the potentially richer premise for studying deviance in modern society. (Lemert, 1967: v)

Edwin Lemert, Howard Becker, John Kitsuse, Edwin Schur and other leading exponents of the labeling perspective tend to deny that there is such a thing as labeling theory. They prefer to see them-

16

selves as having injected some 'sensitizing concepts' into the sociology of deviance. At the same time, however, the writings of labelists are replete with deterministic propositions concerning the impact of labeling on deviance. Whether or not we want to call these collections of propositions a theory, they are central to this analysis, and I am concerned to assess how they stand up to empirical testing, even if some of the labelists are not.

The first labeling theorist was Frank Tannenbaum in his 1938 book, *Crime and the Community*:

The person becomes the thing he is described as being. Nor does it seem to matter whether the valuation is made by those who would punish or by those who would reform. In either case the emphasis is upon the conduct that is disapproved of. The parents or the policeman, the older brother or the court, the probation officer or the juvenile institution... Their very enthusiasm defeats their aim. The harder they work to reform the evil, the greater the evil grows under their hands. The persistent suggestion, with whatever good intentions, works mischief, because it leads to bringing out the bad behavior that it would suppress. The way out is through a refusal to dramatize the evil. The less said about it the better. The more said about something else, still better. (Tannenbaum, 1938: 20)

No statement could be more starkly contradictory to that which is argued in this book. We will come to the position here that, with certain qualifications, 'the more said about crime the better', that low crime societies are those that do 'dramatize the evil'. However, Tannenbaum's pungent analysis, neglected for decades, by the mid-seventies had become extraordinarily influential, indeed the dominant paradigm in textbooks on deviance (Sagarin and Montanio, 1976; see also Cole, 1975). Thus, we saw influential books with titles like *Radical Non-Intervention* (Schur, 1973), conceiving of delinquency as 'just part of growing up'; if we left the kids alone they would be okay. Taylor *et al* (1973: 282), in the final sentence to the most significant criminological book of the decade, took the labeling position one big step further by suggesting that we not only stop officially reacting to criminals, we jettison the whole concept of crime: 'The task is to create a society in which the facts of human diversity, whether personal, organic or social, are not subject to the power to criminalize'.

Of what, then, does labeling consist, and why is it predicted to have dire consequences? Erikson suggests that there are three stages to the labeling process:

The community's decision to bring deviant sanctions against the individual...is a sharp rite of transition at once moving him out of his normal position in society and transferring him into a distinctive deviant role. The ceremonies which accomplish this change of status, ordinarily, have three related phases. They provide a formal confrontation between the deviant suspect and representatives of his community (as in the criminal trial or psychiatric case conference); they announce some judgement about the nature of the deviancy (a verdict or diagnosis for example), and they perform an act of social placement, assigning him to a special role (like that of prisoner or patient) which redefines his position in society.

(Erikson, 1962: 311)

Erikson further suggests that 'An important feature of these ceremonies in our culture is that they are almost irreversible' (1962: 311). The reason is that deviance becomes a master status overriding all other statuses in determining how others will respond to the deviant. Erikson is wrong to suggest that this process is irreversible; many who as young people are labeled as criminals, prostitutes, drug users, have left these deviant statuses well and truly behind them by middle age. On the other hand, a prediction of our theory is that in cultures which rely heavily on punishment, exclusion and stigma for social control, irreversibility is much more of a problem than in cultures characterized by reintegrative shaming.

Once a person is stigmatized with a deviant label, a self-fulfilling prophecy unfolds as others respond to the offender as deviant. She experiences marginality, she is attracted to subcultures which provide social support for deviance, she internalizes a deviant identity, she experiences a sense of injustice at the way she is victimized by agents of social control, her loss of respectability may push her further into an underworld by causing difficulty in earning a living legitimately. Deviance then becomes a way of life that is difficult to change and is rationalized as a defensible lifestyle within the deviant subculture. Labeling theorists differ on the relative importance of each of these deviance amplification processes and on the order in which they occur. The important point for our work is that every version of the labeling perspective holds that social control makes the deviant worse.

Is there a body of empirical evidence to support this fairly straightforward prediction? Tittle (1980) has provided a systematic review of the rather limited data available. He found little evidence from studies with the strongest controls that offenders who are labeled more severely (e.g. by imprisonment rather than probation) are more likely to reoffend, and pointed to evidence from qualitative studies that criminal behavior precedes labeling. Elliott *et al.* (1979: 20–1) and Box (1981) reached a similar conclusion:

Thus six studies offer some support for the view that apprehended but not severely sanctioned juveniles do increase their deviant behaviour, become more negative in their attitudes towards the police, become more involved with delinquent peers and more willing to go along with them, and come to regard themselves as more delinquent (Ageton and Elliott, 1974; Farrington, 1977; Farrington, Osborn and West, 1978; Gold and Williams, 1969; Hirschi, 1969; Jensen, 1972; Klemke, 1978). On the other hand, no support for some or all of these possibilities was reported in four other studies (Fisher, 1972; Fisher and Erickson, 1973; Foster, Dinitz and Reckless, 1972; Hepburn, 1977). One final study (McEachern, 1968) both supported and rejected parts of the argument. (Box, 1981: 214)

Further research since Tittle's review has done little to change his conclusion that the weight of evidence is, if anything, against labeling increasing crime (consider the review by Shoemaker, 1984: 186–249; see also Kwasniewski, 1984:172–5). A recent longitudinal study by Thomas and Bishop (1984) using self-report delinquency data failed to support the conclusion that sanctioning pushes actors toward an acceptance of the label which has been attributed to them, though the results were at least ambiguously consistent with the proposition that sanctioning increases rather than reduces delinquency. More persuasive evidence on the latter point is provided by the Cambridge longitudinal study of delinquency. This study showed that boys who were apprehended for and convicted of delinquent offenses became more delinquent than boys who were equally delinquent to begin with but who escaped apprehension (West and Farrington, 1977: 162). The Cambridge study perhaps amounts to the most convincing empirical support for radical non-intervention, for the notion that juveniles who are 'helped' by the juvenile justice system turn out worse (see also McCord, 1978; Bazemore, 1985; Palmara *et al.*, 1986; but see Junger and Junger (1985) for failure to obtain a similar result on a Dutch sample and Klein (1986) and Ray and Downs (1986) for equivocal results).

It should hardly be surprising that the evidence on the association between labeling and crime is mixed. While the explanations of the labeling theorists as to why deviance should be a product of social control are persuasive, there are also persuasive arguments which run the other way. Stigma is a deterrent; it is something which most people prefer to avoid. A labeled person, far from being pushed into a deviant self-conception, may through confronting the low regard expressed by others, decide that she has a problem with drugs, for example, and needs help. She may be forced to look at herself and she may not like what she sees. Then she may be motivated to rehabilitate herself. Even if labeling produces a criminogenic transformation of a person's identity, role and behavior more often than it prompts a rejection of deviance by the labeled person, stigmatization may still have a general deterrent effect on other persons who witness the misfortune of the outcast.

If the labeling perspective is to be the stimulus to testable propositions with any hope of consistent empirical support, then a strategy is required for predicting the circumstances where labeling will be counterproductive and where it will actually reduce crime. This is the challenge that the theory in this book sets out to meet. Reintegrative shaming is conceived as labeling that reduces crime, stigmatization as criminogenic labeling. It is not that the data show the key prediction from labeling theory to be wrong; it is simply that in working so hard at 'sensitizing' agents of social control to how their efforts can make things worse, labelists neglected to specify the limits of this contention. The result is that the social reaction revolution of the 1960s and 1970s did both great good and great harm. It fostered a justifiable cynicism about a variety of rehabilitative and punitive measures which amounted to net widening without any reason for believing that crime would be reduced. A wholesome liberal tolerance of diversity was encouraged; the community learnt a lot about the dangers of overreacting to deviance that might be transient if left alone.

Yet, at the same time, the labeling perspective fostered a debilitating nihilism that gave no advice about the limits of tolerating diversity. Would it really be counterproductive to label as criminal a drug manufacturer who bribed a health minister to have a ban lifted on a profitable pharmaceutical, or to label a rapist as criminal? If 'moral panic' over petty juvenile offending was anathema to liberal labelists, was moral apathy over some forms of sexual abuse of women and white collar crime equally a cause for celebration? While tolerance of diversity is important for avoiding the excesses of counterproductive cracking down on petty deviance, intolerance of diversity is also critical for crime control. Societies imbued with the ideology of labeling theory will be excessively apathetic about nontrivial crime; to be effective against crime, societies need to be interventionist in a communitarian sense, to be intolerant of crime in a way that is both spiteful and forgiving.

Subcultural Theory

There is a strong link between labeling and subcultural theories of crime. Labelists such as Becker (1963:38) see subculture formation arising in part from the fact that the society creates similar types of outcasts with a common fate who face the same problems. These outcasts therefore commonly band together and create deviant subcultures that provide social support for deviant behavior. The subculture combines a perspective on the world (heroin is all right if sensibly managed) with a set of routine activities (heroin use, dealing, bribery of police).

Subcultural theorists see the motivation behind criminal behavior as essentially similar to the motivation behind conforming behavior – the desire to satisfy the expectations of significant others in a membership or reference group. Subcultural theories derive much of their sustenance from the widely reported finding that persons who associate with criminals or are more strongly attached to delinquent peers are more likely to engage in crime themselves.[1] As Elliott *et al.* (1985: 85–9) show, there are some longitudinal data to support the view that this is not all a matter of 'birds of a feather flocking together'; attachment to delinquent associates precedes increased delinquent behavior (see also Elliott *et al.*, 1979: 16).

The most influential subcultural theories have focused on lower class cultures as generating milieu of male delinquency (Cohen, 1955; Miller, 1958), though there have been theories of criminogenic organizational cultures producing white collar crime (Cressey, 1976). Miller (1958) concluded from his observations of lower class gang behavior that 'trouble', 'toughness', 'smartness', 'excitement', 'fate', and 'autonomy' were the key focal concerns of lower class

[1]See Glueck and Glueck, 1950; Short, 1957; Reiss and Rhodes, 1964; Voss, 1964; Erickson and Empey, 1965; Hardt and Peterson, 1968; Jensen, 1972b; Hindelang, 1973; Kandel, 1973; Elliott and Voss, 1974; Krohn, 1974; Conger, 1976; Jensen and Eve, 1976; Hepburn, 1977a; Rankin, 1977; West and Farrington, 1977; Kandel *et al.*, 1978; Akers *et al.*, 1979; Aultman, 1979; Johnson, 1979; Poole and Regoli, 1979; Matsueda, 1982; Bowker and Klein, 1983; Huba and Bentler, 1983; Thompson *et al.*, 1984; Patterson and Dishion, 1985; Riley and Shaw, 1985; Segrave and Hastad, 1985; Morash, 1986.

culture. The primary motivation of gang delinquency is the attempt to act out these lower class focal concerns.

Miller assumes that class differences in officially recorded delinquency can be explained by the existence of one monolithic set of middle class values, and another monolithic but separate consensus about values among the lower class. Matza and Sykes (1961) point out that many of Miller's lower class focal concerns are almost identical with respectable middle class goals. Courage, easy money, and adventure are values which are equivalent to Miller's 'toughness', 'smartness', and 'excitement'. 'Toughness' can save lives or it can kill people, as Sutherland and Cressey (1978:82) argued:

> Though criminal behavior is an expression of general needs and values, it is not explained by those general needs and values, since non-criminal behavior is an expression of the same needs and values.

Albert Cohen (1955) prefaces his theory of delinquency with the assumption that both lower class and middle class boys begin their school careers with a commitment to traditional success goals; but because lower class socialization equips lower class boys less adequately than their middle class counterparts for success at school, more of the lower class boys become failures in the status system of the school. This failure initially engenders shame and guilt, and perhaps some resentment and bitterness as well.

Having failed in the status system of the school, the student has a status problem and is in the market for a solution. He solves it collectively with other students who have been similarly rejected by the school. The outcasts band together and set up their own status system with values which are the exact inverse of those of the school: contempt for property and authority instead of respect for property and authority, immediate impulse gratification instead of impulse control, apathy instead of ambition, toughness instead of control of aggression. The delinquent's conduct is right by the standards of his subculture precisely because it is wrong by the standards of the school. By participating in this subculture, the poor academic performer can enhance his self-image by rejecting his rejectors. The boy's status problem is solved by the collective creation of a new status system in which he is guaranteed of some success.

There is considerable empirical evidence now that the values inferred by Miller and others from *ex post facto* interpretations of the behavior of delinquent gangs are not endorsed by a majority of either lower class people or delinquents; nor are they consistently more often endorsed by lower class than middle class people. Where values have been isolated which are supported by a larger minority of delinquents than of non-delinquents, commitment to these values is not related to class. Thus class differences in criminogenic values cannot be invoked as an explanation for greater delinquency by lower class youth (Braithwaite and Braithwaite, 1981). Beyond the almost trite statement that delinquents have attitudes somewhat more tolerant of delinquency, there is nothing that the evidence enables us to say with confidence about the relationships between values and delinquency (Kornhauser, 1978: 214–44; Braithwaite and Braithwaite, 1981). Even serious repeat delinquents mostly place higher value on conventional accomplishments than on success at breaking the law (Short, 1964; Short and Strodtbeck, 1965; Short *et al.*, 1965; Lerman, 1968).

The search for widespread subcultural differences in modern Western societies to explain structural differences in crime rates has not been a fruitful one. But this does not mean that there is not an infinite variety of subcultural value systems in a society; it is simply to say that they are not sufficiently consistent in nature to throw up repeated constellations of subcultural values in a large-scale values survey. There probably do exist gangs which exhibit Miller's focal concerns, others which evidence something like Cohen's reaction formation. Perhaps more importantly, there are many juveniles who sustain a joint allegiance to the values of the school and the values of anti-school subcultures:

A modern society contains numerous status systems that are not in competition with one another; acceptance of one need not require repudiation of others. In particular, students who do not reject the value system endorsed by parents and school officials but who do not succeed in its terms can nevertheless accept the value system of a subculture of delinquency (in the sense of Matza (1964)) as a 'second best' alternative on pragmatic grounds.
(Greenberg, 1977: 203)

Downes (1966) in his study of delinquents in Stepney and Poplar found that the typical response to failure is not Cohen's 'reaction formation' but 'dissociation'. Rather than rebelliously turning the values of the school upside down, it is more typical for the delinquent simply to withdraw interest in the work world of the school. Box (1981: 107–8) also suggests that there is no reaction formation because lower class boys often do not internalize the status criteria of the school in the first place; it is simply that the boys 'can't be indifferent to' the status criteria of the school.

For Matza (1964) the intervening variable between failure in a status system and delinquency is 'drift'. The delinquent belongs to a subculture characterized by values which *allow* delinquency but *do not demand it*.

> The delinquent is neither compelled nor committed to deeds nor freely choosing them; neither different in any simple or fundamental sense from the law abiding, nor the same... He is committed to neither delinquent nor conventional enterprise... The delinquent transiently exists in a limbo between convention and crime, responding in turn to demands of each, flirting now with one, now the other, but postponing commitment, evading decision. Thus he drifts between criminal and conventional action.
>
> (Matza, 1964: 28)

Failure in the status system of the wider society fosters this drift. Powerlessness is the most important dimension of this failure: 'Being pushed around puts the delinquent in a mood of fatalism. He experiences himself as effect. In that condition he is rendered irresponsible' (Matza, 1964: 89). Powerlessness is particularly critical when the youth is 'pushed around' in a way which he perceives as unjust or oppressive, because a sense of injustice can abrogate the moral bind of law. 'The subculture of delinquency is, among other things, a memory file that collects injustices' (Matza, 1964: 102). The same might be said of business subcultures of resistance to regulatory or tax laws.

Sykes and Matza (1957) have suggested that the main mechanisms which make drift possible are what they call techniques of neutralization. The five major techniques are (1) *denial of responsibility*, e.g. 'I was drunk'; (2) *denial of injury*, e.g. 'they can afford it'; (3) *denial of victim*, e.g. 'we weren't hurting anyone'; (4) *condemnation of the condemners*, e.g. 'they're crooks themselves'; (5) *appeal to higher loyalties*, e.g. 'I had to stick by my mates'.

> It is by learning these techniques that the juveniles become delinquent, rather than by learning moral imperatives, values or attitudes standing in direct contradiction to those of the dominant society.
>
> (Sykes and Matza, 1957: 668)

Quite likely there are subcultures in modern societies characterized by Miller's focal concerns, Cohen's reaction formation, Downes's dissociation, Box's inability to be indifferent to the status criteria of the school, Matza's drift and techniques of neutralization, and any variety of other idiosyncratic cultural adaptations to rejection by a wider community. The ethnographic literature on delinquency does not show consistent patterns but a tapestry, and the crude techniques of survey research report this rich tapestry of subculturalism as an absence of any evidence of 'a' delinquent subculture or 'a' lower class subculture which is coherently distinguishable from the mainstream.

We cannot say that criminal subcultures do not exist or are not important. The Italian Mafia, British Skin Heads, Japanese Yamaguchi Gumi, American Hell's Angels, Indian Banjaras, New Zealand Mongrel Mob, Chinese Triads, New Guinean Rascals are unusually stigmatized groups which have obvious roles in transmitting criminal subcultures. Without much scratching below the surface of society we can see variegated subcultures of drug use, groups that nurture subcultural behavior patterns such as motor vehicle theft gangs, associations of respectable businesspersons in a particular industry who meet to fix prices illegally, networks of intermediaries who negotiate bribes between vendors and purchasers in industries like aerospace, communities of tax consultants and clients who share knowledge on how to evade and avoid taxes (including geographically segregated subcultures called tax havens).

Much of the stuff of illegitimate opportunities in an increasingly complex society is in the nature of knowledge about how to do it; this knowledge is largely preserved and transmitted by subcultures. Granted, most of the groups that transmit these subcultures are not highly organized. Typically they are loosely structured, even brittle social organizations. Most delinquency is not perpetrated in organized gangs; the majority of juvenile offenses are perpetrated by groups of two or three offenders (Zimring, 1981). Victim surveys suggest that most adult crime, including white collar crime, is a solitary affair (e.g. Braithwaite and Biles, 1980: 49; cf. Reiss, 1980). But even solitary crime is often made possible by a learning process that occurs within loosely coordinated groups that provide support for solitary crime in the form of social approval, neutralization, or transmission of knowledge of how to do it.

Criminal subcultures are therefore central to our understanding of crime. Subculturalism in criminology was dealt an unfair blow by empirical disconfirmation of theories of subculturalism which attempted to be too all-encompassing in the blueprint and the process of formation they posited for criminal subcultures. Most delinquents do not share Miller's focal concerns of lower class culture, and even support for the notion that most delinquents drift or engage in neutralization has not been impressive (Schwendinger and Schwendinger, 1967; Hindelang, 1970, 1974; Austin, 1977; Minor, 1980; Ball, 1983; but see Akers *et al*, 1979; Thurman, 1984; Agnew and Peters, 1986). Because criminal subcultures are disparate, theories of crime that depend upon widely held subcultural value systems are doomed to fail, and have failed.

No theory of crime can be adequate, nevertheless, which fails to account for the way knowledge is passed from one generation to the next on how to organize particular types of offending, how to neutralize the moral bind of the criminal law. Criminological theory should explain why a business group can rationalize pollution while being outraged by dealing in heroin, just as a group of young people can excuse selling heroin as harmless and regard crimes against the environment as sacrilege. It is subcultural theory that can account for why the businessperson opts for one type of crime rather than another.

One of the great contributions of labeling theory, as we saw in the last section, is in showing how stigmatization fosters subculture formation. By segregating and rejecting outcasts, stigmatization fosters a search for, or at least attraction to, others who have been similarly rejected by the wider culture. The coming together of these folk with similar axes to grind accounts for most of the forging of criminal subcultures. The group supplies venues where reinforcement, rationalizing, modeling, and social learning of criminality occur in interaction with other persons. Notwithstanding the central role of deviant groups in giving substantial vitality to subcultures, others quite remote from such groups can be influenced directly and indirectly by the deviant group and play a part in transmitting the rationalizations and behavior patterns of the subculture. Consider the mother in a poor black neighborhood who aspires to respectability but cannot totally reject the rationalizations she hears from members of theft networks in the neighborhood. As Cressey (1960: 49) points out she may at once teach her son that 'Honesty is the best policy' and that 'It is all right to steal when you are starving'. Notwithstanding her respectability, she plays a part in transmitting the subculture by approving rationalizations of crime, a part in transmitting both criminal and anti-criminal attitudes.

Thus, as in labeling theory, in the present theory of stigmatization and crime, stigmatization tends to be criminogenic to the extent that those stigmatized find or are exposed to subcultures which provide social support for delinquency. Stigmatization itself is one of the variables which contribute to subculture formation.

Control Theory

Control theories assume that all individuals are subject to many temptations to engage in rewarding criminal behavior. In the face of these ubiquitous temptations, the question is not 'Why did she do it?', but 'Why did she *not* do it?' Human beings will seek the rewards of crime unless they are held in check, or somehow controlled.

One of the attractive features of control theories is that they do not conceive of human beings as determined creatures:

By stressing the boundlessness of human nature and the necessity for the powerful in an established institutional order to *caress*, *coax* and *convert* newcomers into conformity, control theory reveals that when this objective is not achieved individuals remain at liberty to explore, and that exploration may lead to behaviour labelled deviant by the powerful. Occurrence of special circumstances is not necessary to bring about freedom to deviate; freedom is there all the time as a human possibility. (Box, 1981: 132)

Control theory has a distinguished lineage running from Durkheim (1951) to Reckless (1967) to Reiss (1951) to Hirschi (1969), but it is the latter's version which is contemporarily influential. Hirschi saw social bonding as the key to delinquency control: if social bonds fail to develop or are broken, many will choose to engage in forms of delinquency which are rewarding to them. There are four aspects of the social bond – attachment, commitment, involvement and belief. *Attachment* means the emotional connection one feels toward other people, sensitivity to their opinions, feelings and expectations. *Commitment* is the investment accumulated in relationships, the rational aspect of the social bond, the stake in conformity. *Involvement* refers simply to participation in legitimate activities – the extent to which the individual is tied to appointments, deadlines, working hours, plans. *Belief* means acceptance of the desirability of obeying the rules of society.

In the control theory literature, the concrete social bonds which are repeatedly regarded as important are to the family and the school, and occasionally to the church. The evidence is now quite overwhelming that juveniles with strong attachments to their family are less likely to engage in delinquency.[2] A bivariate association between broken homes and delinquency is also widely reported in the literature,[3] but there is doubt that this holds up after entry of appropriate controls (Wilkinson, 1974; Farnworth, 1984; Wilson and Herrnstein, 1985: 246–53). Attachment of juveniles to parents is often very strong in broken homes, stronger than in many unhappy families which stay together (see Nye, 1958), so control theory does not necessarily predict a strong relationship here.

The evidence on an association between attachment and commitment to the school or its teachers and delinquency is even stronger than with the family. An association between poor school performance and delinquency is universally strong,[4] as is the relationship between not liking school or being weakly attached to school and delinquency (e.g. Jensen and Eve, 1976; Thomas and Hyman, 1978; Johnson, 1979; Wiatrowski *et al*, 1981; Kaplan and Robbins, 1983; Agnew, 1985) and low educational and occupational aspirations and delinquency (e.g. Gold, 1963; Hirschi, 1969; Fredericks and Molnar, 1969; Liska, 1971; Figueira-McDonough, 1984). While some causal effect of school failure on delinquency has been fairly consistently

[2]See Glueck and Glueck, 1950; Nye, 1958; McCord *et al*., 1959; Hirschi, 1969; Gold, 1970; Farrington, 1973; Hindelang, 1973; Elliott and Voss, 1974; Jensen and Eve, 1976; Hepburn, 1977a; Hirschi and Hindelang, 1977; Minor, 1977; Thomas and Hyman, 1978; Aultman, 1979; Hagan *et al*., 1979; Poole and Regoli, 1979; Shover *et al*., 1979; Box, 1981:127; Wiatrowski *et al*., 1981; Canter, 1982; Gove and Crutchfield, 1982; Haskell and Yablonsky, 1982; 1982; Matsueda, 1982; Kaplan and Robbins, 1983; Menard and Morse, 1984; Agnew, 1985; Chapman, 1985; Elliott *et al*., 1985; Junger and Junger, 1985; Liska and Reed, 1985; Patterson and Dishion, 1985; Riley and Shaw, 1985; but cf. Johnson, 1979; Thompson *et al*., 1984.

[3]See Weeks and Smith, 1939; Carr-Saunders, 1942; Kvaraceus, 1945; Schulman, 1949; Glueck and Glueck, 1950; Ferguson, 1952; Monahan, 1957; Toby, 1957; McCord *et al*., 1959; Gold, 1963; Slocum and Stone, 1963; Lunden, 1964; Banks, 1965; West, 1967, 1973; Douglas *et al*., 1968; Bruce, 1970; Empey and Lubeck, 1971; Chilton and Markle, 1972; Datesman and Scarpitti, 1975; Rosen and Neilson, 1978; Wadsworth, 1979; Hamparian *et al*., 1978; Elliott *et al*., 1981; Haskell and Yablonsky, 1982.

[4]See Sullenger, 1936; Kvaraceus, 1945; Glueck and Glueck, 1950; Toby and Toby, 1957; Gold, 1963; Lunden, 1964; Polk, 1965a, 1965b; Polk and Halferty, 1966; Schafer and Polk, 1967; Rhodes and Reiss, 1969; Fisher, 1970; Lanphier and Faulkner, 1970; Burns, 1971; Empey and Lubeck, 1971; Kelly, 1971; Kelly and Balch, 1971; Wolfgang *et al*., 1972; Farrington, 1973; Frease, 1973; Gold and Mann, 1973; Hindelang, 1973; Mugishima and Matsumoto, 1973; Hassall, 1974; Phillips, 1974; Elliott and Voss, 1974; Jensen and Eve, 1976; Thomas *et al*., 1977; Offord *et al*., 1978; Johnson, 1979; Jensen and Rojek, 1980; Figueira-McDonough, 1984; Hartstone and Hansen, 1984.

supported (Phillips and Kelly, 1979), one recent study found delinquency to be more a cause than a consequence of school attachment (Liska and Reed, 1985).

It has been suggested that the correlation between school failure, attachment to the school and delinquency may be spurious, the causal relationship being between low intelligence and delinquency (Wilson and Herrnstein, 1985). On the contrary, the IQ – delinquency association virtually disappears after controlling for school failure and attachment (Hirschi and Hindelang, 1977), and indeed the school failure – delinquency association might itself be almost totally explained by institutional practices such as negative social labeling (Menard and Morse, 1984, 1986; but see Harry and Minor, 1986).

Thus, juveniles who are strongly bonded to their family and the school are less likely to engage in delinquency. While control theory is successful in explaining modest proportions of variance in delinquent behavior, one cannot but wonder if the variance explained would be greater if the theory specified further what it is that socially bonded others do that restrains delinquency. The literature of developmental psychology tells us that parents in loving families do not always use the strong attachments their offspring have toward them to exert effective social control. Loving but laissez-faire families are not very effective at child-rearing (Baumrind, 1971; Patterson, 1982; Hirschi, 1983; Chapman, 1985). Attachment is a necessary but not a sufficient condition for effective social control. Control theory does not adequately answer the question 'attachment for what?' The theory in this book hazards an answer to this question by suggesting that attachments and commitments (interdependency as we conceptualize it) reduce crime when people make use of them to engage in reintegrative shaming.

A second limitation of control theory as articulated by Hirschi is that

it ignores completely the most serious crimes in our society, namely the crimes of the powerful. The crimes of Watergate, of oil-sanction busting in Rhodesia, of illegal war in southeast Asia, of the Great Electrical Conspiracy, of the baby-killer scandal resulting from the promotion and sale of powdered baby milk in the Third World (Chetley, 1979), and so on, ad nauseam, are not even touched by the notions of stake in conformity, attachment to significant others, or beliefs in conventional morality...

(Box, 1981: 153)

Yet if we have an elaboration of control theory which says that the reason that attachment and commitment prevent delinquency is that they make possible certain informal processes of social control, then those informal control processes may well be as relevant to holding white collar crime in check as they are to juvenile delinquency. This is precisely what we claim of reintegrative shaming. Moreover, our theory posits that cultures in which social bonding is intense, with attachment and commitment to the family being the most important kinds of bonding, are cultures which foster reintegrative shaming. These are cultures which can direct effective communitarian control against the most heinous corporate crimes as well as minor delinquencies.

A third limitation of Hirschi's control theory is again best expressed by Box:

it does not claim to explain careers in ordinary conventional crimes – its emphasis on situational subjective factors is at best suited to explaining why many adolescents, and maybe adults, dip into and out of deviant activity without experiencing too much cognitive dissonance or sleepless nights. The behaviour of 'secondary deviants', that is the persistent, habitual, frequent criminal behaviour of self and socially-identified deviants, is not part of its explanatory domain. In this sense, control theory is an explanation of the less serious, comparatively trivial, forms of delinquent behaviour.

(Box, 1981: 153)

To solve this problem, it is necessary to establish a link between control theory (to explain primary deviance) and labeling theory (to explain how stigmatization produces secondary deviance), and subcultural theory (to explain how social support is provided to sustain secondary deviance). The theory of reintegrative shaming supplies these links.

Second, control theory must be complemented by subcultural theory to explain why some uncontrolled persons become race fixers and others street fighters.

Third, and most critically, subcultural theory complements control theory by drawing attention to the fact that some persons direct attachment, commitment, involvement and belief to deviant groups and criminal subcultures as well as to parents and teachers who mostly transmit the anti-criminal dominant culture. Adolescents often have to weigh their stake in conformity to conventional society against their stake in conformity to a delinquent peer group. Business executives regularly must balance their reputation in the wider society and belief in its laws against their loyalty to the company and their ensnarement within its subculture.

Even though control theory is one sided in this way, written narrowly from the standpoint of conventional adult society, it has explanatory power simply because this standpoint is the one with the greatest cultural momentum. We can greatly enhance this explanatory power, however, by accounting for the circumstances where a tipping point is reached beyond which controls exerted by criminal subcultures acquire greater force than controls exerted by the mainstream culture. Such an account is possible if we distinguish reintegrative shaming from stigmatization. Reintegrative shaming keeps most of us on the anti-criminal side of the tipping point most of the time. Stigmatization is required both to create subcultures and to effect a stake in conformity to subcultures which tips differential association in favor of crime. To the extent that stigmatization is strong in the society, there will be more frequent tipping of the balance from favoring a stake in conformity to favoring a stake in deviance. To the extent that reintegrative shaming is strong, control theory explanations will have greater force and subcultural theory explanations lesser force. Partitioning modalities of shaming is therefore the shunt which can connect the main line of control theory and the sidetrack of subcultural theory into an integrated explanatory system.

Opportunity Theory

The seminal work of opportunity theory is Robert K. Merton's *Social Theory and Social Structure* (1957). According to Merton, in any society there are a number of widely shared goals which provide a frame of aspirational reference. The most important of these in America is material success. In addition to cultural goals held up as 'worth striving for', there are defined legitimate institutionalized means for achieving the cultural goals. The legitimate means for achieving the cultural goal of material success are a good education, a good job, investment, and so on.

When an individual has internalized a certain goal, and when the legitimate means for achieving that goal are blocked, the individual is under pressure to resort to illegitimate means to achieve the goal. The child from a poor family learns that he should strive for the cultural goal of material success, but legitimate means of achieving that goal are closed to him because he cannot do well at school, he does not have the 'connections', the 'polish' or the 'presentability' to wangle a good job, and he has no capital for investment. He is therefore in the market for an illegitimate means of achieving the cultural goal he has been taught to value so highly.

Cloward and Ohlin (1960) have been responsible for an important development on the work of Merton in the area of juvenile delinquency. They maintain that if delinquency is to result from the desire to achieve a cultural goal then two things are necessary. First, like Merton, they say legitimate means for achieving the goal must be blocked; but, second, illegitimate means for achieving the goal must be open. Within any given community there may or may not be a system of illegitimate opportunities (a criminal subculture). If, for instance, a lower class adolescent who does not have legitimate access to success goals available to him is sent to live in a respectable middle class suburb with an aging population, he may find that no illegitimate opportunities are available either. There may be no criminal role models and criminal learning structures, no delinquent groups to provide social support for delinquency. Thus having either legitimate paths to success goals open or illegitimate paths closed may be enough to prevent an adolescent from becoming delinquent.

A large number of studies using various awareness of limited opportunity measures have consistently found delinquents to perceive their opportunities as more limited compared to non-delinquents (Elliott, 1961, 1962; Landis, 1962; Short, 1964; Landis and Scarpitti, 1965; Polk, 1965a; Luchterhand and Weller, 1966; Jessor *et al.*, 1968; Wilcox, 1969; McCandless *et al.*, 1972; Brennan and Huizinga, 1975; Datesman *et al.*, 1975; Cernkovich, 1978; Segrave and Hastad, 1985). Short and Strodtbeck (1965:268–9) found that members of delinquent gangs both perceived their legitimate opportunities to be lower than did a sample of non-gang members, and perceived their illegitimate opportunities to be greater compared with the non-gang boys.

A society with large fractions of the population feeling that legitimate opportunities are blocked to them is one with a strain which puts many in the market for illegitimate means of goal attainment. When there is a sufficient density of such people, there is a risk that they will fashion together a criminal subculture that will supply techniques to neutralize guilt over the pursuit of illegitimate opportunities and exchange of information on how to discover and exploit illegitimate opportunities.

Let us imagine, for example, that the government suddenly decides to double sales tax on beer in an effort to discourage consumption. The brewing companies might find as a consequence that legitimate opportunities are blocked for them to achieve their profit or growth targets. They might get together at trade association meetings to curse the government, to begin to suggest to each other that they have no choice but to conspire to fix prices, in other words to fashion a criminal subculture which rationalizes price fixing by blaming the government for it, by appealing to the higher loyalty of saving the jobs of their workers, and which evolves new criminal conduct norms for the industry.

Certain types of societies systematically block legitimate opportunities for fractions of the population, thereby fostering this kind of subculture formation. Societies with adversarial business regulatory cultures where industry is rarely consulted adequately on the design of government regulatory intervention are more likely to regulate in a way which frustrates goal attainment by business. Even where cooperative regulatory styles result in intervention which is equally painful to that resulting under adversarial regulation, the involvement of business in shaping the regulation improves the chances that business will perceive the regulation to be a tolerable frustration. Cooperative regulation is less likely to foster techniques of neutralization which excuse illegitimate means of solving the frustration. In Chapter 9 we consider in more detail the role of adversarial regulation in fomenting business subcultures of resistance to the law.

Societies which systematically deny racial minorities access to a decent or comparable standard of living foster criminal subcultures within those oppressed groups. School systems which systematically block legitimate opportunities to a fraction of the school population by segregation of poor academic performers into stigmatized streams foster delinquent subcultures within that fraction. Once a criminal subculture has formed it can sustain a more generalized reaction against the values of the mainstream culture rather than just the rationalization of illegitimate means to the particular goals which are blocked. Cohen's theory of reaction formation, discussed in the section on subcultural theory, is an example of a theory of generalized rejection of mainstream cultural proscriptions.

Not all blockage of legitimate opportunities has its effect on crime through criminal subculture formation, and not all illegitimate opportunities are created by subcultures. The man who bashes and rapes a woman after she denies consent for legitimate intercourse might be acting as a culturally isolated solitary criminal. On the other hand, the rapist might be influenced by pornographic subcultures of violence toward women which in turn have significant overspills into rationalizations accepted by generally law-abiding citizens (remember the respectable mother who rationalizes stealing if one is hungry). In practice, therefore, it is difficult to disentangle the direct effects of blocked opportunities from effects mediated by subcultures.

Learning about how to exploit illegitimate opportunities, how to rationalize and enjoy social support for doing so, occurs primarily through participation in criminal subcultures. Nevertheless, illegitimate opportunities can be increased in a society in ways that are in no sense mediated by subcultures: motor vehicle ownership rates can rise, increasing opportunities for car theft.

For our present purposes, however, the important point about opportunity theory is that it explains subculture formation. It is this feature of opportunity theory that integrates it with the other great theoretical traditions within the framework of the theory of reintegrative shaming.

Learning Theory

By far the most influential learning theory of crime is Sutherland and Cressey's differential association theory. Differential association maintains that 'a person becomes delinquent because of an excess of definitions favorable to violation of law over definitions unfavorable to violation of law' (Sutherland and Cressey, 1978:81). Essentially, these definitions are acquired in social groups, mostly intimate ones. Motives for crime are not mere rationalizations of fundamental biological drives, but are linguistic constructs; a vocabulary of motives is learnt through differential association. Differential associations vary in frequency, duration, priority and intensity.

Burgess and Akers (1966) were responsible for a behaviorist revision of Sutherland and Cressey as 'differential association – reinforcement theory'. This approach downplayed much of the social element of motives as linguistic constructs which are group products

(Taylor *et al.*, 1973: 130–3) . For Burgess and Akers (1966: 137), 'Criminal behavior is learned according to the principles of operant conditioning'. Such an approach has some impressive empirical support. For example, Akers *et al.* (1979) were able to explain 68 per cent of the variance in marijuana use with questionnaire measures of differential association, differential reinforcement (e.g. praise for not using, perceived probability of punishment), definitions favorable or unfavorable to use (e.g. techniques of neutralization) and imitation ('admired' models who use marijuana).

The most recent learning theory approach to crime, the work of Wilson and Herrnstein (1985), is distinguished from Burgess and Akers by its emphasis on classical as well as operant conditioning. Wilson and Herrnstein's formulation is essentially one of crime as choice. Crime is the choice made by offenders when it is perceived as having consequences preferable to doing something else. The larger the ratio of the net rewards of crime to the net rewards of non-crime, the more likely is crime. The net rewards of crime include a balancing of such things as the likely material gain from crime and social approval of peers against social disapproval of onlookers. The net rewards of non-crime bring in the remunerativeness of legitimate work as an alternative way of employing time to illegitimate work, and the desire to avoid future punishment. This seems a straightforward matter of operant conditioning. However, pangs of conscience are seen as one of the important punishers of crime, and they are seen as a product of classical conditioning. Wilson and Herrnstein believe that conscience differs from calculation and is a powerful force in its own right:

If we were calculators pure and simple, we would realise we can say with impunity anything we wanted while hooked up to the polygraph. A few people are capable of acting this way, but we think them rather odd, as indeed they are: The ability to lie without emotion is a mark of the psychopath. (Wilson and Herrnstein, 1985: 218)

If rules are consistently enforced by parents whose approval is valued by their children, then the experience of conforming to the rules will itself become pleasurable and the thought of breaking them a source of anxiety.

Wilson and Herrnstein rely on operant conditioning to predict that cities will have more crime than rural areas because of the higher density of reinforcers in the former (e.g. more cars to steal), that both the availability of remunerative employment and severe and certain punishment will increase the net rewards of non-crime, that social approval from delinquent friends increases the net rewards of crime. In the next chapter we will see that a number of these predictions are supported by the literature. Wilson and Herrnstein's notion of the ratio of the net rewards of crime to the net rewards of non-crime is essentially a restatement of the principle of differential association.

Classical conditioning is the basis of a number of further predictions which bring in biological causes. 'Persons deficient in conscience may turn out to be persons who for various reasons resist classical conditioning – they do not internalize rules as easily as others' (Wilson and Herrnstein, 1985: 49). Here is one basis for IQ as a correlate of crime. People whose constitution makes them low on conditionability will be both slow to learn (low IQ) and slow to develop a classically conditioned conscience. Criminals are people with autonomic nervous systems that respond more slowly and less vigorously to stimuli.

The rewards of crime are more immediate than the rewards of non-crime, it is argued, so persons who, even with a strong conscience, commit crime, may be persons who have difficulty imagining the future consequences of present action. Again, unintelligent people may have trouble with such imagining. Alternatively, highly impulsive persons may discount very heavily even those consequences they can foresee, and thus resist the operant conditioning that might lead them to choose non-crime over crime. Constitutionally determined IQ and impulsiveness in these and other ways become fundamental causes of crime.

Putting aside measurement problems of IQ tests being biased by class and race, and systematic tendencies for smarter crooks not to get caught, no theory is as blind to the massive reality of white collar crime. White collar criminals are not of low IQ, often they are extraordinarily scheming rather than impulsive. Given the massive volume of white collar crime, it is improbable that the modest IQ and impulsiveness deficits evident in samples of common criminals would survive the inclusion of white collar offenders in accord with the proportion of the offending population they represent. Even when white collar offenders are excluded, it has already been pointed out during the discussion of control theories that the evidence is inconsistent with the conclusion that IQ is causally related to crime.

Wherever we stand on the biological causes of crime, however, we should still be able to accept the core insights of all learning theories that crime is a matter of choices made against a background of reinforcers and punishment. Also we must accept Wilson and Herrnstein's point that human beings are not mere calculators: whether they acquire conscience through classical conditioning or some other process, human beings can and often do choose not to engage in crime when biologically or socially defined rewards of crime seem to exceed costs. They do so out of a commitment to ideas of right and wrong, out of sympathy for others, a sense of justice or equity, and for many other reasons of conscience. A learned conscience is the cornerstone to understanding the potency of reintegrative shaming for explaining law observance.

Unfortunately, however, all of this makes prediction from learning theories problematic. Even knowing fully the balance of intrinsic and socially defined rewards and costs of a particular type of crime does not warrant a prediction because these operant factors might or might not be overwhelmed by classically conditioned conscience.

Cressey (1960:57) has conceded that 'the statement of the differential association process is not precise enough to stimulate rigorous empirical test, and it therefore has not been proved or disproved.' Accordingly Cressey called for future work to specify in more detail the mechanisms which lead to criminal learning. The theory of reintegrative shaming is an attempt to do precisely that. Sutherland and Cressey's (1978: 80–2) nine differential association propositions may be right[5], but unless they are given some specific-

---

[5]The nine propositions are:

1. Criminal behavior is learned; 2. Criminal behavior is learned in interaction with other persons in a process of communication; 3. The principal part of the learning of criminal behavior occurs within intimate personal groups; 4. When criminal behavior is learned, the learning includes (a) techniques of committing the crime, which are sometimes very complicated, sometimes very simple; (b) the specific direction of motives, drives, rationalizations and attitudes; 5. The specific direction of motives and drives is learned from definitions of the legal codes as favorable or unfavorable; 6. A person becomes a delinquent because of an excess of definitions favorable to violation of law over definitions unfavorable to violations of law; 7. Differential associations may vary in frequency, duration, priority and intensity; 8. The process of learning criminal behavior by association with criminal and anticriminal patterns involves all of the mechanisms that are involved in any other learning; 9. While criminal behavior is an expression of general needs and values, it is not explained by those general needs and values, since noncriminal behavior is an expression of the same needs and values (Sutherland and Cressey, 1978: 80-2).

ity of content, they will remain banal, untestable and of limited use for guiding policy. Differential association theory tells us that crime is a function of the ratio of associations favorable to crime and those unfavorable to it. My theory specifies how reintegrative shaming is the process that presents people with behavior patterns unfavorable to crime, and how stigmatization followed by subcultural learning is the process whereby behavior patterns favorable to crime are learned. Chapter 8 shows that this specifies a more genuinely testable theory than differential association, and Chapter 10 reveals that it generates a mix of expected and surprising, uncontroversial and controversial policy predictions that exceed by far those derived from differential association in its basic form.

On Consensus

The theory of reintegrative shaming assumes that there is a core consensus in modern Western societies that compliance with the criminal law is an important social goal. David Ermann (pers. comm., 1987) has pointed out that shaming itself may be one of the factors that creates this consensus. Thus, one might elaborate the theory by suggesting that a society devoid of shaming will not only have rampant crime because of the effects of shaming summarized in Figure 1 (p. 99), but also because without shaming the precondition for those effects to operate will not be met.

Control theory and most learning theories are consensus theories; subcultural theories and differential association assume multiple moralities (dissensus); strain theories like Albert Cohen's or Cloward and Ohlin's assume that juveniles at least start out with a commitment to consensus values, but then strain leads them to seek refuge in subcultures which reject the consensus; labeling theory really makes no assumptions about societal consensus.

Subcultural theories, either in an unadulterated form, or as theories of blocked opportunity leading to subcultural participation, therefore pose a problem in any scheme which sets out to synthesize them with consensus theories. But the extent to which this is a problem depends on what we are assuming consensus about, and on how widely diffused criminal subcultures are believed to be. The theory developed here does not assume consensus on a far-reaching set of mainstream cultural values. We have already argued that value consensus versus dissensus has been an unusually fruitless pursuit in criminological research, thanks to the false leads of grand subculturalists such as Walter Miller. We only assume here consensus over the content of most criminal laws. The facts are that, putting aside a degree of dissensus concerning a small number of victimless crimes like prostitution, homosexuality and marijuana use, there is overwhelming consensus, at least in contemporary democracies, that most acts which are crimes should be crimes. Moreover, different groups – blacks compared with whites, young compared with old, judges and police compared with ordinary citizens, highly educated people compared with the uneducated – support very similar relative rankings of the seriousness of long lists of criminal offenses (r normally > 0.80). These conclusions are now supported by many studies from various countries (Rose and Prell, 1955; Sellin and Wolfgang, 1964; Wright and Cox, 1967a, 1967b; Kutchinsky, 1973; Wilson and Brown, 1973; NSW Bureau of Crime Statistics and Research, 1974; Rossi *et al.*, 1974; Chilton and DeAmicis, 1975; Figlio, 1975; Riedel, 1975; Wellford and Wiatrowski, 1975; Newman, 1976; Thomas *et al.*, 1976; Hamilton and Rytina, 1980; Pontell *et al.*, 1983; Kwasniewski, 1984; Rossi *et al.*, 1985; but note the caveats of Miethe, 1982, 1984 and Cullen *et al.*, 1985).

Thus, extreme versions of subculturalism which posit wholesale rejection of the criminal law by substantial sections of the community simply do not wash. Fagins are very unusual; the evidence is that even parents who themselves have criminal records try to instill respect for the law in their children. As West (1982:49) reported: 'parental attitudes toward delinquency were almost always censorious, regardless of the parents' own delinquent history'. Most criminal subcultures do not suggest that criminal laws are wrong; rather they supply rationalizations of different sorts for why a particular circumstance of offending is not 'really' a crime or not a 'serious' crime.

Glaser (1978: 6) distinguishes predatory crime (where an offender preys on others) from nonpredatory crime. The latter is a clearer concept than victimless crime because of dispute over whether prostitutes are victimized by their occupation, and the like. Both the contemporary survey research evidence and the historical record support Glaser's (1978: 31–2) conclusion that while laws against predatory crime originate in conflict among classes, 'once they are enacted, extensive consensus develops across class lines, making them become cumulative'. Conflict persists, however, over statutes that penalize nonpredatory offenses, and new conflict arises whenever attempts are made to extend the criminal law to previously legal forms of predation.

The consensus therefore is limited to the established accumulation of predatory crimes. If one tried to generalize the theory of reintegrative shaming to a global theory of deviance, instead of just a theory of predatory crime in modern industrialized societies, one would be in deep trouble. Beyond predatory criminal law, analyses rooted in ongoing conflict rather than consensus have the greater merit. However, the criminal law is uniquely designed as a cautious consensus instrument: the pressure to get crimes off the books when there is division over them is considerable, as is the pressure to deal with misbehavior in ways other than criminalization when significant minorities see criminalization as unjust. Jurisprudential opinion leaders are forever warning of the dangers of eroding respect for the criminal law if it strays from that which the overwhelming mass of the populace will accept.

Crude conflict theorists who contend that the criminal law is a manifestation of ruling class interests are simply wrong. As Jock Young (1975:71) has pointed out, working class support for the criminal law is widespread and better explained by the interests which the criminal law does to some extent serve for the working class than by any glib resort to 'false consciousness':

However much the new deviancy theorist talked of diversity and dissensus in society, the ineluctable reality of a considerable consensus over certain matters could not be wished away. This was particularly noticeable, moreover, in the widespread and uniform social reaction against various forms of deviancy (and, especially, against crimes against the person and certain crimes against property).

An effectively functioning criminal law is, if anything, more in the interests of the working class than the ruling class because their lives, if not their property, are at greater risk from crime in the streets (Hindelang *et al.*, 1978; Najman, 1980) and from occupational health and safety offenses (Reiman, 1979; Reasons *et al.*, 1981; Frank, 1985).

In modern capitalist societies there are many more statutes that criminalize the behavior of corporations (anti-pollution laws, occupational health and safety laws, consumer protection laws, antitrust laws, laws to enforce compliance with standards for everything from elevators to cleaning animal cages in laboratories) than there are laws that criminalize the behavior of the poor. Moreover, under many of the business statutes, *mens rea* is not required for proof of guilt; self-incrimination can be forced on defendants; search and seizure without warrant are provided for; and due process protections are generally weak (Grabosky and Braithwaite, 1986).

None of this is to deny the existence of profound class bias in the way laws are often administered. The common disjunction between tough laws against business and weak enforcement of them indicates a need to separate the instrumental and symbolic effects of legislation (Edelman, 1964; Gusfield, 1967; Carson, 1975; O'Malley, 1980; Hopkins and Parnell, 1984). Edelman is undoubtedly correct when he says that unorganized and diffuse publics tend to receive symbolic rewards, while organized professional ones reap tangible rewards.

While the criminal law in action may be massively class biased, the criminal law in the books is difficult to construe this way. Thus, scholarship which takes the law in the books as an authoritative definition of crime (as this book does) cannot fairly be characterized as criminology which legitimates ruling class hegemony. It certainly can be argued that the law in general is structurally, if not instrumentally, in the interests of capital. The *criminal* law in the books, in contrast, is instrumentally and structurally in the interests of the working class. The empirical evidence is voluminous that the community consensus is extraordinarily punitive toward ruling class crime, and that the criminal law more or less adequately crystallizes this consensus.[6] While the criminal law in action can in various ways be characterized as repressive of the working class, the criminal law in the books is more reflective of a progressive consensus which has emerged over the last century for punishing powerful offenders at least as harshly as powerless offenders who do equal wrongs.

This is not to say that the consensus is total or free of *any* class content. For example Miethe (1984:472) showed that within the framework of whites and blacks agreeing on the absolute and rela-

[6]See Newman, 1957; Rettig and Pasamanick, 1959; Joint Commission on Correctional Manpower and Training, 1968; Gibbons, 1969; Time Magazine, 1969; Wilson and Brown, 1973; Carroll *et al.*, 1974; Rossi *et al.*, 1974; Reed and Reed, 1975; Conklin, 1977; Scott and Al-Thakeb, 1977; Australian Law Reform Commission, 1980:28; Schrager and Short, 1980; Wolfgang, 1980; Broadhurst *et al.*, 1981; Cullen *et al.*, 1982, 1983; Salas *et al.*, 1982:512–14; Jones and Levi, 1983; Sebba, 1983; Frank *et al.*, 1984; Grabosky *et al.*, 1987.

tive seriousness of white collar crimes compared with other kinds of crime, whites considered white collar crime *against* business (e.g. embezzlement) as slightly more serious than did blacks, while blacks regarded crimes by business against consumers (e.g. short weight, price fixing, false advertising) as slightly more serious than whites (see also Rossi *et al.*, 1985).

If subculturalism based on wide sectors of the populace rejecting the criminal law, or on most persons at certain locations in the social structure (e.g. the lower class) having distinctive criminogenic values is out, then what kind of subculturalism is acceptable? It is a proliferation of narrowly diffused subcultures, mostly transmitted by disorganized groups which approve disparate, even idiosyncratic, value commitments and behavioral repertoires. Some tiny subcultures might go close to a wholesale rejection of the morality of all criminal law and substitution of pro-criminal values; but more often, as argued earlier, they foster 'drift', 'neutralization' or 'dissociation', or single issue negation of the moral claims of criminal law (e.g. drug use, toxic waste dumping (Block and Scarpitti, 1985)).

Even Hirschi's (1969) control theory accepts, against the background of adult consensus over criminal law, the notion of significant numbers of juveniles becoming delinquent because of a temporary loosening of 'belief' in the desirability of staying within the confines of the law, though Hirschi denies, mistakenly I think, that this suspension of 'belief' has much to do with collective support from delinquent peers.

Second, the conception of subculturalism in the theory of reintegrative shaming suggests in Chapter 4 that the groups which transmit subcultures of predatory crime are not numerically strong. Subcultures do not have to be omnipresent to play a vital role in criminological theory. As Box (1981) has argued, the concepts of control theory, and, one might add, opportunity theory, do a reasonable job of explaining primary or episodic deviance. Secondary deviance, or persistent patterns of criminality, particularly of a sort which require extensive job training in the illegitimate labor market, necessitate the explanatory concepts of labeling and subcultural theories.

Most of us have engaged in episodic acts of delinquency that can be explained by a loosening of controls. While most of us may have experimented with illegal drugs in our youth, generally we do not continue to do so as mature adults; we never establish ongoing relationships with the subculture of drug distribution, corruption, property crime and social support for use. Because secondary deviance is exceptional, subcultures that enjoy support from only a tiny minority can do a reasonable job of explaining it.

Those who support control theory and disparage subcultural and labeling theories are rather too forgetful of the fact that episodic acts of primary delinquency are the much less important part of the crime problem compared to the activities of people who find networks of support for permanent part-time work in the illegitimate job market and even full-time illegitimate work. The methodology of self-reported delinquency, which is swamped by minor acts of episodic delinquency, seduces much empirical criminology into allowing the more measurable to drive out the more important.

In short, the tension between 'consensus-based' control theory and 'dissensus-based' subcultural theory can be reconciled by a realistic perception of how isolated,but nevertheless important, criminal subcultures are in the wider society. Thus, we do need control theory to bring young offenders to the doorstep of criminal subcultures; stigmatization (labeling theory) to open the door; and we need subcultural and learning theory to maintain the house as a rewarding place for secondary deviants to stay in. In Chapter 4 we begin the task of putting these elements together in the theory of reintegrative shaming; but first we must be clear on the facts our theory of crime must fit.

3

Facts a theory of crime ought to fit

The theory of reintegrative shaming was developed not only to generate new predictions and new policy implications about crime, but also to explain as adequately as possible what are the well-established strong relationships between crime and other variables. Below are a list of what I believed to be, in developing the theory, the strongest and most consistently supported associations in empirical criminology, bearing in mind that we are concerned with a general theory and not with propositions relevant only to specific types of crime. Any credible theory would at least have to be consistent with these findings, and preferably would offer an explanation for most of them.

1. *Crime is committed disproportionately by males.*

   In most, if not all, societies men constitute over 90 per cent of adult prison populations. Arrest and court data also consistently show in all countries (e.g. Simon and Sharma, 1979)a massive overrepresentation of men in criminal statistics, while self-report measures tend to show much more modest gender differences in offending rates (e.g. Braithwaite, 1977: 26; Smith and Visher, 1980; Canter, 1982; Warner, 1982; Ouston, 1984; McGarrell and Flanagan, 1985:340–1; Morash, 1986; Riley, 1986). Smith and Visher's (1980) review of forty-four studies suggests that the more serious the type of offense, the greater the gender differences in rates of offending.

   Following up on modest gender differences in self-report studies, some have suggested that women benefit from a 'chivalry' factor in enforcement and criminal sentencing (Krohn *et al.*, 1983; Zingraff and Thompson, 1984; Staples, 1984), but this has been hotly disputed in the literature (Scutt, 1979; Hancock, 1980). Any evidence of 'chivalry' in the criminal justice system

44

is certainly insufficient to explain a finding of twenty times as many male as female homicide offenders in a nation's prisons (Walker and Biles, 1985: 13, 60–1).

Some contend that the gap between male and female offending rates is shrinking (Adler, 1975; Smith and Visher, 1980), while others conclude that any such increases have been modest or restricted to property offenses of the type traditionally engaged in by females (Steffensmeier, 1978; Steffensmeier and Steffensmeier, 1980; Mukherjee and Fitzgerald, 1981; Challinger, 1982; Ageton, 1983; Box and Hale, 1983). What is beyond doubt is that massive gender differences remain (Ramsay, 1984).

The other source of data consistently confirming this is victim surveys, where victims are asked to recall, where possible, the gender of their offender(s). The first Australian National Crime Victims Survey, for example, found the ratio of male to female victim-reported offenders to range from 6 to 20 depending on the type of offense (Braithwaite and Biles, 1980: 51). American victim surveys suggest female crime as a proportion of total crime quite similar to that derived from Uniform Crime Reports (Hindelang, 1979). Even observational data on as 'traditionally female' an offense as shoplifting has shown men proportionally twice as likely to shoplift as women (Buckle and Farrington, 1984).

As Smart (1976) and many others have pointed out, traditional criminological theory has tended to concentrate on male delinquency and has failed utterly in explaining why massive gender differences in offending persist in all societies at all points of time for which data exist.

2. *Crime is perpetrated disproportionately by 15-25 year olds.*
Data on persons found guilty or cautioned in England and Wales for indictable offenses show that offenses per 100,000 population increase sharply from age 10 to peak at age 15-18 and then decline sharply to reach low levels by the late 20s, which gradually become even lower for the remainder of the life cycle (Riley and Shaw, 1985: 3). A similar pattern with minor variations can be seen in all societies (e.g. FBI, 1981: 200–1). Hirschi and Gottfredson (1983) conclude that this age structure of offending has been essentially invariate across cultures and historical periods and for different types of crime. Greenberg has

challenged the sweeping nature of this claim by suggesting that youth in some historical and societal contexts are more marginalized and more prone to crime than others (Greenberg, 1977, 1985; but see Hirschi and Gottfredson, 1985).

There is a more fundamental problem with the seemingly uncontroversial conclusion that crime is perpetrated disproportionately by 15-25 year olds. This is that for the major category of crime barely captured in criminal statistics – white collar crime – the opposite is probably true. People under 25 are the least likely age group to engage in white collar crime because to do so requires incumbency in high status occupational roles which most under-25s have yet to attain. Here we are following the conventional definition by Sutherland (1983: 7) of white collar crime as 'a crime committed by a person of respectability and high status in the course of his occupation'. Arguably, income tax evasion and some other types of fraud against government (e.g. welfare cheating) do not fit this definition. Interestingly, Rowe and Tittle (1977) found self-reported tax cheating among 33 per cent of 15-24 year olds, 28 per cent of 25-44 year olds, 14 per cent of 45-64 year olds and 8 per cent of 65-93 year olds.

Thus, a more appropriately qualified expression of this generalization from the literature would be that *for those offenses which persons of all ages have opportunities to commit, crime is committed disproportionately by 15-25 year olds*; or a more precise formulation might be, *for those offenses which do not require incumbency in high status occupational roles, crime is committed disproportionately by 15-25 year olds.*

3. *Crime is committed disproportionately by unmarried people.*
The same qualification about white collar crime applies here. Nevertheless, putting aside white collar crime, there can be no doubt about the strong and consistent bivariate association between being unmarried and higher offending (Martin *et al.*, 1979, Parisi *et al.*, 1979: 628; South Australian Office of Crime Statistics, 1980; Wolfe *et al.*, 1984).

Unfortunately, however, the literature has devoted little attention to the question of the extent to which married people have lower crime rates because they are older on average than unmarried persons. The Cambridge study found only a very modest tendency for those who had married by age 21 or 22 to engage in fewer subsequent offenses by age 24 (West, 1982:100–4). Sutherland and Cressey (1978:226) report residual marital status effects after some controls for age. In the face of these limited data, the question of whether the marriage effect is no more than a consequence of the age effect must remain open.

4. *Crime is committed disproportionately by people living in large cities.*
Crimes are reported to the police at a higher rate in larger cities than in smaller cities, at a higher rate in smaller cities than in rural areas, and within larger cities at a higher rate in the core cities than in the suburbs (e.g. Clinard and Abbott, 1973; Ames, 1981: 61; FBI, 1985: 145–6; cf. Archer and Gartner, 1984: 98–117). Victim surveys also support the association between large city life and high crime rates (Braithwaite and Biles, 1980; McGarrell and Flanagan, 1985: 286), as do self-reported delinquency surveys (McGarrell and Flanagan, 1985: 373). In the United States there is a positive correlation between city size and the proportion of the population which is black; however, an association between urbanism and crime does remain after controlling for percentage black (Laub, 1983). There are no systematic data on the ecological distribution of white collar crime, but almost all instances described in the literature occur in cities, mostly large cities where financial and industrial activity is concentrated (but see Lane, 1953).

5. *Crime is committed disproportionately by people who have experienced high residential mobility and who live in areas characterized by high residential mobility.*
Geographical mobility was a key variable in the social disorganization school; Shaw and McKay (1969) and their University of Chicago followers felt that mobile individuals who were liable to move at any time did not feel concerned about enforcing informal social control in the neighborhood, and were in turn less susceptible to informal controls exercised by others. From the 1930s an impressive body of evidence accumulated associating residential mobility and crime (Sullenger, 1936; Longmoor and Young, 1936; Porterfield, 1948; Reiss, 1951; Nye, 1958; Eaton and Polk, 1961; Clinard, 1964; Lunden, 1964; Shaw and McKay, 1969; Clinard and Abbott, 1973; Sampson *et al.*, 1981; Crutchfield *et al.*, 1982).

6. *Young people who are strongly attached to their school are less likely to engage in crime.*

We have already covered the strong evidence for this association in the discussion of control theory in Chapter 2 (pp. 28-9). This is the first of a number of propositions which only have application to juvenile offenders, in this case because adults rarely attend school.

7. *Young people who have high educational and occupational aspirations are less likely to engage in crime.*

The overwhelming evidence for this has also already been discussed in Chapter 2 (pp. 28-9).

8. *Young people who do poorly at school are more likely to engage in crime*

See earlier discussion in Chapter 2 at (pp. 28-9).

9. *Young people who are strongly attached to their parents are less likely to engage in crime.*

See earlier discussion in Chapter 2 at (pp. 27-9).

10. *Young people who have friendships with criminals are more likely to engage in crime themselves.*

See earlier discussion in Chapter 2 at (p. 21).

11. *People who believe strongly in the importance of complying with the law are less likely to violate the law.*

This association, as mentioned in Chapter 2, has been consistently supported in the literature (Short and Strodtbeck, 1965; Hirschi, 1969; Hindelang, 1970, 1974; Siegal *et al*, 1973; Silberman, 1976; Hepburn, 1977; Minor, 1977; Thomas and Hyman, 1978; Akers *et al*, 1979; Grasmick and Green, 1980; Braithwaite and Braithwaite, 1981; Wiatrowski *et al*, 1981; Thurman, 1984; but see Rankin, 1977). There has been limited attention in the literature to the possibility that law-breaking behavior causes a diminution in respect for the law, rather than the reverse. With self-report studies there has also been a neglect of the likelihood that social desirability bias might cause the error in reports of respect for the law and reports of law breaking to be negatively correlated.

12. *For both women and men, being at the bottom of the class structure, whether measured by socio-economic status, socio-economic status of the area in which the person lives, being unemployed, being a member of an oppressed racial minority (e.g. blacks in the US), increases rates of offending for all types of crime apart from those for which opportunities are systematically less available to the poor (i.e. white collar crime).*

This used to be uncontroversial, but became controversial in the 1960s and 1970s with a large number of self-report studies of delinquency which produced slight and statistically non-significant class differences or differences between blacks and whites in the United States. Tittle *et al.* (1978) have been the main proponents of the view that class is at best an inconsequential correlate of crime, while I have been on the other side of this debate (Braithwaite, 1979, 1980). My contention is that self-report measures have biases which exaggerate the proportion of delinquency perpetrated by middle class juveniles, and that massive class and race differences for officially recorded offenses of high reportability such as homicide and car theft cannot be explained away. It is also difficult to explain away the finding that 'surveys of victims of crimes [in the US] reveal that of the offenders whose racial identity could be discerned by their victims, about half were black; for the most serious offenses two-thirds were black' (Wilson and Herrnstein, 1985: 29). Nevertheless, this is perhaps the most controversial entry on our list.

13. *Crime rates have been increasing since World War II in most countries, developed and developing. The only case of a country which has been clearly shown to have had a falling crime rate in this period is Japan.*

Interpol statistics and other sources (e.g. Gurr, 1977a; Gurr *et al.*, 1977; Mukherjee, 1981: 32; Landau, 1984) suggest that, apart from the classic case of Japan, which will be discussed in Chapter 4, crime rates from countries for which reasonably reliable data are available have tended to increase in the period since World War II. Apart from Japan, Switzerland is the only country that might be construed as having an overall fall in the crime rate since World War II (Gurr, 1977b; but see Clinard, 1978). As Wilson and Herrnstein (1985:416–17) conclude, the general increase can be partly explained by the changing age structure of the population; but, controlling for age, 'between 1960 and 1973, the arrest rate for homicide of persons in the age group fifteen to twenty-four increased by 69 per cent [in the US]'.

The trend has not in all cases been continuously upward and consistently reflected for all types of offenses. For example, between 1980 and 1984 the rate of reported index offenses in the United States dropped 15 per cent, but even so in 1984 it was still higher than it was in the mid-seventies and much higher than before the crime explosion of the 1960s (FBI, 1985: 43). In some countries, crime trends during the twentieth century might be conceived as conforming to a U-curve, with decreases early in the century, a mid-century trough, and then the post-war increase. Consider Mukherjee's (1981) work on Australia, for example (see also Wilson and Herrnstein, 1985: 409–10). Evidence on crime trends across the nineteenth and twentieth centuries for a small number of countries will be discussed further in Chapter 8. The data from most countries are simply not available to make generalizations on longer term trends. The only generalization we can make with confidence about historical crime trends is one of a general post-war increase.

The Failure of the Dominant Theories to Explain These Findings

Most of the entries on this checklist would be uncontroversial to those familiar with the criminological literature. Most debate would center on what else should be added to a list of what we most confidently know. I do not propose to aggravate the reader by raking through the entire literature of criminology to dis-count why other relationships are insufficiently strong or insuffi-ciently consistently supported to justify inclusion on the list.

The contention in the conclusion to this work will be that the theory developed here better explains these thirteen powerful associations than any other in the literature. It is amazing that such basic, potent and uncontroversial correlates of crime as age and sex remain totally untouched by most of the dominant theories.

Opportunity theories measure up badly against this list. The class-crime association, school failure and crime association, and perhaps the urbanity–crime association, are the only items from our list on which opportunity theories make an impression. Females have low crime rates, yet suffer more profound oppor-tunity blockages than males.

The most influential subcultural theories (Cohen, 1955; Mil-ler, 1958; Cloward and Ohlin, 1960; Wolfgang and Ferracuti, 1967) are driven by a concern with the criminality of lower class subcultures, and for similar reasons to opportunity theory do not make much of an impression on our list.

Control theory clearly does well in explaining points 6 to 9. As for labeling theory, it would require quite a bit of development to explain any of the items on the list; but then its defenders would point out that the labeling perspective is not about explaining the 'facts of crime', it is about rendering those facts problematic. Ironically, however, the theory in this book begins its effort to explain as many of these associations as it can through refining the concepts of the labeling perspective.

Learning theories do best at accounting for these facts. Sutherland and Cressey (1978: 77–298) have devoted a lot of space to explaining some of them in differential association terms. The lack of specificity of differential association, however, makes explanation possible only by invoking many variables not explicitly included in the theory. For example, low female rates of offending are explained by the fact that females become pregnant, resulting in closer supervision of girls and less emphasis in their socialization on being rough and tough (Sutherland and Cressey, 1978: 135). I do not propose to go through Sutherland and Cressey's account of how differential association theory can explain the best known facts of crime. The point is that I agree with them that differential association provides a framework which can be used to do so. The difficulty is in how you put the specificity required into the framework so that the explanations are explicitly incorporated into a refutable theory.

In their learning theory, Wilson and Herrnstein (1985) have not provided an account *in terms of the theory* of why females should engage in less crime. Unlike the other theorists, Wilson and Herrnstein do provide an account linked to their theory of the age–crime association that is persuasive and that overlaps the explanation provided in the theory of reintegrative shaming:

The rise in crime in childhood and early puberty accompanies the awakening of major sources of reinforcement for delinquent behavior – money, sex, and peers who value independence of, or even defiance of, conventional morality. At the same time, the growing child is becoming literally, as well as psychologically, independent of powerful adults (parents etc.) who might enforce conventional standards. Given energy, strength, potent new sources of drive but few legitimate means of consummation, a lack of economic and social skills, and peers who are similarly vigorous and frustrated, the adolescent years are destined to foster a rise in delinquency.   (Wilson and Herrnstein, 1985: 146)

Wilson and Herrnstein do not provide an account of the association between crime and marital status (proposition 3). The city-size–crime link is accounted for by the greater density of rewards for crime (opportunities) in big cities (proposition 4). Young people who are more attached to their parents are seen as more susceptible to punishment by social disapproval of parents (proposition 9). Residential mobility is seen as threatening the attachment to and social disapproval of neighbors (proposition 5). Propositions 6 to 8 are largely, though not totally, viewed as a by-product of the more fundamental associations between IQ, impulsiveness and delinquency.

The association with delinquent friends proposition (10) is also obviously supported by all learning theories. Belief in the importance of complying with the law (proposition 11) is explained by the punishing effect of pangs of conscience in altering the net rewards of crime. Poverty reduces the net rewards of non-crime (proposition 12). Wilson and Herrnstein even provide an account of rising post-war crime rates which we will discuss in Chapter 9 in some detail.

Learning theories can do much better than the other dominant theories in accounting for what we know about crime, and they can do this without resort to constitutional determinants. Indeed, by jettisoning a concern with Wilson and Herrnstein's constitutional determinants, and instead focusing upon the *learning* elements of their theory, it is possible to provide an account of gender and crime within the theory, and a superior account of some of the other well-known correlates of crime, The theory of reintegrative shaming attempts to do this.

My theory is partly a learning theory of crime. It is one that aspires to do an even better job than existing learning theories of explaining what we know, and it seeks to do so with much more specific propositions which are more refutable than the existing rather vague theories. The specificity and testability is achieved by dissecting shaming as the reinforcer of crime and conformity which is more critical than other reinforcers. The capacity to enhance explanation of what we know is also achieved by integrating control, subcultural, opportunity and labeling theory into a cognitive learning theory framework organized around the partitioning of reintegrative shaming from stigmatization.

4

The family model of the criminal process: reintegrative shaming

After an empirical study of *The Impact of Publicity on Corporate Offenders*, Brent Fisse and I concluded:

> If we are serious about controlling corporate crime, the first priority should be to create a culture in which corporate crime is not tolerated. The informal processes of shaming unwanted conduct and of praising exemplary behavior need to be emphasized.   (Fisse and Braithwaite, 1983: 246).

However, in that book, and in an earlier contribution with Gilbert Geis, a sharp distinction was made between the merits of shaming for controlling corporate crime and its demerits with crime in the streets.

> A major risk in apprehending the traditional criminal is that the stigmatizing process will push him further and further into a criminal self-concept. This is the contention of labeling theory. Evidence such as that from the Cambridge longitudinal study of delinquency has been interpreted as support for the labeling hypothesis. This study showed that boys who were apprehended for and convicted of delinquent offenses became more delinquent than boys who were equally delinquent to begin with but who escaped apprehension... These labeling arguments cannot readily be applied to corporate offenders. They are likely to regard themselves as unfairly maligned pillars of respectability, and no amount of stigmatization is apt to convince them otherwise. One does meet people who have a mental image of themselves as a thief, a safecracker, a prostitute, a pimp, drug runner, and even a hit man, but how often does one meet a person who sees himself as a corporate criminal? The young black offender can often enhance his status back on the street by having done some time, but the reaction of the corporate criminal to incarceration is shame and humiliation.
> (Braithwaite and Geis, 1982: 300–1)

The purpose of this book is to show that the conclusions of these two earlier works about the efficacy of shaming for controlling corporate crime do in fact apply to common crime as well. Cultural commitments to shaming are the key to controlling all types of crime. However, for all types of crime, shaming runs the risk of counterproductivity when it shades into stigmatization.

The crucial distinction is between shaming that is reintegrative and shaming that is disintegrative (stigmatization). Reintegrative shaming means that expressions of community disapproval, which may range from mild rebuke to degradation ceremonies, are followed by gestures of reacceptance into the community of law-abiding citizens. These gestures of reacceptance will vary from a simple smile expressing forgiveness and love to quite formal ceremonies to decertify the offender as deviant. Disintegrative shaming (stigmatization), in contrast, divides the community by creating a class of outcasts. Much effort is directed at labeling deviance, while little attention is paid to de-labeling, to signifying forgiveness and reintegration, to ensuring that the deviance label is applied to the behavior rather than the person, and that this is done under the assumption that the disapproved behavior is transient, performed by an essentially good person. Quoting Suchar, Page (1984: 10) sees the defining characteristic of stigmatization as assignment of a deviant characteristic to the person as a master status.

The individual...is assigned a 'master status trait': homosexual, drug addict, prostitute, juvenile delinquent, or others... this label will dominate all other 'characteristics' of the individual; 'good athlete', 'good conversationalist', 'good dancer', and the like are subordinated to or negated by this trait which is immediately felt to be more central to the 'actual' identity of the individual.

One might think that, notwithstanding the criminogenic consequences of assignment to a deviant master status, stigmatization might still be more useful for crime control than reintegrative shaming because being made an outcast is a more terrible sanction than being shamed and then forgiven. The theory will come to reject this view because the nub of deterrence is not the severity of the sanction but its social embeddedness; shame is more deterring when administered by persons who continue to be of importance to us; when we become outcasts we can reject our rejectors and the shame no longer matters to us. We will see in the next chapter that the deterrence literature supports the view that the severity of sanctions is a poor predictor of the effectiveness of social control, while the social embeddedness of sanctions is an important predictor.

The Family Model

The best place to see reintegrative shaming at work is in loving families. Griffiths has described a 'family model' of the criminal process as one in which, instead of punishment being administered within the traditional framework of disharmony and fundamentally irreconcilable interests, it is imposed within a framework of reconcilable, even mutually supportive interests:

> Offenses, in a family, are normal, expected ocurrences. Punishment is not something a child receives in isolation from the rest of his relationship to the family; nor is it something which presupposes or carries with it a change of status from 'child' to 'criminal child'. When a parent punishes his child, both parent and child know that afterward they will go on living together as before. The child gets his punishment, as a matter of course, within a continuum of love, after his dinner and during his toilet training and before bed-time story and in the middle of general family play, and he is punished in his own unchanged capacity as a child with failings (like all other children) rather than as some kind of distinct and dangerous outsider.
>
> (Griffiths, 1970: 376)

Family life teaches us that shaming and punishment are possible while maintaining bonds of respect. Two hypotheses are suggested: first, families are the most effective agents of social control in most societies partly because of this characteristic; second, those families that are disintegrative rather than reintegrative in their punishment processes, that have not learnt the trick of punishing within a continuum of love, are the families that fail at socializing their children.

The second hypothesis is consistent with the child development literature (consider, e.g., Berkowitz, 1973; Patterson, 1982). Perhaps the classic studies in this genre are those of Baumrind (1971, 1978). She found an 'authoritative' child rearing style which combined firm control (setting clear standards and insisting on compliance with them) with nurture and encouragement more likely to secure superior control of undesirable behavior such as aggression than 'authoritarian' (close control by parents who were cold and detached) or 'permissive' (loose control by nurturant parents) child rearing styles.

For social learning theory reasons alone, families in which disapproval rather than approval is the normal state of affairs are incapable of socializing children by withdrawal of approval. Trasler explains why the effectiveness of shaming depends on continued social integration in a relationship sustained by social approval:

The contrast between the ordinary enjoyment of [parents'] approval and the distress of being temporarily out of favour is essential; if the child is constantly fearful and insecure in his relationship with his parents, the withdrawal-of-approval technique will not succeed in establishing a specific avoidance response. (Trasler, 1972: 144)

Our theory predicts that cultures in which the 'family model' is applied to crime control both within and beyond the family will be cultures with low crime rates. The family analogy forces us to think more clearly about what we mean by shaming, however.

What is Shaming?

Developmental psychologists sometimes like to make distinctions between soclization by shaming and by guilt-induction (Dienstbier *et al.*, 1975; see also French, 1985). Shaming, according to this distinction, follows transgressions with expressions of the lower esteem the offense has produced in the eyes of external referents like parents and neighbors; guilt-induction responds to transgressions with admonitions concerning how remorseful the child should feel within herself for perpetrating such an evil act. The distinction is rather too fine for our theoretical purposes because 'guilt-induction' always implies shaming by the person(s) inducing the guilt and because, as we will argue later, in broader societal terms guilt is only made possible by cultural processes of shaming. For our purposes, to induce guilt and to shame are inextricably part of the same social process. This is not to deny the distinction which Benedict (1946) and others make between guilt as a failure to live up to the standards of one's own conscience and shame as a reaction to criticism by other people. But you cannot *induce* guilt without implying criticism by others. In other words, from the perspective of the offender, guilt and shame may be distinguishable, but guilt *induction* and sham*ing* are both criticism by others. Equally, the old distinction between shame and guilt cultures has no place in my theoretical framework because the consciences which cause us guilt are, according to the theory, formed by shaming in the culture.

Of what, then, does shaming consist? It can be subtle: a frown, a tut-tut, a snide comment, a turning of the back, a slight shaking of the head, a laugh; it can be a direct verbal confrontation in which the offender is admonished about how guilty she should feel or how shocked her relatives and friends are over her conduct; it can be indirect confrontation by gossip which gets back to the offender; it can be broadcast via the mass media or by a private medium (as when the feminist paints a slogan on the front fence of a rapist); it can be officially pronounced by a judge from the bench or by a government which names a wrongdoer in an official report or in the chamber of the legislature; it can be popularized in mass culture by a film which moralizes about a certain act of wrongdoing.

The modalities of shaming are often culturally specific: in republican Rome criminals had the doors of their house burned, and persons who had been wronged followed their offenders about dressed in mourning clothes and with dishevelled hair, sometimes chanting against the person at home or in public places (Lintott, 1968; cited in Bayley, 1985: 22). In Cuban or Chinese Peoples' Courts, ordinary citizens verbally denounce wrongdoing as part of the trial process. Freidson and Rhea (1972) showed that the almost universal sanction applied to clinic doctors who engaged in professional deviance was for colleagues and administrators to 'talk to them', first 'man to man', then if this did not work, by enlisting the aid of other talkers, up to the ultimate sanction of a talking-to by a formal committee of colleagues. Under the time-honored naval tradition of 'Captain's mast', a seaman who fell asleep on watch, for example, could be denounced by the captain in the presence of members of the ship's company assembled on deck for the purpose of shaming him. In Crow Indian culture, shaming is effected by a polite mocking of another's inappropriate behavior called 'buying-of-the-ways'.

One Indian recalled a childhood occasion when he became angry and reacted by laying on the ground and pouting, not in and of itself unusual. However, another playmate laid on the ground next to him and imitated his pouting, thereby 'buying his ways'. Through such mimicry, the first pouting child sees his own action and is reminded of his inappropriate behavior....

On occasion, and particularly among adults, the correcting scenario of ridicule is accentuated by the 'buyer-of-the-ways' actually approaching the rule violator and offering a small token of money (i.e., several dollars) which is supposed to be graciously accepted, even if with embarrassment. The buyer then announces to onlookers what has taken place and what is about

to take place, at which time the buyer rather dramatically repeats the
inappropriate behavior.   (Austin, 1984: 36)

Though shaming is often associated with a formal punishment, it
does not have to be, as in this Crow example where shaming
(informal punishment) is actually associated with a tangible reward.

The Uncoupling of Shame and Punishment

Western theorizing on deterrence often refers to the greater importance of the shame associated with punishment than of the punishment itself. Andenaes (1974:78) put it this way:

That the offender is subjected to the rejection and contempt of society serves
as a deterrent; the thought of the shame of being caught and of the subsequent conviction is for many stronger than the thought of the punishment
itself.

Andenaes continued that the ducking stool, the stocks and the
pillory were 'not only instruments of corporal punishment but were
used to reduce the status of the offender as well' (Andenaes, 1974:
78-9)

Yet the recent history of Western punishment practices has
amounted to a systematic uncoupling of punishment and public
shaming. The public visibility of the pillory and the chain-gang were
replaced by penal practices to warehouse offenders away from public view. Public executions and flogging became private executions
and floggings.

Viewed in a narrow historical context, this uncoupling was a good
thing. Public exhibitions of state acts of brutality against other
human beings perhaps did as much to legitimate brutality as it did
to delegitimate crime. In differential association terms, they involved the state in communicating definitions favorable to violence.
More critically to the present analysis, most of the shaming was
stigmatizing rather than reintegrative, as von Hippel concluded on
Continental punishment during the Middle Ages:

Public executions of capital, mutilating, corporal and dishonoring punishments, often aggravated by horrible methods of inflicting them, dulled the
aim of deterrence and harmed general deterrence by brutalizing the conscience of people. Equally disastrous was the effect of this penal law from the
point of view of individual prevention. The outlawed, the banished, the

mutilated, the branded, the shamed, the bereft of honor or stripped of power it expelled from the community of decent people and thus drove them out on the highway. Therefore the penal law itself recruited the habitual and professional criminals, who flourished in those days. (von Hippel, 1925: 158)

Branding on the cheek of offenders was abandoned in eighteenth-century England because it had 'not had its desired effect by deterring offenders from the further committing of crimes and offences, but, on the contrary, such offenders, being rendered thereby unfit to be entrusted in any service or employment to get their livelihood in any honest and lawful way, become the more desperate' (Pike, 1876:280–1).

While compassionate people must applaud the demise of these practices, the revulsion from them has produced a pervasive uncoupling of punishment and shaming in some Western societies. In my home state of Queensland, it used to be common for pubs which sold watered-down beer to be ordered by the court to display signs prominently indicating that the proprietor had recently been convicted of selling adulterated beer. The practice was stopped because it was regarded as 'Dickensian', and because adverse publicity was regarded as having uncertain impacts that undermined the proportionality of sentences determined by the courts. Shoham 1970:12–13) has described a number of shame-based or 'poetic' punishments' that have now diappeared, such as a baker being required to walk in the public square with underweight loaves hung around his neck.

Shearing and Stenning have shown that one of the most important trends in contemporary criminal justice is its privatization. Private security officers are fast becoming more pervasive agents of social control than public police. A characteristic of this private enforcement is its total rejection of a moral conception of order and the control process.

Within private control, order is conceived primarily in instrumental rather than moral terms. Order is simply the set of conditions most conducive to achieving fundamental community objectives. Thus in a business corporation, for instance, order is usually whatever maximizes profit.

(Shearing and Stenning, 1984: 339)

The corporate security division will typically respond to a detected embezzler by getting the money back and sacking the employee. No thought is given to the fact that the non-public nature of this enforcement, free of any moral content, might mean that the embezzler will be thrown back on to the labor market only to be picked up by, and to victimize, another private actor.

One contention of this book is that the uncoupling of shame and punishment manifested in a wide variety of ways in many Western countries is an important factor in explaining the rising crime rates in those countries. Equally, if we look at the only clear case of a society which has experienced a downward trend in crime rates since World War II, Japan, it might be argued that this was a result of the re-establishment of cultural traditions of shaming wrongdoers, including effective coupling of shame and punishment. The decline was not simply an immediate post-war phenomenon: between 1976 and 1980 the number of murders in Japan fell 26 per cent; during the same period in the United States, murders increased by 23 per cent (Fenwick, 1983: 83). The Japanese crime rate is probably the lowest of any developed country (Ames, 1981).

Reintegrative Shaming in Japan

Following World War II, the Japanese suffered from anomie, in the Durkheimian sense of a general breakdown of norms governing group and individual behavior: 'The more weakened the groups to which [the individual] belongs, the less he depends on them, the more he consequently depends only on himself and recognizes no other rules of conduct than what are founded on his private interests' (Durkheim 1951:209). According to Dahrendorf (1985), a similar anomie characterized Germany in the immediate aftermath of the humiliation of defeat in World War II. But Japan did not meekly follow the blueprint for Westernization of their criminal justice system which the occupying Americans attempted to impose following the war. In this the Japanese may have been fortunate, if one is to heed Bayley's conclusion from his comparative study of Japanese and United States police:

Searching for an explanation of the remarkably different crime rates in Japan and the United States, it is a mistake to write off as fortuitous the fact that Japanese, compared with Americans, are less combative in confrontation with authority; that offenders against the law are expected to accept the community's terms for resocialization rather than insisting on legal innocence and bargaining for the mitigation of punishment; that individual character is thought to be mutable, responsive to informal sanctions of proximate groups; that government intervention in social life is more acceptable and that individuals feel a moral obligation to assist actively in preserving moral consensus in the community.   (Bayley, 1976: 1)

Japan might be expected to have a high crime rate according to its demographics. It modernized at an extraordinarily rapid rate; it is highly urbanized in densely packed cities. The proportion of Japanese employed in agriculture declined from 30 per cent in 1960 to 10 per cent in 1980. On the other hand, it has enjoyed lower unemployment rates than other countries and it is culturally homogeneous. Its criminal justice system is efficient (in the sense of apprehending a high proportion of offenders) but extremely lenient (it sends very few of them to prison). George (1984:52) reports that in 1978 Japanese police cleared 53 per cent of known cases of theft, but only 15 per cent of the 231,403 offenders involved were arrested. Prosecution only proceeds in major cases or more minor cases where the normal process of apology, compensation and forgiveness by the victim breaks down. Fewer than 10 per cent of those offenders who are convicted receive prison sentences, and for two-thirds of these, prison sentences are suspended. Whereas 45 per cent of those convicted of a crime serve a jail sentence in the US, in Japan the percentage is under two (Haley, 1982:273). Even 27 per cent of murder cases result in suspended sentences of imprisonment in Japan. Moreover, the average length of sentence has reduced over the years (Bayley, 1976: 141; Adler, 1983: 102). Recalling World War II and the modern-day exploits of the 'Red Army' and other protest groups, it is difficult to argue that the Japanese have a genetic or cultural legacy of non-violence.

The conclusions of the leading scholars who have studied the social context of Japan's low and declining crime rate (Clifford, 1976; Bayley, 1976; Adler, 1983; Fenwick, 1985) can be read as support for the notion of high interdependency in Japanese society (with employers and neighbors as well as families), highly developed communitarianism, and these two characteristics fostering a shaming of offenders which is reintegrative. Consider this further conclusion from Bayley:

The feeling that security consists in acceptance is transferred from the family to other groups,allowing them to discipline members through the fear of exclusion. This accounts for the ability of the police to discipline their own members so effectively. By enwrapping the officer in family-like solicitude, the organization raises the psychological costs of expulsion. Similarly, a Japanese accepts the authority of law as he would the customs of his family. The policeman is analogous to an elder brother who cautions against offending the family...

In psychological terms, the system relies on positive rather than negative reinforcement, emphasizing loving acceptance in exchange for genuine repentance. An analogue of what the Japanese policeman wants the offender to feel is the tearful relief of a child when confession of wrongdoing to his parents results in a gentle laugh and a warm hug. In relation to American policemen, Japanese officers want to be known for the warmth of their care rather than the strictness of their enforcement.   (Bayley, 1976: 156)

Here is the family model writ large. Shaming as a feature of Japanese culture is well known to even the most casual observers of Japan. What is not so widely known is the reintegrative nature of this shaming. The fact that convicted American offenders are more than twenty times as likely to be incarcerated as convicted Japanese offenders says something about the respective commitments of these societies to outcasting versus reintegration.

When an individual is shamed in Japan, the shame is often born by the collectivity to which the individual belongs as well – the family, the company, the school – particularly by the titular head of the collectivity.

When a young constable raped a woman in Tokyo several years ago, his station chief resigned. In this way, junior and senior ranks express a shared commitment to blameless performance. This view of responsibility is part of Japanese culture more largely. When a fighter aircraft struck a commercial airliner, causing it to crash, the minister of defence resigned. Parents occasionally commit suicide when their children are arrested for heinous crimes...

Japanese policeman are accountable, then, because they fear to bring shame on their police 'family', and thus run the risk of losing the regard of colleagues they think of as brothers and fathers.   (Bayley, 1983:156)

Families are of course the key social units which take responsibility for reintegrating the convicted offender. Beyond the family, however, are a staggering proliferation of community volunteers. Japan is covered by 540,000 local liaison units of Crime Prevention Associations and 10,725 Vocational Unions for Crime Prevention, 126,000 volunteer cooperators for Juvenile Guidance (doing street work with juveniles), 8,000 Big Brothers and Sisters for delinquents, 320,000 volunteers in the Women's Association for Rehabilitation, 80,000 members of the Voluntary Probation Officers Association,

1,640 voluntary prison visitors, 1,500 'Cooperative Employers' willing to provide jobs for probationers and parolees, 2,028 Police–School Liaison Councils, plus many others (see references cited in Adler, 1983: 104–5; and Clifford, 1976). The national commitment to reintegration is even written into Article 1 of the Offenders' Rehabilitation Law:

The objective of this law is to protect socially and promote individual and public welfare by aiding the reformation and rehabilitation of offenders ...and facilitating the activities of crime prevention. All the people are required to render help according to their position and ability, to accomplish the objective mentioned in the previous paragraph.

The crime prevention associations and other voluntary groups are linked with a system of informal local government that extends into every household, and with a neighborhood-based form of policing. Even popular culture underlines the notion of shame followed by reintegration:

Betty Latham [1967], an American anthropologist, has shown that Japanese folktales stress repentance and reform whereas Western folktales stress punishment and often death. Western societies seem to give up more quickly on people than Eastern ones. In a Japanese translation of 'Little Red Riding Hood', for example, the wicked wolf falls on his knees and tearfully promises to mend his ways. In the Western version, the wolf is simply killed.   (Bayley, 1985: 105)

Apology has a central place in the aftermath of Japanese legal conflicts (Wagatsuma and Rosett, 1986; Haley, 1986). Ceremonies of restoration to signify the reestablishment of harmony between conflicting parties are culturally pivotal; the best way for this reconciliation to occur is by mutual apology, where even a party who is relatively unblameworthy will find some way in which he contributed to the conflict to form the basis of his apology.

There are a multitude of cultural bases for Japanese aversion to outcasting and commitment to reintegration. According to Wagatsuma and Rosett (1986) apology in Japan amounts to dissociation from that evil part of oneself that committed an unacceptable act. Japanese idiom frequently accounts for wrongdoing with possession by a 'mushi' (worm or bug). Criminals are therefore not acting according to their true selves; they are victims of a 'mushi' which can be 'sealed off', 'thus permitting people to be restored to the community without guilt' (Wagatsuma and Rosett, 1986: 476). The cultural assumption of basic goodness and belief in each individual's capacity for eventual self-correction means that 'nurturant acceptance' ('amayakashi') is the appropriate response to deviance once shame has been projected to and accepted by the deviant. Thus, Bayley explains the distinctive pattern of police-offender encounters in Japan:

An American accused by a policeman is very likely to respond 'Why me?' A Japanese more often says 'I'm sorry'. The American shows anger, the Japanese shame. An American contests the accusation and tries to humble the policeman; a Japanese accepts the accusation and tries to kindle benevolence. In response, the American policeman is implacable and impersonal; the Japanese policeman is sympathetic and succoring. (Bayley, 1976: 150)

Japan's crime control achievements may of course be purchased at a cost (see, e.g., Fataba, 1984). The interdependency, the shaming, the communitarian mobilization to resocialize wrongdoers, are ingredients of a culture in which duties to the community more often than in the West overwhelm the rights of individuals. We will return to this potential policy dilemma in Chapter 10. Critics also sometimes suggest that Japan's high suicide rate shows that the effective suppression of crime simply means that personal problems manifest themselves in other ways. However, the evidence of an inverse relationship between the intra-punitiveness and extra-punitiveness of societies is weak (Cohen and Fishman, 1985), and Clifford (1976: 141) has shown that while the Japanese suicide rate may seem high compared to the crime rate, it is fairly average in international terms. This is in spite of the fact that Japanese culture grants a degree of approval to suicide that other cultures do not. Expanding the theory in this book to other forms of deviance beyond crime would lead to the prediction that forms of deviance which are most socially approved (least subject to reintegrative shaming), like suicide in Japan, will be most common. Or, if there is less shame for women entering the mentally ill role and more shame for women in entering the criminal role, the theory could be used to predict a higher ratio of mental illness to crime for women than for men – a finding that occurs in Japan and all other societies.

Shaming and Subcultures

In Chapter 2 it was argued that subcultures that provide various degrees of social support for illegal behavior do exist in all societies. Even Japan has some 2,500 highly organized criminal gangs, as well as many motorcycle gangs and other groups which transmit criminal subcultures (Clifford, 1976: 117–24). Sometimes these subcultures are in opposition to the mainstream culture in the sense of promoting values which are the antithesis of mainstream values; sometimes they provide a social environment which is merely more tolerant of deviations from societal norms when opportunities arise to choose between gratification and compliance; sometimes they foster a 'drift' between the conventional and the deviant.

Even when all these levels of subculturalism are incorporated into the analysis, groups with strong and visible commitment to subcultural behavior patterns are numerically weak in most societies. This means that subcultural groups are not readily on tap with recruitment centers in each suburb as are the armed forces. Most citizens would know how to make contact with the army should they want to join up, but most Americans would have no idea of how to become an associate of the Mafia or to join the Hell's Angels. Consequently, even when life circumstances make criminal subcultures very attractive to individuals, more often than not those life circumstances have changed by the time the individual is exposed to an opportunity to be recruited into a subcultural group which engages in activities attractive to the individual.

If individuals were not choosy about the kind of deviant subculture they would find gratifying, subcultures would of course be more accessible in practical terms than they are. If I could imagine my own circumstances of life changing so that I would be atttracted to participation in a deviant subculture, I might imagine first confronting an opportunity to participate with others in illicit drug use. But since I once had a frightening experience with marijuana interacting with alcohol, even soft drug use would not appeal to me in the least. An opportunity to smash things does not appeal either, so a vandalism opportunity would be a bore; an opportunity to rape a woman would overwhelm me with disgust rather than pleasure. On the other hand, the prospect of being $1,000 richer and my bank $1,000 poorer sounds like a result which would please me, so maybe if my life circumstances rendered me amenable to crime, fraud would appeal to my taste. The point is that criminological theory, like economic theory, systematically forgets that people have different tastes. Just because my social controls are loosened and I encounter an illegitimate opportunity, I will not take it unless it appeals to my taste. Thus, if subcultural groups are numerically weak to start with,

I will not experience opportunities to associate with many of them during my periods of suspended commitment to conventional society, and I will encounter even fewer opportunities to share in a subculture which offers those particular kinds of satisfactions which appeal to my tastes.

Stigmatization is the most important of those life circumstances that increase the attraction of individuals to criminal subcultures. As Albert Cohen (1955) told us, when a student is rejected by the status system of the school – is labeled incorrigible or a failure – he has a status problem and is in the market for a solution. Cohen suggests that he solves it collectively with other students who have similarly been rejected by the school. The outcasts band together and set up their own status system with values the exact inverse of those of the school.

Such extreme oppositional criminal subcultures as Cohen's or the Hell's Angels do not need to be invoked, though they are part of the scene, for the stigmatization hypothesis to be relevant. Young people who are constantly hammered by the family and the school with shaming that puts them in a position of mainstream rejection may find solace in a group of heroin users. Now the only thing which distinguishes that subculture from the mainstream culture may be heroin use; in all other respects those involved might be quite average in their law-abidingness, at least initially. All that is being suggested is that, when individuals are shamed so remorselessly and unforgivingly that they become outcasts, or even begin to think of themselves as outcasts it becomes more rewarding to associate with others who are perceived in some limited or total way as also at odds with mainstream standards. Once labeling and rejection have occurred, further attempts at admonishing association with the group which provides social support for deviance have no force.

However, we have said that subcultural groups, even broadly conceived as groups that provide any kind of systematic social support for illegality, are often thin on the ground. Most delinquency is at least to begin with a social rather than a solitary activity: drug use necessitates association with a supplier, vandalism or street fighting usually requires an audience, car theft needs someone to teach you the ropes (Zimring, 1981; Wilson and Herrnstein, 1985: 292–3). It often happens, therefore, that outcasts who are in the market for illegitimate opportunities do not encounter those opportunities, at least not opportunities of a kind which appeal to them.

Either the opportunities are not encountered or a choice is made to reject them. Thus, the outcome of disintegrative shaming will often be that the outcast will reintegrate herself. We must not assume that reintegration only occurs at the hands of those who do the shaming. Individuals make choices in the light of the social structural realities they confront; they are not empty vessels totally determined by these realities.

Alternatively, outcasts who find no subcultural support for offending, or who choose to reject the subculture, remain more likely to commit crime (as lone offenders) than those who are reintegrated, though they should be less likely to become persistent offenders than those who do discover subcultural support.

In summary, then, stigmatization by the family, the school, and other sources of social control increases the attraction of outcasts to subcultural groups which provide social support for crime, and weakens social control by the former against criminal activities. However, if attractive opportunities for participation in subcultures are not encountered, stigmatization will, on balance, have a crime preventive impact. This is because there is a chance in these circumstances that the outcast will tire of a life of rejection and seek to prove himself worthy of reconciliation with the primary groups which have labeled him. Stigmatization will then have effected rehabilitation just as well as reintegrative shaming might have done. On the other hand, stigmatization still runs a risk of solitary deviance, including suicide, which is probably greater than with reintegrative shaming. At the same time, it must be remembered that irrespective of whether stigmatization is worsening or improving the prospects of crime by the outcast, at a societal level it is making a contribution to crime prevention. At a societal level shaming will still have the pluses we will discuss later of dramatizing wrongdoing for all to see, of strengthening social solidarity, of deterring others from the stigmatized conduct.

All of this means two things:

1. Reintegrative shaming is superior to stigmatization because it minimizes risks of pushing those shamed into criminal subcultures, and because social disapproval is more effective when embedded in relationships overwhelmingly characterized by social approval.

2. Whether disintegrative shaming is superior to no shaming at all is uncertain, depending largely on the density of criminal subcultures in the society.

5

Why and how does shaming work?

The Deterrence Literature

The criminological literature on deterrence provides one important motivation for turning to informal methods of social control such as shaming for the key to explaining crime. This literature shows reasonable support for an association between the certainty of criminal punishment and offending, but little support for the association between crime and the severity of punishment (Waldo and Chiricos, 1972; Bailey and Lott, 1976; Kraut, 1976; Silberman, 1976; Teevan, 1976a, 1976b, 1976c; Anderson *et al.*, 1977; Meier and Johnson, 1977; Minor, 1977; Cohen, 1978; Jensen and Erickson, 1978; Bishop, 1984; Williams, 1985; Paternoster and Iovanni, 1986; Piliavin *et al.*, 1986). Deterrence research is now demonstrating a much stronger effect of informal sanctions on deviance than formal legal sanctions (Burkett and Jensen, 1975; Kraut, 1976; Anderson *et al.*, 1977; Meier and Johnson, 1977; Jensen and Erickson, 1978; Akers *et al.*, 1979; Tittle, 1980b; Meier, 1982; Paternoster *et al.*, 1983a, 1983b; Bishop, 1984; Williams, 1985; Paternoster and Iovanni, 1986; but see Piliavin *et al.*, 1986).

It would seem that sanctions imposed by relatives, friends or a personally relevant collectivity have more effect on criminal behavior than sanctions imposed by a remote legal authority. I will argue that this is because repute in the eyes of close acquaintances matters more to people than the opinions or actions of criminal justice officials. As Blau (1964: 20) points out: 'a person who is attracted to others is interested in proving himself attractive to them, for his ability to associate with them and reap the benefits expected from the association is contingent on their finding him an attractive associate and thus wanting to interact with him'.

A British Government Social Survey asked youths to rank what they saw as the most important consequences of arrest. While only

69

10 per cent said 'the punishment I might get' was the most important consequence of arrest, 55 per cent said either 'What my family'
or 'my girlfriend' would think about it. Another 12 per cent ranked
'the publicity or shame of having to appear in court' as the most
serious consequence of arrest, and this was ranked as a more serious
consequence on average than 'the punishment I might get' (Zimring
and Hawkins, 1973: 192). There is clearly a need for more empirical
work to ascertain whether the following conclusion is too sweeping,
but Tittle would seem to speak for the current state of this literature
when he says:

> social control as a general process seems to be rooted almost completely in
> informal sanctioning. Perceptions of formal sanction probabilities or sever-
> ities do not appear to have much of an effect, and those effects that are
> evident turn out to be dependent upon perceptions of informal sanctions.
> (Tittle, 1980b: 241)

Only a small proportion of the informal sanctions which prevent
crime are coupled with formal sanctions, so this literature in a sense
understates the importance of informal sanctions. These studies are
also by no means tests of the theory of reintegrative shaming – how
to test the theory is discussed in Chapter 10 – but they certainly
suggest that we are looking in the right place for an explanation of
crime. To quote Tittle (1980b: 198) again, they suggest that 'to the
extent that individuals are deterred from deviance by fear, the fear
that is relevant is most likely to be that their deviance will evoke
some respect or status loss among acquaintances or in the community as a whole'. In the rational weighing of the costs and benefits of
crime, loss of respect weighs more heavily for most of us than formal
punishment. Yet in learning theory terms this rational weighing
results from the operant conditioning part of learning. There is also
the much more important effect of consciences which may be classically conditioned by shame (see Chapter 2, pp. 35–8).

A related reading of the deterrence literature is that it shows it is
not the formal punitive features of social control that matter, but
rather its informal moralizing features. The surprising findings of a
classic field experiment by Schwartz and Orleans (1967) has fostered such a reading. Taxpayers were interviewed during the month
prior to the filing of income tax returns, with one randomly selected
group exposed to an interview stressing the penalties for income tax
evasion, the other to an interview stressing the moral reasons for tax

compliance. Whereas the moral appeal led to a significant increase in the actual tax paid, the deterrent threat was associated with no significant increase in tax paid compared to a control group.

Beyond Deterrence, Beyond Operant Conditioning: Conscience and Shaming

Jackson Toby (1964: 333) suggests that deterrence is irrelevant 'to the bulk of the population who have introjected the moral norms of society'. People comply with the law most of the time not through fear of punishment, or even fear of shaming, but because criminal behavior is simply abhorrent to them. Most serious crimes are unthinkable to most people; these people engage in no rational weighing of the costs and benefits of crime before deciding whether to comply with the law. Shaming, we will argue, is critical to understanding why most serious crime is unthinkable to most of us.

The unthinkableness of crime is a manifestation of our conscience or superego, whatever we want to call it depending on our psychological theoretical preferences. For Eysenck (1973: 120) conscience is a conditioned reflex. As infants we have many experiences where minor acts of deviance are associated with smacks, rejection, spells in the corner, reprimands, and other unpleasant stimuli. These experiences attach conditioned fear and anxiety reponses to the deviant behavior. Names like 'bad' and 'naughty' also become associated with these unpleasant events and in time also produce a conditioned anxiety response. This verbal labeling is the key to a process of generalization that groups together a variety of types of misbehavior as 'bad' and 'naughty' that all elicit conditioned anxiety; in time the generalization proceeds further, with the more abstract concept of 'crime' being defined as 'naughty' or 'evil'. We will leave it to the psychologists to debate how much the acquisition and generalization of conscience is a conditioning or a cognitive process. The point is that conscience is acquired.

For adolescents and adults, conscience is a much more powerful weapon to control misbehavior than punishment. In the wider society, it is no longer logistically possible, as it is in the nursery, for arrangements to be made for punishment to hang over the heads of persons whenever temptation to break the rules is put in their path. Happily, conscience more than compensates for absence of formal control. For a well socialized individual, conscience delivers an anxiety response to punish each and every involvement in crime – a more systematic punishment than haphazard enforcement by the police. Unlike any punishment handed down by the courts, the anxiety response happens without delay, indeed punishment by anxiety precedes the rewards obtained from the crime, while any punishment by law will follow long after the reward. For most of us, punishment by our own conscience is therefore a much more potent threat than punishment by the criminal justice system.

Shaming is critical as the societal process that underwrites the family process of building consciences in children. Just as the insurance company cannot do business without the underwriter, the family could not develop young consciences in the cultural vacuum which would be left without societal practices of shaming. Shaming is an important child-rearing practice in itself; it is an extremely valuable tool in the hands of a responsible loving parent. However, as children's morality develops, as socialization moves from building responsiveness to external controls to responsiveness to internal controls, direct forms of shaming become less important than induction: appealing to the child's affection or respect for others, appealing to the child's own standards of right and wrong. There is indeed some evidence that, as children develop, reliance on direct forms of shaming may be less effective than reliance on induction (Dienstbier *et al.*, 1975), just as there is a great deal of evidence that excessive reliance on punishment or power-assertion parenting is associated with later delinquency, probably because it inhibits the maturation of internal controls at the expense of external controls (Hoffman and Saltzstein, 1967; Feshbach, 1970; Hoffman, 1970; Eron and Leftkowitz, 1971, Eron *et al.* 1974; Welsh, 1976; Maccoby, 1980: 385; Agnew, 1985).

However, the external controls must still be there in the background. If the maturation of conscience proceeds as it should, direct forms of shaming, and even more so punishment, are resorted to less and less. But there are times when conscience fails all of us, and we need a refresher course in the consequences of a compromised conscience. In this backstop role, shaming has a great advantage over formal punishment. Shaming is more pregnant with symbolic content than punishment. Punishment is a denial of confidence in the morality of the offender by reducing norm compliance to a crude cost–benefit calculation; shaming can be a reaffirmation of the morality of the offender by expressing personal disappointment that the offender should do something so out of character, and, if the shaming is reintegrative, by expressing personal satisfaction in seeing the character of the offender restored. Punishment erects barriers between the offender and punisher through transforming the relationship into one of power assertion and injury; shaming produces a greater interconnectedness between the parties, albeit a painful one, an interconnectedness which can produce the repulsion of stigmatization or the establishment of a potentially more positive relationship following reintegration. Punishment is often shameful and shaming usually punishes. But whereas punishment gets its symbolic content only from its denunciatory association with shaming, shaming is pure symbolic content.

Nevertheless, just as shaming is needed when conscience fails, punishment is needed when offenders are beyond being shamed. Unfortunately, however, the shameless, the remorseless, those who are beyond conditioning by shame are also likely to be those beyond conditioning by punishment – that is, psychopaths (consider, for example, the work of Mednick on conditionability and psychopathy – which would seem equally relevant to conditioning by fear of shame or fear of formal punishment (Mednick and Christiansen, 1977; Wilson and Herrnstein, 1985:198–204)). The evidence is that punishment is a very ineffective ultimate backstop with people who have developed beyond the control techniques which were effective when they were infants. This is the problem with behavior modification (based on either rewards or punishment) for rehabilitating offenders. Offenders will play the game by reverting to pre-adolescent responsiveness to reward–cost social control because this is the way they can make their life most comfortable. But when they leave the institution they will return to behaving like the adults they are in an adult world in which punishment contingencies for indulging deviant conduct are remote.

The conscience-building effects of shaming that give it superiority over control strategies based simply on changing the rewards and costs of crime are enhanced by the participatory nature of shaming. Whereas an actual punishment will only be administered by one person or a limited number of criminal justice officials, the shaming associated with punishment may involve almost all of the members of a community. Thus, in the following passage, when Znaniecki refers to 'punishment', he really means the denunciation or shaming associated with the punishment:

Regardless of whether punishment really does deter future violation of the law or not, it seems to significantly reinforce agreement and solidarity among those who actively or vicariously participate in meting it out... Opposing the misdemeanours of other people increases the conformity of those administering the punishment, thus leading to the maintenance of the systems in which they participate.   (Znaniecki, 1971: 604)

Participation in expressions of abhorrence toward the criminal acts of others is part of what makes crime an abhorrent choice for us ourselves to make. Moreover, in the next chapter, through discussing gender and reintegrative shaming, I will argue that, through frequently being an instrument of reintegrative shaming, one is more likely to be susceptible to reintegration when one is shamed oneself. The female role, which is partly about *doing* reintegration in families, renders its exponents more committed to the view that *being* reintegrated is desirable, should one find oneself at risk of becoming an outcast.

When we shame ourselves, that is when we feel pangs of conscience, we take the role of the other, treating ourselves as an object worthy of shame (Mead, 1934; Shott, 1979). We learn to do this by participating with others in shaming criminals and evil-doers. Internal control is a social product of external control. Self-regulation can displace social control by an external agent only when control has been internalized through the prior existence of external control in the culture.

Cultures like that of Japan, which shame reintegratively, follow shaming ceremonies with ceremonies of repentance and reacceptance. The nice advantage such cultures get in conscience building is two ceremonies instead of one, but, more critically, confirmation of the moral order from two very different quarters – both from those affronted and from him who caused the affront. The moral order derives a very special kind of credibility when even he who has breached it openly comes out and affirms the evil of the breach.

This is achieved by what Goffman (1971: 113) calls disassociation:

An apology is a gesture through which an individual splits himself into two parts, the part that is guilty of an offense and the part that disassociates itself from the delict and affirms a belief in the offended rule.

In cultures like that of Japan which practise disassociation, the vilification of the self that misbehaved by the repentant self can be much more savage than would be safe with vilification by other persons: 'he can overstate or overplay the case against himself, thereby giving others the task of cutting the self-derogation short' (Goffman, 1971: 113). So in Goffman's terms, reintegrative shaming is achieved by splitting the self first into a blameworthy part which is the target for the specific and general deterrent effects, and the moral educative effects, of shame, while the second part of the self stands back and joins with the community as an instrument of blame-giving to help achieve these effects. This second part of the self is also the part that is forgiven, reintegrated. Goffman's interpretation of Japanese reintegrative shaming might therefore be disassociation of the 'real' self which is both an instrument of shaming and an object of reintegration, from an evil part of the self which is the object of shaming.

In summary then, shame operates at two levels to effect social control. First, it deters criminal behavior because social approval of significant others is something we do not like to lose. Second, and more importantly, both shaming and repentance build consciences which internally deter criminal behavior even in the absence of any external shaming associated with an offense. Shaming brings into existence two very different kinds of punishers – social disapproval and pangs of conscience.

The Mechanics of Gossip

We said earlier that shaming is more important as a wider cultural process than as a concrete child-rearing tactic because, without shaming, the building of consciences would be impossible. It is the presence of shaming in the society which gives socialization its content. I remember learning about how terrible murder is when our next-door neighbor was killed by the local butcher over a gambling disagreement. I remember my mother moralizing about the incident – shaming the butcher, talking about what a disgrace it was to his parents. No doubt this shaming was going on in every house in the neighborhood, and new content was being put into young consciences in the process.

I doubt if anyone in the neighborhood actually confronted the family with its shame. They did not need to. The butcher's family would have known that moralizing and gossip were rife. Instead people tended to express sympathy to the family that something so terrible should have happened. An exception was Eddie, an intellectually impaired young man, who would be hushed up by embarrassed customers in the butcher shop when he insisted on exclaiming: 'I know why "x" doesn't work in the shop any more. I know what he did.'

In other words, apart from Eddie, the shaming did not reach the ears of the family concerned, but the gestures of reintegration did. This is how reintegrative shaming so often works: gossip with which the deviant or his family are never confronted (but which they know is inevitably occurring) combined with openly expressed efforts to reintegrate, to indicate acceptance, regret, the need to put it behind the offender and the family and make a new start. Secret indirect gossip is combined with open direct gestures of reintegration.

Gluckman (1963) is the leading exponent of an anthropological tradition of studying gossip which fits this analysis. According to Gluckman, gossip is critical for crystallizing and reinforcing community values. Yet these anthropologists have shown that in many societies there is a studious avoidance of gossiping about a person to her face (e.g. Campbell, 1964: 265). They argue that if community members did, gossip would be divisive, indeed would often provoke a violent response. Instead gossip furthers the coherence and unity of the group.

This is an overly functionalist account. Gossip is often the stuff of conflict rather than of social integration. As Campbell (1964: 272), for example, concluded from his study of a Greek mountain community: 'And since the downfall of one family validates and in some sense improves the status of other families, men attempt by every means of allusive gossip and criticism of conduct to deny each other their pretensions to honour'.

Yet the valuable contribution of this tradition is showing how gossip *can* foster social integration by avoiding open criticism. It will not always be so. The central mission of this book, after all, is to show that shaming can be both reintegrative and disintegrative, and that much turns on this distinction.

Through listening to and participating in secretive gossip directed at others we learn the circumstances by which people suffer loss of reputation through gossip. Thus, when we engage in comparable behavior ourselves we know that others will be gossiping about us even though we do not hear it directly. We have learnt the culture.

Shaming in the community is thus a more mediated, subtle process than it is within the family. However, we should not underestimate the extent to which reintegrative shaming is achieved even within the family by indirect expressions of disapproval combined with direct expressions of reacceptance. The mother complains to a father or a sibling that she is disappointed in her child. Perhaps the father or the sibling then passes on to the deviant family member the message that mother is disappointed. The child apologizes to mother and she directly expresses forgiveness. Even more subtly, mother is seen to have been crying. This reminds the child of a similar occasion in the past when mother told her she was crying because her other daughter had 'let her down'. The child, seeing the moist eyes, suspects that it is she who is now being similarly shamed in discussions between other members of the family. She asks forgiveness: she is shamed by a tear and reintegrated with a hug. This is partly what we mean by saying that shaming and guilt induction are indistinguishably part of the same social process.

The Curriculum of Crimes

Community-wide shaming is necessary because most crimes are not experienced within the average household. Children need to learn about the evil of murder, rape, car theft, and environmental pollution offenses through condemnation of the local butcher or the far away image on the television screen. But the shaming of the local offender known personally to children in the neighborhood is especially important, because the wrongdoing and the shaming are so vivid as to leave a lasting impression.

Much shaming in the socialization of children is of course vicarious, through stories. Because they are not so vivid as real-life incidents of shaming, they are not so powerful. Yet they are necessary because so many types of misbehavior will not occur in the family or the neighborhood. A culture without stories for children in which morals are clearly drawn and evil deeds clearly identified would be a culture which failed the moral development of its children. Because human beings are story-telling animals, they get much of their identity from answers to the question 'Of what stories do I find myself a part?' 'Deprive children of stories and you leave them unscripted, anxious stutterers in their actions as in their words' (MacIntyre, 1984: 138).

Essentially, societal processes of shaming do three things:
1. They give content to a day-to-day socialization of children

which occurs mainly through induction. As we have just seen, shaming supplies the morals which build consciences. The evil of acts beyond the immediate experience of children is more effectively communicated by shaming than by pure reasoning.

2. Societal incidents of shaming remind parents of the wide range of evils about which they must moralize with their children. Parents do not have to keep a checklist of crimes, a curriculum of sins, to discuss with their offspring. In a society where shaming is important, societal incidents of shaming will trigger vicarious shaming within the family so that the criminal code is eventually more or less automatically covered. Thus, the child will one day observe condemnation of someone who has committed rape, and will ask a parent or other older person about the basis of this wrongdoing, or will piece the story together from a series of such incidents. Of course societies which shame only half-heartedly run a risk that the full curriculum of crimes will not be covered. Both this point and the last one could be summarized in another way by saying that public shaming puts pressure on parents, teachers and neighbors to ensure that they engage in private shaming which is sufficiently systematic.

3. Societal shaming in considerable measure takes over from parental socialization once children move away from the influence of the family and the school. Put another way, shaming generalizes beyond childhood principles learnt during the early years of life.

This third principle is about the 'criminal law as a moral eye-opener' as Andenaes (1974: 116–17) calls it. As a child, I may have learnt the principle that killing is wrong, but when I leave the familiar surroundings of the family to work in the unfamiliar environment of a nuclear power plant, I am taught by a nuclear safety regulatory system that to breach certain safety laws can cost lives, and so persons who breach them are treated with a comparable level of shame. The principle that illegal killing is shameful is generalized. To the extent that genuine shame is not directed against those who defy the safety rules, however, I am liable to take them much less seriously. Unfortunately, societal shaming processes often do fail to generalize to organizational crime.

Recent years in some Western societies have seen more effective shaming directed at certain kinds of offenses – drunk driving, occupational health and safety and environmental offenses, and political corruption, for example (see references at p. 39–41). This shaming has for many adults integrated new categories of wrongdoing (for which they had not been socialized as children) into the moral frameworks pre-existing from their childhood.

While most citizens are aware of the content of most criminal laws, knowledge of what the law requires of citizens in detail can be enhanced by cases of public shaming. Through shaming directed at new legal frontiers, feminists in many countries have clarified for citizens just what sexual harassment, rape within marriage, and employment discrimination mean. Social change is increasingly rapid, particularly in the face of burgeoning technologies which require new moralities of nuclear, environmental and consumer safety, responsible use of new technologies of information exchange and electronic funds transfer, ethical exploitation of new institutions such as futures exchanges, and so on. Shaming is thus particularly vital in sustaining a contemporarily relevant legal and moral order.

Biographical references to barbaric dictators as caring husbands and sons or 'model family men' provide regular enough reminder that our societal processes for generalizing conscience from family situations to situations in the wider society are less than perfect.

The Problem of Discontinuity in Socialization Practices

The most fundamental problem of socialization in modern societies is that as children mature in the family we gradually wean them from control by punishment to shaming and reasoned appeals to internal controls. The transition from family to school involves a partial reversion back to greater reliance on formal punishment for social control. The further transition to social control on the streets, at discos and pubs by the police is an almost total reversion to the punishment model. A discontinuity with the developmental pattern set in the family is established by the other major socializing institutions for adolescents – the school and the police.

We have seen that Japanese society handles this discontinuity much better than Western societies by having a criminal justice system (and a school system) much more oriented to catalyzing internal controls than ours. Japanese police, prosecutors and courts rely heavily on guilt-induction and shaming as alternatives to punishment. If appeals to shame produce expressions of guilt, repentance and a will to seek reunification and forgiveness from loved ones (and/or the victim), this is regarded as the best result by all actors in the drama of criminal justice. The Japanese phenomena of neighborhood police, reintegrative shaming at work and school as alternatives to formal punishment processes, have two effects. First, they put social control back into the hands of significant others, where it can be most effective. Second, they soften some of the discontinuity between the increasing trust to inner controls of family life and the shock of a reversion to external control in the wide world. Just as the evidence shows that aggression and delinquency is the reaction to excessive use of punishment and power assertion as the control strategy within the family, we might expect rebellion against a demeaning punitiveness on the street to be all the more acute when families have eschewed authoritarianism in favor of authoritativeness.

This lesson is not only one that applies to police relations with juveniles. Government regulatory inspectorates which deal with businesspeople often provoke the same kind of rebellion, 'an organized culture of resistance' (Bardach and Kagan, 1982; Braithwaite, 1985a), by imposing a punishment model of social control as a first approach rather than as a last resort on people who are accustomed to being treated as moral agents capable of responding to appeals to their better nature. This theme will be expanded in Chapters 9 and 10.

In short, societies which replace much of their punitive social control with shaming and reintegrative appeals to the better nature of people will be societies with less crime. These societies will do better at easing the crushing discontinuity between the shift away from punitive control in home life and the inevitable reversion to heavier reliance on punitive control in the wider society.

Conclusions

We have seen that the micro process of shaming an individual has consequences far beyond the life of that individual. The social process of gossip links a micro incident into a macro pattern. A shaming incident reinforces cultural patterns which underwrite further cultural products like a moralistic children's story, a television program, a schoolteacher's homily. The latter modalities of public (societal) shaming exert pressure for further private (individual) shaming.

The reasons why reintegrative shaming works in preventing crime might be summarized as follows:

1. The deterrence literature suggests that specific deterrence associated with detection for criminal offending works primarily through fear of shame in the eyes of intimates rather than fear of formal punishment.

2. Shame not only specifically deters the shamed offender, it also generally deters many others who also wish to avoid shame and who participate in or become aware of the incident of shaming.

3. Both the specific and general deterrent effects of shame will be greater for persons who remain strongly attached in relationships of interdependency and affection because such persons will accrue greater interpersonal costs from shame. This is one reason why reintegrative shaming makes for more effective social control than stigmatization.

4. A second reason for the superiority of reintegrative shaming over stigmatization is that the latter can be counterproductive by breaking attachments to those who might shame future criminality and by increasing the attractiveness of groups that provide social support for crime.

5. However, most compliance with the law is not achieved through either specific or general deterrence. Most of us comply with the law most of the time, not because we rationally weigh our fear of the consequences of detection against the benefits of the crime, but because to commit the crime is simply unthinkable to us. Shaming is the social process which leads to the cognition that a particular type of crime is unthinkable. Cultures where the social process of shaming is muted are cultures where citizens often do not internalize abhorrence for crime.

6. A third reason for the superiority of reintegrative shaming over stigmatization is that a combination of shame at and repentance by the offender is a more powerful affirmation of the criminal law than one-sided moralizing. A shaming ceremony followed later by a forgiveness and repentance ceremony more potently builds commitment to the law than a shaming ceremony alone. Nothing has greater symbolic force in community-wide conscience-building than repentance.

7. Because shaming is a participatory form of social control, compared with formal sanctioning which is more professionalized than participatory, shaming builds consciences through citizens being instruments as well as targets of social control. Participation in expressions of abhorrence toward the criminal acts of others is

part of what makes crime an abhorrent choice for us ourselves to make.

8. Once consciences have been formed by cultural processes of shaming and repentance, pangs of conscience become the most effective punishment for crime because whereas conscience delivers a timely anxiety response to every involvement in crime, other negative reinforcers, including shame, are delivered unreliably or with delay.

9. Shaming is therefore both the social process which builds consciences, and the most important backstop to be used when consciences fail to deliver conformity. Formal punishment is another backstop, but a less effective one than reintegrative shaming.

10. Gossip within wider circles of acquaintances and shaming of offenders not even known to those who gossip are important for building consciences because so many crimes will not occur in the direct experience of limited groups like families. Societal incidents of shaming remind parents and teachers of the need to moralize with their children across the whole curriculum of crimes.

11. Public shaming puts pressure on parents, teachers and others to ensure that they engage in private shaming which is sufficiently systematic, and public shaming increasingly takes over the role of private shaming once children move away from the influence of the family and school. The latter is one reason why public shaming by courts of law has a more important role to play with strictly adult offenses like crimes against the environment than with predominantly juvenile offenses like vandalism.

12. Public shaming generalizes familiar principles to unfamiliar or new contexts. It integrates new categories of wrongdoing, which may arise from technological change into pre-existing moral frameworks. Public shaming transforms the loss of life in a battle at My Lai into a 'war crime' and a 'massacre', and through our distant involvement in the incident of shaming, the moral category of illegal killing acquires some expanded meanings.

13. Cultures with heavy emphasis on reintegrative shaming establish a smoother transition between socialization practices in the family and socialization in the wider society. Within the family, as the child grows, social control shifts from external to internal controls; punishment-oriented cultures set this process more starkly in reverse in the public domain than do shame-oriented cultures. To the extent that crime control can be made to work by continuing to

catalyze internal controls it will be more effective; this is precisely why families are more effective agents of social control than police forces.

14. Gossip and other modalities of shaming can be especially effective when the targets of shame are not directly confronted with the shame, but are directly confronted with gestures of forgiveness or reintegration. Citizens who have learnt the culture do not have to be shamed to their faces to know that they are the subject of gossip, but they may need to be directly offered gestures of acceptance before they can be confident that they are again part of the community of law abiding citizens. In other words, shaming which is excessively confrontational renders the achievement of reintegration a tall order. There is thus something to be said for hypocrisy: our friends are likely to recover from a suspicion that we have stabbed them in the back, but stabbing them in the front can be divisive!

15. The effectiveness of shaming is often enhanced by shame being directed not only at the individual offender but also at her family, or her company if she is a corporate criminal. When a collectivity as well as an individual is shamed, collectivities are put on notice as to their responsibility to exercise informal control over their members, and the moralizing impact of shaming is multiplied. For reasons which will be elaborated in the next chapter, a shamed family or company will often transmit the shame to the individual offender in a manner which is as reintegrative as possible. From the standpoint of the offender, the strategy of rejecting her rejectors may resuscitate her own self-esteem, but her loved ones or colleagues will soon let her know that sinking deeper into the deviant role will only exacerbate the shame they are suffering on her behalf.

6

Social conditions conducive to reintegrative shaming

The Comparative Literature

In this chapter we will argue that the fundamental societal conditions conducive to cultural processes of reintegrative shaming are communitarianism and interdependency. These are the characteristics which the criminologists who have studied the Japanese crime situation have concluded to be at the heart of Japanese success in securing low and declining crime rates (see Chapter 4). Clinard (1978) concluded that the decentralization and communitarianism of the Swiss canton system, with its heavy reliance on citizen assumption of responsibility for crime control, was important in understanding the low Swiss crime rates, a conclusion endorsed by Adler (1983).

Adler's *Nations Not Obsessed With Crime* is the most ambitious comparative study of countries believed to have low crime rates. It can justifiably be criticized as a work based on shaky foundations (Mukherjee, 1985) though the totally unsatisfactory state of comparative data on crime rates is of course not the fault of Adler, who studied ten countries which she believed (largely on the basis of a United Nations survey) to have low crime rates: Switzerland, Ireland, Bulgaria, the German Democratic Republic, Costa Rica, Peru, Algeria, Saudi Arabia, Japan and Nepal. She concluded that a Durkheimian condition of social solidarity, which she called 'synnomie', was a characteristic these low crime countries shared. These conclusions were based on very limited data, to say the least. However, Adler's synnomie is very similar to the communitarianism which other comparativists like Bayley, Clifford and Clinard have discussed.

Adler's low crime societies were characterized by social cohesive-

84

ness, a strong family system, and social control systems which 'do not aim to control by formal restraint', or, in the terms of this book, which do aim to control by reintegration into cohesive networks. Effective shaming is an implied product of this synnomie. For example in discussing Bulgaria, Adler suggests: 'Particularly effective appears to be the public reprimand, expressed before a social group to which the offender belongs' (Adler, 1983: 42).

Speculative though so much of the work from this comparativist tradition is, it is part of the stimulus for the proposition that communitarianism and interdependency are the crucial conditions for effective reintegrative shaming. This is as it should be in the progress of social science. Qualitative comparative case studies should supply the heuristics for coherent theorizing; then these theories, if they prove valuable as theories, should be put to systematic empirical test.

Defining Communitarianism

Communitarianism and interdependency are highly related concepts. While communitarianism is a characteristic of societies, interdependency is a variable applied to the individual level of analysis, though of course a society of highly interdependent individuals can be described as an interdependent society. The aggregation of individual interdependency is the basis for societal communitarianism. Yet we can be in relationships of interdependency with people without sharing a community with those people in any genuine sense of mutual help and trust. The relationship between judge and convicted criminal, for example, is one of interdependency with great potential for shaming, but no sense of community.

For a society to be communitarian, its heavily enmeshed fabric of interdependencies therefore must have a special kind of symbolic significance to the populace. Interdependencies must be attachments which invoke personal obligation to others within a community of concern. They are not perceived as isolated exchange relationships of convenience but as matters of profound group obligation. Thus, a communitarian society combines a dense network of individual interdependencies with strong cultural commitments to mutuality of obligation. Individual interdependencies are interpreted within the framework of group loyalties – father–son interdependencies are symbolically part of family obligation, employer–

employee interdependencies part of company loyalty. In summary, there are three elements to communitarianism: (1) densely enmeshed interdependency, where the interdependencies are characterized by (2) mutual obligation and trust, and (3) are interpreted as a matter of group loyalty rather than individual convenience. Communitarianism is therefore the antithesis of individualism.

Communitarianism and Shaming

Most Western societies might be characterized more by individualism than communitarianism. Nisbet (1979) has been among many observers of the declining capacities of families, churches and residential communities to exert informal social control. The ideology of individualism dismantles the sanctioning capacities of these intermediate groups between the individual and the state. Ironically, as Bayley (1985) suggests, this gives individualistic societies nowhere to turn for dealing with burgeoning crime problems but to the coercive apparatus of the state. In crime control, the ideology of individualism spawns state interventionism. But the decline of communitarianism is much more than a product of ideology. It is a consequence of urbanization, for example, though, as Japan shows, not quite an inevitable consequence. World population growth progressively increases the average size and density of the communities in which most of us live. Industrialization and declining labor-intensiveness of agriculture in most parts of the world exacerbate this tendency further. An associated phenomenon is increasing residential mobility. People do not live in one place for as long as they used to. Anonymity becomes a characteristic of mobile urban communities; neighbors cease to be significant others, relatives become geographically separated, even school and church affiliations become more transient, not only because parishioners and students are moving more often, but the teachers and preachers are more mobile as well.

Shaming can of course be applied by the state in individualistic cultures which hand over more or less total responsibility for social control to the state. Shaming by the state is important. Individualistic societies in which the state engages in a great deal of shaming should have less crime than individualistic societies in which the state seeks to achieve social control through clinically administering punishment without associated moralizing and denunciation. Communitarian societies with much state shaming should have less crime than communitarian societies without state shaming, if the latter exist. But communitarian societies can deliver more than state shaming, they can also deliver shaming by neighbors and relatives and congregation members in a way that individualistic societies cannot. Shaming by significant others should be more potent than shaming by an impersonal state. Most of us will care less about what a judge (whom we meet only once in our lifetime) thinks of us than we will care about the esteem in which we are held by a neighbor we see regularly. Moreover, frequency of contact means that even if state shaming, being more authoritative, is more potent, it will be less efficacious than community shaming because of regularity of imposition. I may have to put up with the stony stare of my neighbor every day, while the judge will get only one chance to stare stonily at me.

Communitarianism and Reintegration

Communitarian societies not only have a capacity to deliver more potent shaming, they can also deliver shaming which is more reintegrative. Shaming often works in communitarian societies through formal pronouncements of shaming being made directly by the state through the court system and indirectly by the community through scandal and gossip which is not expressed openly to the offender. Reintegration, in contrast, is often the job of the family and close friends; their task is a nurturant one – to show that even though the blow to reputation has been severe, the offender is forgiven and still accepted by her loved ones, and her loved ones are by her side to provide practical support in getting on with life.

Richard Erickson's (1977) study of offenders released from prison empirically supported the conclusion that the more socially distant a person is from the ex-offender, the more likely she will react to him in a stigmatic fashion. Contrary to Goffman's (1968) predictions, the offender's family, 'rather than removing the contamination by dissociating themselves from their son...join the stigmatised individual in a collective effort at seeking a conventional identity' (Erickson, 1977: 22). Similarly, ex-inmates contrasted the acceptance of close friends with the tendency of socially distant people (including probation officers) to react to them as criminals: 'Me mates know what I'm really like. They know many sides of me, whereas others just think of the criminal side first, sort of thing' (Erickson, 1977: 23).

The same capacity to shame reintegratively applies to communitarian corporations. A director of Japan's largest oil company, when interviewed by Brent Fisse and myself about how the company found a new job in head office for a refinery general manager disgraced following a fatal accident, said: 'We are like a family. If a young son commits a crime, the father must bear blame.'

A critical feature of communitarian societies is that they are both more capable of potent shaming which amounts to stigmatization and less willing to cast out their deviants. As Wilkins (1964) has pointed out, people who live in village cultures have much more complex experience of each other as total personalities; or, as Christie (1981: 81) has argued:

All other things being equal, though obviously they are not, it seems to be a plausible hypothesis that the greater the amount of information on the totality of the life of the relevant system members, the less useful (and needed) are generalized concepts such as 'sickness', 'madness',— and 'crime'. The system members come to know so much about each other, that the broad concepts in a way become too simple. They do not add information, they do not explain.

Thus, in an anonymous urban community it is easier to label a neighbor as 'mentally subnormal' and therefore 'dangerous' than it is in a communitarian village to put in a deviant category Jack, 'who is so kind, so complex, who has problems enough, whose total biography many know' (Christie, 1981: 90); 'Maybe he drools, but he is also known to be harmless, and his father was a good workman' (Wilkins, 1964: 68).

This means that, in communitarian societies, while pressures for shaming are greater because people are so much more involved in each others' lives, for the same reason pressures for stigmatization are less. People are shamed for their particular sins rather than through lumping them into crude master categories. There is more gossip, more scandal, more shame but more empathy, less categorical stigma, and therefore ultimately less criminal subculture formation. Effective crime control is likely to occur in communities where offenders are not confronted as criminals but as whole persons. Interpersonal encounters with the offender and his family encompass the whole person rather than the label, and are reintegrative (as with the butcher who murdered my neighbor). Yet indirect shaming by gossip is much more focused on the deviant label, on wild

condemnations which sensitive citizens would never directl
the offender.

Communitarian societies can in some sense, therefore, h
cake and eat it. They can get reintegration by overt confrontations
which treat people as whole complex personalities, and can reinforce
morality by covert gossip which treats offenders much more as
simple sinners. The overt encounters reflect a more rational, fair-
minded account of the offender compelled by the need to continue
interacting with him; the covert gossip reflects the irrepressible
capacity of human beings to affirm their own normalcy, to enhance
their own relative repute, by merciless and simplistic devaluations of
others. Communitarian societies can deliver both sides of this
hypocritical equation with a force which atomized societies cannot
match. The anthropological fieldwork literature amply illustrates
the paradox of communitarian village life in which vicious gossip is
rife but practical tolerance of the 'village idiot' and other deviants is
high. In the extreme case of an atomized society, people are not
interested enough in each other to engage in malicious gossip, and,
when forced to interact with offenders, they are not *knowledgable*
enough about them to respond to them other than according to the
appropriate deviant stereotype.

Predictors of Interdependency

We now switch backwards a level of analysis from the societal
condition conducive of reintegrative shaming (communitarianism) to the individual-level variable which is the building block
of communitarianism (interdependency). We have already argued
that individuals are more susceptible to shaming by other individuals when they are in relationships of interdependency. The
permanence and intensity of a relationship, how wide ranging are
the concerns in which one is dependent on the other, determine the
strength of interdependency. On all these dimensions, for example,
parents usually have stronger interdependencies with their children
than do their peers. Thus parents generally, though not invariably,
have a greater capacity than peers to shame their children. But the
strength of the interdependency also depends on the respect and
obligation associated with the relationship. When parents lose the
respect of their children, it is peers who often come to have the

greater capacity to shame. The task now is to understand what individual characteristics are associated with interdependency.

Unemployment

Persons who leave school and then do not find employment are set free from the interdependencies associated with schooling without establishing the new set of interdependencies associated with work. Shaming by employers has some special potency, whether effected by a snide remark in front of workmates or by some other means. If the employee is dependent on the job, she cannot walk away from the shaming. Unemployed people are not susceptible to this kind of shaming which is especially important in cultures like Japan where relationships with the boss are rather permanent and have wide ramifications.

Commitment

Teachers are dependent on students for a job and students are dependent on teachers for education and certification of their competence to enter the labor market. But if students have a weak commitment to education and have given up on labor market aspirations, the capacity of teachers to shame, or of the school as an institution to shame, will be weak. Hirschi's (1969) control theory is very much about the failure of this kind of interdependency arising from weak commitments to educational and occupational advancement.

Age and Marital Status

The most important correlate of interdependency is stage in the life cycle. Well socialized children establish strong relationships of interdependency with their family of orientation, their school, and, depending on how communitarian the culture, with the neighborhood of their family of orientation. By mature adulthood, these relationships of interdependency have been substantially cut and replaced by a new set of interdependencies with the nuclear family of procreation, the neighborhood in which that family lives, and the workplace.

Between the severing of the first set of interdependencies and the establishment of the second set is a transition. There can be many years between severing relations with a school which is capable of shaming and settling into a steady job with its new possibilities for shaming – years of casual relationships in which shaming is a signal for breakup and starting afresh with someone else, years in transient rented dwellings indulging in wild parties which upset neighbors whom one does not know or care about. Adolescents tend to cut their interdependency with parents, school, and 'the old fogey next door' very rapidly, while they slowly and tenuously develop new interdependencies. As we go back in history, this becomes less true; adolescent culture is essentially a twentieth century concept: 'In the early nineteenth century, children became adults as soon as they began to work, and that was at a very early age, indeed' (Wilson and Herrnstein, 1985: 435).

The period of tenuous interdependency has been extended by a number of features of modern societies; the expanded duration of education (tertiary institutions, with a passing parade of teachers, supply less effective interdependencies than junior schools), growing youth unemployment (Greenberg, 1977), and delayed marriage and childbearing. The latter is possibly the most important inter-dependency of all. As Silberman suggests: 'The most compelling reason for going straight is that young men fall in love and want to marry and have children; marriage and the family are the most effective correctional institutions we have' (Silberman, 1978; quoted in Bayley, 1985: 113).

The age–crime association has proved a difficult nut to crack for criminology, so much so that Hirschi and Gottfredson were moved to conclude that 'efforts to explain the age effect with the theoretical and empirical variables currently available to criminology are doomed to failure' (Hirschi and Gottfredson, 1983: 567). Rowe and Tittle (1977) attempted to explain the age–crime association on a limited self-reported criminality measure with scales to measure social integration, moral commitment, sanction fear and the utility of crime for the subject. The combined effect of these controls was to explain away the age–crime association for only four of eight types of crime. The 'social integration' measure is an approximation of my interdependency concept, though some items in the scale do not tap it (e.g. 'amount of personal pride the respondent felt in the US today'). While 'social integration' did slightly better than the other scales in explaining the age-crime association, controling for 'social integration' alone effected only very modest reductions in the association, and could explain it away for only one of eight comparisons.

Gender

The transition between interdependencies for females is very different from that for males. In a patriarchal culture men are expected to break away from dependency on the family of procreation, to become 'men-of-the-world', even to 'sow their oats', and then to 'settle down' to create their own family of procreation. Women, on the other hand, are expected to swap one form of dependency (on the family of orientation) for another (on the family of procreation). Women are under no imperative to 'cut free from their mother's apron strings' and certainly not to 'sow their oats'. In summary, in patriarchal cultures, the sanctioned sequence for males is one set of interdependencies, followed by a period as a free agent, followed by the man building a new set of interdependencies. For females, to the extent that society is patriarchal, it is one set of dependencies, followed by accepting the terms of another set of dependencies established by a male partner. The female is thus always more socially integrated, always more susceptible to shaming by those on whom she is dependent, and never quite as free to make deviant choices as the male.

The empirical evidence on female delinquency is consistent with this view. As Box (1981) concludes from this literature, the correlates of female delinquency seem pretty much the same as those of male delinquency (Jensen and Eve, 1976; Hagan *et al.*, 1979; Johnson, 1979; Shover *et al.*, 1979; Smith, 1979; Canter, 1982;Thornton, 1982; McCarthy and Hoge, 1984; Elliott *et al.*, 1985; Segrave and Hastad, 1985; but see Ray and Downs, 1986). It is just that females are on average more attached to and effectively controlled by their parents than males, have fewer delinquent friends, and have less of most characteristics associated with delinquency for both sexes.

Jensen and Erickson (1978) reported from a study of 3,000 high school students consistent associations between self-reported delinquency and a variety of items tapping how much the student 'would worry' following apprehension as a delinquent over 'how your parents might react', over the possibility that 'your teachers might think badly of you', etc. Consistent with the prediction of the theory of reintegrative shaming, Jensen and Erickson (1978: 29–30) reported:

Females were significantly more concerned about every possible consequence of labeling than males, and the relationships were much more impressive than for other background variables: Gamma coefficients ranged from −.14 to −.37. Two of the most impressive differences involved parental reaction and self-respect. Eighty percent of the females felt that their parents would definitely be upset, as compared with 63% of the males. Forty-seven percent indicated they definitely might think badly of themselves as compared to 28% of the males.

From an early age, daughters are socialized to accept an ongoing status of dependency (which becomes interdependency as soon as they are old enough to care for younger children), while male socialization is more oriented to preparation for breaking away and asserting dominance. As Udry (1974: 54) concludes: 'By age three, the boy will begin to perceive that some new requirements go with being male. Males are not supposed to be passive, compliant and dependent, but on the contrary, are expected to be aggressive, independent and self-assertive.'

Hagan *et al.* (1979: 25) theorize and empirically support the position that 'women are more frequently the instruments and objects of *informal* social controls, while men are more frequently the instruments and objects of *formal* social controls'. Women are not only the prime objects of dependency upon the family, they are also the main instruments of transmitting sexually stratified dependency into the next generation: 'Young girls, used to relying on older siblings and adults ("seeking help"), soon give this help ("offer help and support") to younger children' (Chodorow, 1971).

Reintegrative shaming in the family is more effective with girls because, as suggested by the control theory literature on female delinquency, they are more attached to their parents, and more concerned to be respected by their parents, than are boys. Perhaps partly for this reason, formal social controls are more often resorted to with boys, not only in the way demonstrated by Hagan *et al.* (1979) of boys suffering higher risks of police intervention, but also for example through the greater resort by schools to corporal punishment for boys. Elaborating the seminal work of Hagan *et al.* (1979), we predict that females will be more often the objects and the instruments of reintegrative shaming, while males will be more often the objects and instruments of stigmatization. That is, it will be more often boys than girls who will be cast out from the family for acts of deviance, and it will be more often fathers who will be involved in the banishment; mothers, even in the face of outcasting, will more often be struggling to achieve reintegration to the extent possible in the circumstances.

Just as it is through participating in gossip that we become sensitive to being targets of gossip, there is a reciprocal relationship between being an instrument and an object of reintegrative shaming. Socialization to engage in reintegrative shaming as the preferred method of social control renders a person more susceptible to being reintegrated by shaming. To understand the lower crime rates of women, we need to understand the structurally differentiated mission of women to secure social integration in the family. It is much more difficult for women than for men to have a period in their life cycle where they make a break with that mission by cutting ties of interdependency.

The expanding time-out from interdependency of males since World War II, and the comparative absence of time-out for females, are, respectively, neglected explanations for rising post-war crime rates and for the much lower crime rates of females compared with males.

Cultural Homogeneity

There is a case for positing cultural homogeneity as a precondition for effective social control, including reintegrative shaming (e.g. Grabosky, 1984: 173–5; Bayley, 1985). Of course the theory already incorporates cultural diversity as a key concept through the importance of criminal subcultures. The theory rejects the notion that American blacks as a group exert more shaming to secure violation of the law than shaming to secure compliance; but it accepts that there may be subcultures which are totally black which use shame to foster crime rather than conformity, just as there are subcultures of Anglo-Saxon businessmen which do this.

While cultural diversity is incorporated into the theory through this key role of subcultures, the theory does not take the further step of arguing that there is less likely to be shaming in a society that is culturally fragmented (and less likely to be shaming which is reintegrative).

If the theory were a general theory of deviance one would be tempted to take this further step. Here we are building a theory of predatory crime, however. In the most culturally fragmented societies, the different cultural fragments can generally agree on this – that almost all criminal laws to protect the persons and property of citizens are justified, and offenses against them worthy of disapproval. Australian Aboriginals might reject the white man's criminal justice system, might believe that it discriminates viciously against blacks, might have a different view of the punishments appropriate (e.g. support for corporal punishment), might view their traditional justice system as superior, but at least there is general agreement between Aboriginals and whites in Australia that the behavior criminalized by white man's law should be criminalized. This cross-cultural agreement is what distinguishes the core values of the criminal law from the dissensus over values involved in the disapproval of other forms of deviance and the approval of 'pro-social' forms of behavior.

If there is at least consensus among major cultural fragments of the society that rape, murder, theft and fraud are criminal and should be disapproved, then there is not a strong basis for assuming that culturally fragmented societies will be less prone to shame effectively. The different cultural groups may shame their own in their own way to secure the compliance with the criminal law which they all view as desirable.

To the extent that a society is culturally divided, then interdependencies will not form across cultural groups. Interdependencies will not disappear; they will simply become more culturally segregated; people will not marry less, but blacks will marry blacks and whites will marry whites.

Different cultural groups will of course differ in their traditions of shaming. Minority groups do not necessarily shame less potently than the majority group. In this regard, it is worth contemplating the behavior of Jews, Japanese and Chinese in the United States. If, on the other hand, one wished to contend that blacks and Chicanos in the US make for an opposite picture, it should be contemplated whether the high crime rates of these groups might have less to do with shaming and belief in the law than with the systematically blocked opportunities they endure in the American class system.

Why should we expect the poor to be less committed to the criminal law than the rich, when, as pointed out in Chapter 2, the poor are those most likely to be victims of the most serious types of both common crime and white collar crime? It makes little sense for the rich to be more committed to the criminal law than the poor when there are more crimes on the statute books which criminalize the behavior of business than laws which criminalize the behavior of the poor, even if the powerful can generally secure practical immunity from its enforcement. The evidence suggests, even excluding white collar crime from consideration, that there are not significant class differences in tolerance of law breaking: values have not been identified that distinguish the working class from the middle class and that are also correlated with delinquency (Braithwaite, 1979: 77–84; Braithwaite and Braithwaite, 1981). The degree of inequality in society is important to the explanation of crime rates (Braithwaite, 1979; Braithwaite and Braithwaite, 1980; Carroll and Jackson, 1983; Sampson, 1985; but see Messner, 1982; Bailey, 1984). However, structured differences in legitimate and illegitimate opportunities between the classes are a more promising basis for connecting crime and inequality than is the pursuit of value differences between classes.

Cultural groups surely do vary in the extent to which they shame their own effectively. Cultural heterogeneity only undermines shaming over values which are the subject of cross-cultural consensus to the extent that the constituent cultural groups shame impotently. Adding a new cultural group to a society (reducing societal homogeneity) may reduce crime rates if the new group is more effective at informal social control than the majority group. Most immigrant groups in Australia, for example, show lower crime rates than native-born Australians (Francis, 1981); Sutherland and Cressey (1978:148-9) found below-average crime rates for foreign-born citizens in a number of countries, including the United States.

On the other hand, cultural heterogeneity may well weaken the state-based part of shaming. While I have argued that this is less important than shaming by proximate groups, the solemn pronouncements of blame by courts of law are still very important. To the extent that minority groups do not identify with the majoritarian criminal justice system, pronouncements of shame by courts will have less force.

Whether or not the theory would be better if cultural homogeneity were posited as a condition conducive to reintegrative shaming is an empirical question. It is not a major modification to the theory to add cultural homogeneity as an extra variable to the top right corner of Figure 1, p. 99. However, one would have to be careful in how one went about testing it. There are many societies in which minority groups push up crime rates; in most of these cases the minorities have fewer legitimate opportunities for achieving success goals than citizens from the majority group. Disentangling the effects of pursuing illegitimate opportunities as a response to closed legitimate opportunities from the effects of attenuated shaming of crime may be a tall order. The solution summarized in the next chapter seems best: cultural minorities are only posited as central to the understanding of crime in so far as they are minorities subject to systematically blocked legitimate opportunities, in which case the existence of those oppressed minorities fosters criminal subculture formation.

Conclusion

While shaming by the state is less potent than shaming by proximate communities, effective state shaming is one of the factors which assist societies to maintain low crime rates. This is so because state shaming can trigger much of the community shaming, and because the state is needed to shame incidents of such low frequency and high seriousness as to be otherwise beyond the direct experience of most community members. Moreover, reintegrative shaming is often achieved through state punishment (combined with community gossip thereby triggered) delivering most of the shame, and intimates delivering most of the reintegration.

Communitarianism is the societal characteristic most critical not only for fostering shaming, but also shaming which is reintegrative. Stigmatization is less likely in communitarian cultures because the complex experience that people have of each other makes it more difficult to squeeze the identities of offenders into crude master categories of deviance. Communitarianism therefore not only fosters gossip, shame and reintegration; it may also inhibit criminal subculture formation in the society through granting less credence to outcast master statuses.

7

Summary of the theory

Figure 1 provides a schematic summary of the theory. In the first part of this chapter clear definitions are attempted for the key concepts in Figure 1. The cluster of six variables around interdependency at the top left of Figure 1 are characteristics of individuals; the three at the top right are characteristics of societies; while high levels of crime and shaming are variables which apply to both individuals and societies. The theory as summarized in Figure 1 thus gives an account both of why some kinds of individuals and some kinds of societies exhibit more crime.

We could get a more parsimonious theory by collapsing the similar constructs of interdependency (an individual-level variable) and communitarianism (a societal variable) into a single construct, but then we would no longer have a framework to predict both which individuals and which societies will have more crime. On the desirability of being able to do this I can only agree with Cressey (see also Chapter 8, pp. 109–11):

A theory explaining social behavior in general, or any specific kind of social behavior, should have two distinct but consistent aspects. First, there must be a statement that explains the statistical distribution of the behavior in time and space (epidemiology), and from which predictive statements about unknown statistical distributions can be derived. Second, there must be a statement that identifies, at least by implication, the process by which individuals come to exhibit the behavior in question, and from which can be derived predictive statements about the behavior of individuals. (Cressey, 1960:47)

Key Concepts

Interdependency is a condition of individuals. It means the extent to which individuals participate in networks wherein they are depen-

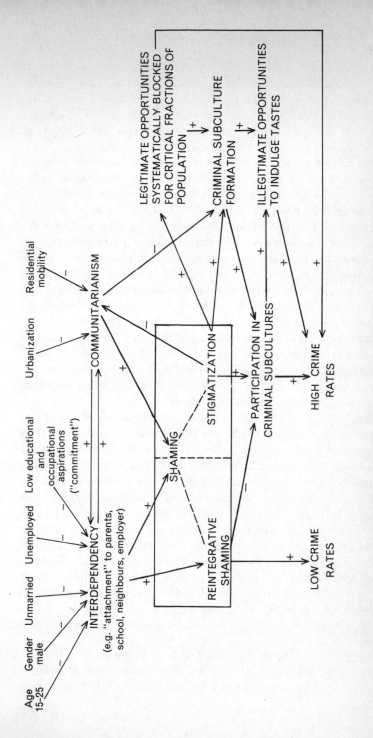

Figure 1: Summary of the Theory of Reintegrative Shaming

dent on others to achieve valued ends and others are dependent on them. We could describe an individual as in a state of inter-dependency even if the individuals who are dependent on him are different from the individuals on whom he is dependent. Inter-dependency is approximately equivalent to the social bonding, attachment and commitment of control theory.

Communitarianism is a condition of societies. In communitarian societies individuals are densely enmeshed in interdependencies which have the special qualities of mutual help and trust. The interdependencies have symbolic significance in the culture of group loyalties which take precedence over individual interests. The inter-dependencies also have symbolic significance as attachments which invoke personal obligation to others in a community of concern, rather than simply interdependencies of convenience as between a bank and a small depositor. A communitarian culture rejects any pejorative connotation of dependency as threatening individual autonomy. Communitarian cultures resist interpretations of de-pendency as weakness and emphasize the need for mutuality of obligation in interdependency (to be both dependent and depend-able). The Japanese are said to be socialized not only to *amaeru* (to be succored by others) but also to *amayakasu* (to be nurturing to others) (Wagatsuma and Rosett, 1986).

Shaming means all social processes of expressing disapproval which have the intention or effect of invoking remorse in the person being shamed and/or condemnation by others who become aware of the shaming. When associated with appropriate symbols, formal punishment often shames. But societies vary enormously in the extent to which formal punishment is associated with shaming or in the extent to which the social meaning of punishment is no more than to inflict pain to tip reward–cost calculations in favor of certain outcomes. Shaming, unlike purely deterrent punishment, sets out to moralize with the offender to communicate reasons for the evil of her actions. Most shaming is neither associated with formal punishment nor perpetrated by the state, though both shaming by the state and shaming with punishment are important types of shaming. Most shaming is by individuals within interdependent communities of concern.

Reintegrative shaming is shaming which is followed by efforts to reintegrate the offender back into the community of law-abiding or respectable citizens through words or gestures of forgiveness or ceremonies to decertify the offender as deviant. Shaming and rein-tegration do not occur simultaneously but sequentially, with rein-tegration occurring before deviance becomes a master status. It is shaming which labels the act as evil while striving to preserve the identity of the offender as essentially good. It is directed at signifying evil deeds rather than evil persons in the Christian tradition of 'hate the sin and love the sinner'. Specific disapproval is expressed within relationships characterized by general social approval; shaming cri-minal behavior is complemented by ongoing social rewarding of alternative behavior patterns. Reintegrative shaming is not neces-sarily weak; it can be cruel, even vicious. It is not distinguished from stigmatization by its potency, but by (a) a finite rather than open-ended duration which is terminated by forgiveness; and by (b) efforts to maintain bonds of love or respect throughout the finite period of suffering shame.

Stigmatization is disintegrative shaming in which no effort is made to reconcile the offender with the community. The offender is out-cast, her deviance is allowed to become a master status, degradation ceremonies are not followed by ceremonies to decertify deviance.

Criminal subcultures are sets of rationalizations and conduct norms which cluster together to support criminal behavior. The clustering is usually facilitated by subcultural groups which provide systematic social support for crime in any of a number of ways – supplying members with criminal opportunities, criminal values, attitudes which weaken conventional values of law-abidingness, or techniques of neutralizing conventional values.

Short Summary of the Theory

The following might serve as the briefest possible summary of the theory. A variety of life circumstances increase the chances that individuals will be in situations of greater interdependency, the most important being age (under 15 and over 25), being married, female, employed, and having high employment and educational aspira-tions. Interdependent persons are more susceptible to shaming. More importantly, societies in which individuals are subject to extensive interdependencies are more likely to be communitarian, and shaming is much more widespread and potent in communita-rian societies. Urbanization and high residential mobility are societ-al characteristics which undermine communitarianism.

The shaming produced by interdependency and communitarianism can be either of two types – shaming that becomes stigmatization or shaming that is followed by reintegration. The shaming engendered is more likely to become reintegrative in societies that are communitarian. In societies where shaming does become reintegrative, low crime rates are the result because disapproval is dispensed without eliciting a rejection of the disapprovers, so that the potentialities for future disapproval are not dismantled. Moreover, reintegrative shaming is superior even to stigmatization for conscience-building (see the fifteen points at the conclusion to Chapter 5).

Shaming that is stigmatizing, in contrast, makes criminal subcultures more attractive because these are in some sense subcultures which reject the rejectors. Thus, when shaming is allowed to become stigmatization for want of reintegrative gestures or ceremonies which decertify deviance, the deviant is both attracted to criminal subcultures and cut off from other interdependencies (with family, neighbors, church, etc.). Participation in subcultural groups supplies criminal role models, training in techniques of crime and techniques of neutralizing crime (or other forms of social support) that make choices to engage in crime more attractive. Thus, to the extent that shaming is of the stigmatizing rather than the reintegrative sort, and that criminal subcultures are widespread and accessible in the society, higher crime rates will be the result. While societies characterized by high levels of stigmatization will have higher crime rates than societies characterized by reintegrative shaming, the former will have higher or lower crime rates than societies with little shaming at all depending largely on the availability of criminal subcultures.

Yet a high level of stigmatization in the society is one of the very factors that encourages criminal subculture formation by creating populations of outcasts with no stake in conformity, no chance of self-esteem within the terms of conventional society – individuals in search of an alternative culture that allows them self-esteem. A communitarian culture, on the other hand, nurtures deviants within a network of attachments to conventional society, thus inhibiting the widespread outcasting that is the stuff of subculture formation.

For clarity of exposition the two types of shaming have been presented as a stark dichotomy. In reality, for any society some deviants are are dealt with in ways that are more stigmatic while others receive more reintegrative shaming. Indeed, a single deviant will be responded to more stigmatically by some, more reintegratively by others. To the extent that the greater weight of shaming tends to stigmatization, the crime-producing processes on the right of Figure 1 are more likely to be triggered; to the extent that the balance of shaming tips toward reintegration, informal processes of crime control are more likely to prevail over these crime-producing processes.

The other major societal variable which fosters criminal subculture formation is systematic blockage of legitimate opportunities for critical fractions of the population. If black slum dwellers are systematically denied economic opportunities because of the stigma of their race and neighborhood, then criminal subcultures will form in those outcast neighborhoods. It can be seen that stigmatization (as opposed to social integration) as a cultural disposition may contribute to the systematic blockage of these economic opportunities; but cultural variables like stigmatization will be of rather minor importance compared with structural economic variables in determining opportunities. I have argued that the blockages in this part of the theory are not restricted to closed opportunities to climb out of poverty; systematically blocked opportunities for ever greater wealth accumulation by the most affluent of corporations often lead to corporate criminal subculture formation (see Chapter 9).

Criminal subcultures are the main mechanism for constituting illegitimate opportunity structures - knowledge on how to offend, social support for offending or communication of rationalizations for offending, criminal role models, subcultural groups which assist with the avoidance of detection and which organize collective criminal enterprises. However, illegitimate opportunities are greater in some societies than others for a variety of further reasons which are not incorporated within the theory. While the effects of legitimate and illegitimate opportunities on crime are mostly mediated by participation in criminal subcultures, the blockage of legitimate opportunities combined with the availability of illegitimate opportunities can independently increase crime. Whether illegitimate opportunities to engage in crime are supplied by participation in criminal subcultures or otherwise, they must be opportunities that appeal to the tastes of tempted individuals for them to result in crime.

This summary is crudely simple because it ignores what goes on within the shaming box in Figure 1. That is, it ignores the treatment in Chapters 5 and 6 of the social processes that combine individual acts of shaming into cultural processes of shaming which are more or less integrative: gossip, media coverage of shaming incidents, children's stories, etc. In turn, the summary has neglected how these macro processes of shaming feed back to ensure that micro practices of shaming cover the curriculum of crimes.

Ecological Fallacies?

In a theory which simultaneously provides an account of individual behavior and societal behavior, one can slip variables across from one level of analysis to the other. Thus, when testing the theory at the individual level of analysis, one can code individuals according to whether they live in large cities or whether they have been residentially mobile. That is, the two societal variables at the top right of Figure 1 can be translated into individual-level variables.

Equally, an individual-level variable like 'age 15-25' can become a societal variable – percentage of the population of the society aged 15-25. However, in making these shifts it is possible to perpetrate the ecological fallacy – to assume glibly that what is true at the individual level of analysis will be true at the societal level. A society is more than the sum of its individual parts. Thus, when a society accumulates unusually high numbers of young people, the behavior of *older* people may change in response – they might vote for increased investment in education or police juvenile aid bureaux, for example. There is some evidence, for example, that while unemployment is a strong predictor of individual criminality, societies with high unemployment rates do not necessarily have high crime rates (Braithwaite, 1979; but see Chiricos, 1987). Gender is another variable which does not usefully shift from the individual to the societal level of analysis because societies do not vary in the proportion of their population which is female.

Apart from these two, I can see no sound theoretical or empirical reason why the variables in Figure 1 cannot move between both the individual and societal levels of analysis.

Capacity of the Theory to Explain What We Know About Crime

Chapter 3 set out consistently supported strong correlates of crime. What is the capacity of the theory to explain these relationships? Some indeterminacy arises over the different effects of reintegrative shaming versus stigmatization. For example, what does the theory predict should be the association between gender and crime? Figure 1 shows that being female increases interdependency, which in turn fosters shaming. If the extra shaming produced is reintegrative, being female is associated with low crime rates. However, if the extra shaming amounts to stigmatization, higher crime rates become possible where subcultural support is found for the outcast status.

To solve this problem we make a rather modest assumption. This assumption, as argued earlier, is that in most societies criminal subcultures are minority phenomena – narrowly diffused – so that stigmatization will in only a minority of cases be followed by an opportunity to participate in a subculture which is attractive to the individual. It follows that the level of shaming should be unambiguously negatively related to the crime rate because most shaming will be either reintegrative shaming, or stigmatic shaming which does not lead to subcultural attachments, and both of these options will reduce crime. In any case, as is clear from Figure 1, variables (like gender) which increase interdependency have their effect on shaming partly through increasing communitarianism, and shaming which is a product of communitarianism is most likely to be reintegrative. Interdependency both increases the prospects of shaming and decreases the chances that such shaming as occurs will be stigmatic.

Thus the characteristics associated with low interdependency – being male, 15-25 years of age, unmarried, unemployed, and with low educational and vocational aspirations – should all be associated with high involvement in crime. Urbanization and high residential mobility are also predicted by the theory as correlates of crime. It was concluded in Chapter 3 that all of these characteristics are strong and consistent correlates of crime.

In establishing the relationship between communitarianism and crime, we rely far too heavily on qualitative evidence from Japan and more doubtful qualitative evidence from a handful of other societies. The association between interdependency as a characteristic of individuals and crime, on the other hand, is well established. Control theory has spawned impressive evidence that young people who are 'attached' to their parents and to the school are less likely to engage in delinquency (see Chapter 2).

There is not such an impressive and unambiguous literature on 'attachment' to neighbors and crime (see Chapter 10, pp. 171–3). The recent review of sixty-five studies of religiosity and deviance by Tittle and Welch (1983) suggests the possibility, contrary to some conventional wisdom in criminology, that interdependency via church affiliation may reduce crime. Tittle and Welch (1983: 654) concluded that 'the evidence seems remarkably consistent in suggesting that religion is related to deviant behavior. Indeed, only a few variables in social science (possibly gender and age) have proven to be better predictors of rule breaking' (see also Ellis, 1985).

Thus, through examining the corollaries of the theory we can explain most of the well-established strong correlates of crime discussed in Chapter 3. Specifically, we have already accounted for propositions 1-6 and proposition 9 on pages 44–8. What of the propositions we have not explained?

An account is given of propositions 7 and 8 if we are willing to assume that young people with low educational and occupational aspirations and who do poorly at school are less attached to (interdependent with) their school. The theory of reintegrative shaming provides an explanation for why unemployed people should engage in less crime in terms of their loss of interdependency (proposition 12). Beyond unemployment, being at the bottom of the class structure means blocked legitimate opportunities and an increased likelihood of access to certain kinds of subcultures which supply illegitimate opportunities (proposition 12).

The theory offers a convincing explanation of why crime rates have been increasing in most Western societies since World War II. The recent development of Western societies has been associated with a decline of interdependency and communitarianism and a progressive uncoupling of punishment and shaming. This has been a period when urbanization, residential mobility, delayed marriage and marriage breakdown, and an explosion of the 15-25 age group have occurred in most countries.

Finally, proposition 10 on page 48, that young people who associate with criminals are more likely to engage in crime themselves, approximates one of the propositions of the theory – that participating in a criminal subculture leads to crime. Sharing a criminal subculture was argued to be a route to crime partly because the subculture transmits qualifications or neutralizations to belief in the importance of complying with the law (proposition 11).

In summary, the theory accounts for twelve of the thirteen best established findings of criminology as corollaries of the theory and one as a postulate of the theory.

Shunting the Colliding Locomotives of Criminological Theory

This sharp contrast with the inability of the existing dominant theories to explain much of what we know about crime is achieved, ironically, through the addition of just one element – the partitioning of shaming – as a shunt to connect these diverging theoretical tracks. Through putting the old theoretical ingredients together in a new way, we can do better at accounting for the facts than can any of these traditions separately (compare Chapter 3, pp. 50–2). Moreover, we can do better compared with adding together their separate (contradictory!) elements as partial explanations within an atheoretical multi-factor model.

The top left of Figure 1 incorporates the key variables of control theory; the far right – opportunity theory; the middle and bottom right – subcultural theory; the bottom, particularly the bottom left – learning theory; the right side of the middle box – labeling theory. With one crucial exception (reintegrative shaming), there is therefore no originality in the elements of this theory, simply originality of synthesis.

Through the effect of interdependency in reducing crime, we can capture the explanatory successes of control theory in accounting for primary deviance. Through shunting stigmatization away from other forms of shaming (as that sort of shaming which triggers subcultural participation) we proffer a more promising approach to the explanation of secondary deviance in labeling and subcultural theory terms. We achieve a more specified theory of differential association with conventional others versus others who share a subculture. Conceived another way, it is a theory of differential shaming. Most shaming is by conventional others on the anticriminal side of a tipping point. When stigmatization produces secondary deviance, it is because the balance of shame has tipped; for those who share the subculture there is sufficient approval for crime, sufficient shaming for going straight, to outweigh the shaming of conventional society.

8

Testing the theory

The purpose of this chapter is to describe the different levels of analysis at which the theory of reintegrative shaming might be confronted with data collected systematically with a view to testing the theory. In turn, we shall discuss ethnographic, historical, and survey research, macrosociological studies based on official statistics, and experimental designs.

Ethnographic Research

The first test any theory should confront is for researchers to observe and talk to actors who routinely deal with the phenomena addressed in the theory. If the phenomena posited in the theory are never observed to happen, if grey-haired people with long experience of them say 'They never heard of that happening' (Macaulay, 1986) or 'they never heard of it happening like that', then there is reason to cast serious doubt on the explanatory framework of the theory.

Single case studies are useful in testing theories that generate many interdependent predictions about how things happen, such as the theory of reintegrative shaming. The ethnographic researcher can disconfirm the theory when most of them do not happen; the theory is tested with multiple degrees of freedom arising from the multiple implications of a single theory for a single research site. 'The process is a kind of pattern-matching in which there are many aspects of the patterns demanded by theory that are available for matching with his observations on the local setting' (Campbell, 1979: 57).

In Japan ethnographic work is thus needed which explicitly sets out to assess whether reintegrative shaming is something that Japanese families, schools, corporations and criminal justice agencies actually do, or whether this is a flawed interpretation of existing studies that were really conducted with other purposes in mind. Similar studies might then be conducted in other cultures known to have unusually low or high crime rates.

There is already, of course, a rich ethnographic literature on gossip in modern urban societies which suggests that it makes very little impression on people (Hannerz, 1967; Liebow, 1967; Bott, 1971; Merry, 1984) and a literature based on the study of small-scale societies that accords gossip a central position in informal social control (e.g., Radcliffe-Brown, 1933; Benedict, 1934; Gluckman, 1963; Kluckhohn, 1967). Even within modern urban contexts, there is ethnographic evidence that gossip has an effect on people when it occurs within close-knit networks (high interdependency) while it is a minor concern to people who are mobile or keep a distance from their neighbors (Young and Wilmott, 1957; Suttles, 1968; Bott, 1971). Merry (1984: 296) sees the considerable accumulation of ethnographic evidence about gossip as pointing to four hypotheses:

1. The impact of gossip and scandal is greater in more bounded social systems in which the costs of desertion or expulsion are higher and the availability of alternative social relationships less.
2. The impact of gossip and scandal is greater in social settings where the members of the local social system are more interdependent for economic aid, jobs, political protection, and social support.
3. The impact of gossip and scandal is greater when it has the potential of producing a community consensus that can be converted into a variety of collective actions such as public shaming, ridicule, expulsion, or death.
4. The impact of gossip and scandal is greater when normative consensus about the behavior in question is more extensive.

One can point to such conclusions from the ethnographic literature as a kind of support for certain important elements of the theory of reintegrative shaming, but they can never amount to very persuasive support. They are certainly no match for fieldwork explicitly designed to record observations in such a way that the theory can be refuted. It should go without saying that the relevant observational test of the theory would occur in the ethnographic tradition of putting families in the context of their culture rather than the developmental psychology tradition of observing simply the impact of family practices of reintegrative shaming on individuals. This is so because the theory is not only about reintegrative shaming controlling crime through an impact on the individual target of the shame, but is more fundamentally about the wider cultural impact mediated through all individuals who become aware of the incident of shaming.

Sociology must address the widening gulf between theories at the level of methodological holism (macro-macro associations) and empirical research in a limited tradition of methodological individualism (micro-micro or macro-micro associations) (Coleman, 1986). Most empirical psychological research explores micro-micro associations between one form of individual behavior and another, while much sociological survey research is macro-micro, where the dependent variable is simply the sum of individual behavior scores. The theory of reintegrative shaming is about how certain macro variables (e.g. urbanization, communitarianism) and micro variables (e.g. age, interdependency) affect choices to engage in various forms of purposive social action (shaming, stigmatizing, reintegrating) and how these choices affect other micro choices (to participate in a subculture, to engage in crime, to reintegrate oneself). Finally, the theory is about how micro choices to shame reintegratively combine to constitute a culture of intolerance and understanding, that in turn becomes a macro constraint on choices to engage in crime. In short, the theory rejects a crude methodological holism that explains one structural variable by another without reference to purposive individual action; and it rejects a crude methodological individualism that accepts an understanding of how society behaves from a simple aggregation of how individuals behave.

The most illuminating theories of social phenomena are likely to be those which explain both how macro variables shape purposive individual action, and how these individual choices combine to constitute other macro variables which further constrain individual action, moving backwards and forwards between the macro and the micro in a way that sees human beings as neither totally determined by structural variables nor totally unconstrained in their choices.

Ethnographic research methods clearly provide the sharpest tools for assessing whole theories that move back and forth between structural and individual variables in this way. But this is not to deny that other research strategies can supply superior tests of *parts* of such theories. For example, while survey research cannot test propositions about how macro variables are constituted from individual social action, it can often provide superior data on the effects of macro independent variables on individual behavior because larger, more random samples of individuals are possible compared with ethnographic research.

Historical Research

If a theory can jump the hurdle of making sense of, and not being refuted by, what we can observe of existing societies, then we should confront it with what we can read of past societies. One of the attractions of the theory of reintegrative shaming is that it seems to have promise in interpreting the history of crime over the past two centuries, at least in English-speaking countries.

One of the things that I found persuasive about Wilson and Herrnstein's (1985) *Crime and Human Nature* was, curiously enough, their account of historical variations in crime trends. The trends to be explained since crime statistics became adequate enough to be usable in England, the United States and Australia are sufficiently clearly and consistently supported to give some confidence in the following broad patterns. (Warner, 1934; Ferdinand, 1967; Lane, 1967, 1969, 1979, 1980; Graham, 1969; Richardson, 1970; Gatrell and Hadden, 1972; Skogan, 1975; Gurr *et al.*, 1977; Grabosky, 1977; Peirce *et al.*, 1977; Gatrell, 1980; Gurr, 1981; Mukherjee, 1981; Monkkonen, 1981a, 1982; Hewitt and Hoover, 1982; Wilson and Herrnstein, 1985). Crime was on an upward trend in the late eighteenth and early nineteenth centuries; from about the second quarter of the nineteenth century, though somewhat later in some places, crime rates began a long decline which was halted by about the second quarter of the twentieth century; in the third quarter of the twentieth century crime rates rose strongly again. An important departure from this pattern in the United States would seem to be a sharp up-turn in recorded crime, probably mainly black crime, at the time of the Civil War and persisting into the 1870s (Hindus, 1980; Gurr, 1981; Monkkonen, 1981b:76–77).

Of course, there are no time-series data on white collar crime, though there is evidence that the long decline in common crime of the Victorian era was also a period when bribery and corruption declined in Britain (Wraith and Simpkins, 1963; Scott, 1972; Thompson, 1986; cf. Bourne, 1986). Also some of the new regulatory agencies of the Victorian era had some striking successes. The Alkali Inspectorate, established in 1863, had been credited by 1865 with reducing emissions of acidic fumes from 13,000 to 43 tons per week (Vogel, 1986:240). The new food and drug regulation of the Victorian era was associated with a drop in the percentage of food and drug samples found to be adulterated from 19 per cent in 1873 to 9 per cent in 1898 (Paulus, 1978:454). By the end of the Victorian era coal mine fatalities per 1,000 miners decreased to less than a third of the level prevailing before the appointment of a Mines Inspectorate under the *Coal Mines Inspection Act* 1850 (Braithwaite, 1985a:85). However, Bartrip and Fenn (1980) concluded that while there was a marked reduction in fatal factory accidents after the British Factory Inspectorate was given powers to regulate safety by the *Factory Act* of 1844, fatal accidents increased again later.

Wilson and Herrnstein account for the rising crime of the early nineteenth century in terms of the 'new and threatening dimension' that urban migration of young men leaving farms took in that period:

In the past, a young person who had gone off to seek his fortune had not only worked but lived with his patron family – a large landholder, a village craftsman, a town merchant. In the early nineteenth century, however, cities were growing so rapidly and the productive processes were changing so radically that young men (and later, young women) who left home now went off to live in boardinghouses with other young persons [Johnson, 1978]. As a result, adult supervision of young men was weakened, not because the family had weakened but because the necessary alternative to family life was no longer under adult control [Kett, 1977].
Young male workers living in cities suddenly acquired an autonomous social life. The opportunities of the cities, magnified by the mutual urgings of peers and the absence of restraints once supplied by family admonitions, became irresistible.   (Wilson and Herrnstein, 1985: 431)

In short, the hypothesis is that early nineteenth-century urbanization was criminogenic in a way the past had not been because it severed ties of interdependency more surely than anything that had occurred previously. For Wilson and Herrnstein, the long decline in crime that followed might be accounted for by 'Victorian morality' with its emphasis on conscience development ('the ethic of self-control'), and the post-World War II rise by the new ascendancy of the ethic of self-expression and spontaneity; avoiding guilt became more important than inculcating shame.

In the mid-nineteenth century, child-rearing advice emphasized the importance of inculcating moral and religious principles so as to make the child 'at
an early age a self-maintaining moral being.' [Sunley, 1955]. This view
persisted into the early part of the twentieth century, but beginning in the
1920s it was partially replaced by a different one. Whereas the child was
once thought to be endowed by nature with dangerous impulses that had to
be curbed, he was now seen as equipped with harmless instincts that ought
to be developed. Earlier, the popular advice had stressed the child's moral
development; now, the literature began to emphasize his capacity for enjoyment. [Wolfenstein, 1955]. In 1890, 1900 and 1910, one-third of the child-
rearing topics discussed in a sample of articles from *Ladies' Home Journal,
Woman's Home Companion,* and *Good Housekeeping* were about character development; in 1920, only 3 per cent were. By 1930, articles on character
development had by and large been replaced with ones on personality
development.   (Wilson and Herrnstein, 1985: 420)

Victorian society saw the development of a proliferation of voluntary associations and public institutions designed to instill character
and teach self-control. The Sunday school was perhaps the most
important of these: between 1821 and 1851, Sunday school enrol-
ments tripled in England, accounting for over half all children aged
five to fifteen; by 1929 in New York 40 per cent of children aged four
to fourteen were said to attend Sunday school (Laqueur (1976) and
Boyer (1978) cited in Wilson and Herrnstein, 1985: 432). According
to Wilson and Herrnstein, as the Freudian revolution began to
percolate into popular consciousness, doubts increased about the
risks of children being taught to repress their instincts. Thus, even
institutions like the YMCA lost their moral mission, becoming over
time little more than that part of the post-industrial economy offering gymnasium services.

The strong decline in crime during the Victorian era in England,
the United States and Australia is a major challenge for theories of
crime: this after all was an era of massive urbanization, industrialization, immigration, a widening gulf between the classes, and
mounting class conflict. Perhaps declining birth rates and the rapid
growth of police forces can take some of the credit, though one might
think that the latter would have more effect in pushing up the
detection and recording of previously unrecorded crime, thus creating a more muted picture of the real decline that occurred. Gurr
(1981) has pointed to some of the evidence that more sophisticated
policing may indeed have pushed up the recording of previously
unrecorded crime:

Gatrell observes that English coroners and police became better able to identify death from unnatural causes during the nineteenth century and offers other evidence that homicides were increasingly likely to come to police attention as the century progressed (1980, pp.247-48). Lane reports on nineteenth-century Philadelphia that 'late in the century a number of [manslaughter] cases were prosecuted that earlier would have been tolerated or overlooked' (1979, p.76).   (Gurr, 1981: 300)

Critics of Wilson and Herrnstein contend that they downplay the hypocrisy of Victorian morality. Hypocrisy there certainly was. But for our present purposes we should bear in mind that reintegrative shaming is in considerable measure a policy of hypocrisy; it is a policy of leaving guilty people unpunished, a policy of symbolic shame followed by tangible mercy (see Chapter 10). Victorian morality no less than the policy of reintegrative shaming recognized that any attempt consistently and equitably to punish all infractions of norms would not only be an attempt at the impossible but would also endanger the legitimacy of those norms.

The Victorian era can be interpreted as more than a triumph of the symbols of shame over those of tolerance; it might also be interpreted as a triumph of the policy of integration over that of casting out. Victorian England inherited a criminal class which 'is in fact a recognised section, and a well-known section too, in all towns of great magnitude... It constitutes a new estate in utter estrangement from all the rest' (1854 journal article cited in Tobias, 1979: 57).

The social policies of pre-Victorian and early Victorian England were the policies of outcasting and stigmatization of the criminal class. Capital punishment was increasingly replaced by transportation to colonies such as Australia. Australia in turn inherited its criminal class by transportation from England. While this was also true in a minor way of pre-Victorian America, its criminal class was more fundamentally created by waves of free European immigration in the North and the slave trade in the South (Hindus, 1980).

Transportation and capital punishment were not the only means by which pre-Victorian and early Victorian policy attempted to cast out the criminal classes from the cities. Slum clearance of the criminal areas was vigorously prosecuted in London in the 1850s and 1860s; Saffron Hill, the alleged home of Fagin, for example, was wiped out in the Farringdon Road clearances. The policy was simply to clean the city of what Matthew Arnold described in *Culture and*

Anarchy as 'those vast, miserable, unmanageable masses of sunken people'.

The ecological segregation of the criminal classes reached its peak in the mid-nineteenth century by which time the desertion by the wealthy and middle classes of close proximity to these areas was complete (Stedman Jones, 1984: 247). But at the same time as advocates of policies to remove outcast London from the centre to satellite workmen's townships were getting a better hearing, so were those who favored policies to integrate the 'unemployable' residuum into mainstream British life. Perhaps partly because of bourgeois and aristocratic fears of revolution, nineteenth-century Britain saw a decisive triumph of the policies of integration over those of outcasting, as Stedman Jones has documented:

Historians have generally discussed this question in a rather one-sided and teleological manner. Looking forward to the creation of the welfare state, they have concentrated upon proposals for old-age pensions, free education, free school meals, subsidized housing, and national insurance. They have virtually ignored parallel proposals to segregate the casual poor, to establish detention centres for 'loafers', to separate pauper children from 'degenerate' parents or to ship the 'residuum' overseas. Yet, for contemporaries, both sorts of proposals composed parts of a single debate.

(Stedman Jones, 1984: 313–14)

The Victorian era might be conceived as one when the policies of outcasting were gradually replaced by integrative policies, first in the form of private charities which attempted to make the poor reputable and deserving through the supervision of 'lady rent collectors' and others, and finally by the integrative ideology of the embryonic welfare state. Concomitantly, criminal justice policies became more humane and integrative: capital punishment was eliminated as a penalty for more and more offenses; flogging was abolished for women and replaced gradually for men; transportation ended; Victorian criminal justice reflected the belief of Victorians in progress, in the perfectability of human beings and of human institutions; the rehabilitative ideal began to overtake the retributivism of classical criminology as the dominant penal ideology, though at times the policies to reintegrate offenders were as misguided and even as inhumane as those they had replaced. The Victorian period saw the exclusionary institution of the prison complete its rise to pre-eminence in criminal justice policy and commence a rapid collapse of confidence. The humanitarian shift continued into the

Edwardian era, with Liberal governments introducing law reforms that saw the number of prison receptions decline between 1905 and 1918 from 200,000 to 25,000 per year (Peirce *et al.*, 1977: 149).

The imprisonment rate for England and Wales, which had trebled between 1775 and 1832, declined by almost 20 per cent between 1832 and 1880 (a period when British prisons had to absorb offenders previously transported), and then plummeted sharply and consistently until in the 1930s it reached about a seventh of the imprisonment rate per 100,000 population of a century earlier. Most of the decline in the use of imprisonment occurred in the late-Victorian period (Ramsay, 1982). In Australia, imprisonment rates increased until just past the middle of the nineteenth century, when there was a massive downward trend which continued to 1920 (Braithwaite, 1980). Similar trends are evident in France, Germany and Belgium, though Italy had a substantial rise in imprisonment for the first thirty-three years of the twentieth century (Rusche and Kirchheimer, 1939). The United States is the most striking exception, evidencing a strong rise in imprisonment rates from 1880 to the present without ever experiencing a period when imprisonment rates fell substantially (Calahan, 1979).

The rehabilitative criminal justice policies developed in the Victorian era perhaps were on balance more effective and humane than the retributive and stigmatizing policies they replaced, but this is not the point. The theory of reintegrative shaming would interpret the rise of the rehabilitative ideal as a symptom of a cultural transformation that saw Victorian society refine the power of shaming while increasingly rejecting the principle of casting out. According to the theory, that cultural transformation would be the nub of Victorian success in crime control. Similarly, the decline in the rehabilitative ideal in the West, if not in the East, over the past two decades, would not be interpreted as a cause of our growing crime rates, but as a symptom of our disenchantment with these Victorian values, of our cynicism about even the improvability, let alone the perfectability, of human beings and their institutions, of a resignation to casting out offenders for longer periods of exile as the only resort, an excision of the very word shame from our daily vocabulary (see Lynd, 1958).

To date, we have not been successful in explaining most of the Victorian decline and the post-war jump in crime rates by changing age and opportunity structures. We may yet do so, however, and

interpretations of these historical trends in terms of the theory of reintegrative shaming may then seem redundant. Much more systematic reconstruction of the historical evidence is needed to test competing theories. It is a task which could well bear considerable rewards for empirical criminology.

It is probably uncontroversial to contend that Victorian preoccupation with personal responsibility for protecting one's reputation, with shaming, preceded most of the century-long decline in crime which was halted by the second quarter of this century. However, the timing of the shift toward reintegrative values is controversial. While Garland (1985) sees some earlier Victorian tendencies for the dominant ideology to shift from despising and outcasting criminals to pitying and reclaiming them, for him the most decisive changes in this direction occurred between 1895 and 1914 – after most of the decline in crime. This interpretation, however, is at odds with that of Foucault (1977) who believed that a hundred years earlier punishment had changed from a demonstration of the awesome power of the sovereign to inflict vengeance on the body of the offender to a procedure for requalifying guilty individuals as subjects. The waters are rather muddied, no doubt partly because none of the trends analysed in the historical literature are singular or uniform.

There are many more questions unanswered than answered by the existing historical work. Did the United States and Australia undergo a similar transition from a culture based on retribution and stigma to one based on shame and integration under the ideology and social policies of the welfare state? Clearly the transition to the welfare state was never as complete in the United States, and while slaves were emancipated in the Victorian era, the integration of American blacks was more partial than that of the British residuum. But then perhaps American crime rates declined to settle at very much higher levels than English rates precisely because blacks remained partially stigmatized. Those of England's outcasts who survived the Australian penal system were also eventually emancipated, and were increasingly accepted by the free community. Whether this happened under the influence of emerging Victorian ideals of rehabilitation and whether this contributed to the sharp decline of crime rates that occurred in the middle of the nineteenth century awaits more focused historical work.

Does an interpretation of the history of crime in terms of the theory of reintegrative shaming make any sense for other countries? Calcutta (Hula, 1977), Germany and France (Zehr, 1976) would seem to exhibit crime patterns in the nineteenth century quite different from those evident in England, the United States and Australia. But then would we expect an Anglo-Saxon analysis based on 'Victorian values' to apply to those countries? On the other hand, Stockholm evidences a pattern for the two centuries broadly similar to those of the Anglo-Saxon countries (Gurr *et al.*, 1977). Each country requires its own detailed analysis of how public and private social control practices varied between tolerance and shame, outcasting and integration, and how these changes related to broad variations in crime rates.

Testing the theory against historical data is more feasible than one would expect given a healthy cynicism about official crime statistics because the broad trends we are discussing are so substantial as to be fairly robust:

Official records of offenses against persons and property in London, Stockholm, and Sydney show remarkably similar trends during the past 150 years. From around 1840 to 1930, indicators of common crime fell by an average ratio of 8:1. Since then, especially since 1950, they have increased by similar ratios.   (Gurr, 1977a:114)

Survey Research

Measuring shaming is a tricky business. This is so because of the subtlety, cultural diversity and indeed idiosyncrasy with which shame can be communicated. There are many non-verbal ways of shaming – a sneer, a stare, a sideways glance. Ethnographic research designs can begin to come to grips with these shared meanings, but the sheer variability of shaming modalities creates great problems for cruder forms of data collection such as survey research.

Social survey approaches to testing the theory will likely be limited to respondents' perceptions of having been shamed or of having shamed rather than to reports of specific types of shaming behavior. It is not a great challenge to form attitude scales to measure shaming on the basis of reports that the subject felt she had been shamed because of parents and other intimates learning about an act of delinquency. It is also not such a challenge to measure reintegration by asking questions about whether the incident had been forgiven by the intimates, whether a wedge had been driven between them as a result of it, whether bonds of affection were as strong since the delinquent act had been discovered.

Survey research is the best strategy for measuring the effect of all the individual-level variables in Figure 1 which it is argued foster preconditions for reintegrative shaming – age, marital status, gender, unemployment, educational and employment aspirations, interdependency (attachment to parents, school, neighbors). It is also possible to code the ecological characteristics of the area in which each individual lives that are suggested as correlates of communitarianism – urbanity and residential mobility. Directly measuring communitarianism as it is defined in the theory of reintegrative shaming is a greater challenge. Using variables like the frequency of neighboring in a community is a very crude indicator of its communitarianism because it tells us nothing about the symbolic significance of these activities to those involved; that is, it is difficult in survey research to assess whether attachments have meanings which invoke personal obligations to others in a community of concern. To assess this one really needs to participate in the symbolic worlds of actors via ethnographic research methods.

Communitarianism is the only variable in Figure 1 which poses substantial difficulties of operationalization by survey research methods, however. Participation in criminal subcultures can be operationalized, if somewhat crudely, by variables such as number of delinquent friends, tolerance of friends toward delinquent behavior, and gang membership. At the individual level of analysis, perceptions of legitimate opportunities as blocked and illegitimate opportunities as available have been widely used in the delinquency literature. Of course crime itself can be measured by self-reports of crime or by adding data from official records of crime to the survey results.

The nice thing about survey research methods, therefore, is that they enable an operationalization of all but one variable in Figure 1, so that one can assess the proportion of the variance in individual criminality explained by the theory (less one of its key elements). The variance explained for the theory of reintegrative shaming can then be compared with that for competing theories.

However, we should not forget that the theory of reintegrative shaming is only partly about reintegrative shaming having a specific deterrent effect upon the criminal behavior of the person shamed. In the theory, the effect of shaming in producing specific deterrence is less important than its effect on general deterrence and this in turn is less important than its moral educative impact (the classical as opposed to instrumental conditioning effects, as the learning theorists would put it). That is, reintegrative shaming has most of its impact in reducing crime rates by its effect on many other people who witness or become aware of the shaming event beyond the single person who is shamed. Moreover, a specific act of shaming an individual reinforces cultural patterns that underwrite further cultural products such as a television program that shames the same type of conduct. Survey research methods unfortunately limit us to assessment of the immediate individual effects of shaming to the exclusion of its collective or cultural effects. To assess the latter, we need more macro-sociological research strategies which take the society or community as the unit of analysis rather than shamed individuals within it.

Macrosociological Studies Based on Official Statistics

Unfortunately, it is not an affordable research design to measure the level of communitarianism and reintegrative shaming in a large sample of different societies (either by ethnographic or survey research methods) and then correlate these with societal crime rates.

Even to do so for a reasonable sample of communities within one nation would be logistically challenging. The school provides probably the most feasible, though hardly the most appropriate, unit for this kind of analysis. Observational or survey research could be deployed in a sample of schools or classes within schools to assess which were most based on social control by reintegrative shaming and which had the highest levels of delinquency among its members.

Another possibility is to look for some proxies for the level of shame in the society. For example, one might be willing to assume that in societies where shame over criminal offending is felt more acutely, more murderers will commit suicide following their offense. Thus, the ratio of murderers who committed suicide before being arrested to all convicted murderers might be a proxy for the presence of shame in the culture. A partial test of the theory would observe whether this ratio is higher in countries with higher crime rates.

Across time within one country, this kind of test is already available. Wolpin (1978) found that in England the ratio of murderers who committed suicide before being arrested to all convicted murderers fell fairly steadily from three out of four in 1929 to one in four in 1967. Thus, there is a time-series association for England between a drop in such a proxy for shame over criminal offending and an increase in crime. However, one would want to be cautious with inferences from such data. For example, while the decline in murder–suicides preceded the abolition of capital punishment in 1967, it is still possible that declining use of capital punishment reduced incentives to suicide in order to avoid the torment of waiting for execution. A regression analysis could, however, look at the effect of the shaming proxy on crime net of the effect on crime of declining use of capital punishment and other potentially confounding variables.

Other proxies for shame over breaches of the criminal law might be considered, such as the proportion of offenses cleared by the offender going to the police and confessing, but these, like the murder–suicide proxy, involve imposing a single simple interpretation on action which will have different meanings in different cases.

Experimental Research Designs

Experimental research on reintegrative shaming is more feasible than one might at first imagine. The researcher could obtain the agreement of a school counselor or principal to report to parents or guardians random offenses at school that would not normally be reported to them. That is, once the school had decided a detected offense was not of a type that involved a responsibility on the school to inform parents, a coin would be tossed: heads the parents would be sent a standard letter informing them of the wrongdoing and requesting them to discuss the offense with their child, tails no action would be taken.

At this point, a self-report delinquency instrument would be administered to all offenders to measure the level of offending over the previous year. A year later, self-reports would measure the level of offending for the twelve months following the report to parents for the experimental group, and the rise or fall in delinquency would be compared to that of the control group of offenders over the same period. Police or court records of delinquency for the two year period could also be used in the same way.

Within the experimental group one would use questionnaire

methods to measure the perceived level of shaming by parents and others as a result of the target offense, and the extent that this shaming was perceived as reintegrative or stigmatizing. Parents could be interviewed as well. One would then compare the subsequent delinquency of those who were reintegratively shamed with those whose offending was ignored or stigmatized.

Within this design, some offenders who were constantly in trouble at school would likely be randomly allocated to second and third incidents of reporting to parents. One would of course compare their increase or decrease in offending with those reported only once.

The basic design might be elaborated within the school by having teachers randomly allocate students to be sent or not sent to the principal for a reprimand which could vary randomly between stigmatizing and reintegrative modalities.

Such experiments would be ethically acceptable to many school authorities because randomly notifying parents of something of which they would not normally be notified is hardly an oppressive or contentious form of social intervention.

The problem with the research design again is that it only tests the specific deterrence part of the theory. The effect of the shaming on brothers, sisters, neighbors and friends of the offender in terms of general deterrence and moral education would not be captured. On the other hand, it might be possible to measure within-school general deterrent and moral educative effects of shaming. Conceivably one might randomly allocate whole schools to programs of reintegrative shaming, versus stigmatization, versus tolerance, and observe follow-up school delinquency rates. It would be extremely difficult to secure the agreement of educational administrators to such a macro-sociological experimental design, however, and it would be very expensive research.

Conclusion

It is clear that substantial opportunities for empirical refutation of the theory exist through ethnographic, historical, social survey, experimental and macro-sociological research based on official statistics. All of these methods have different kinds of weaknesses, just as participant observation, self-reports, victim surveys and official records of crime have different kinds of biases in the measurement of crime. Sometimes these biases operate in different directions (for example, the possibility that police statistics exaggerate the proportion of crime committed by working class offenders, while self-reports exaggerate the proportion committed by middle class juveniles (Braithwaite, 1981)). To the extent that opposite biases do exist, there can be strength in the convergence of weaknesses when a multi-method approach to theory testing is adopted. So biased and defective are our measures of such a covert phemonenon as criminal behavior, that in criminology, more than in any science, it is a mistake to take very seriously a single test that is said to support or refute a theory.

9

Reintegrative shaming and white collar crime

The theory of reintegrative shaming is unlike other theories of crime in the literature, with the notable exception of differential association, in that it does not exclude white collar crime from that which is to be explained. There is of course nothing wrong with having a theory of a subset of crime, so long as a theory of rape, for example, is described as a theory of rape rather than as a general theory of crime. However, there has been a tendency in criminology to present as explanations of crime in general, theories that adopt a class-biased conception of crime that excludes white collar offenses. The latest example is Wilson and Herrnstein's (1985) theory of low IQ and impulsiveness, *inter alia*, as central to the 'human nature' of crime. Since one would expect most white collar criminals to be intelligent and scheming rather than stupid and impulsive, Wilson and Herrnstein's decision to be wilfully blind to the vast reality of white collar crime causes them to present as a general explanation of crime something which could not be sustained if confronted with the totality of the patterns of crime in society rather than with a class-biased subset of criminal behavior.

A theory of general applicability has arisen in this case because it was a theory generated originally out of my work on white collar crime with Brent Fisse and others. The purpose of this chapter is to outline how the theory of reintegrative shaming applies to white collar crime. A special chapter is justified because most criminologists are less informed about the more complex world of crime in the suites than they are about crime in the streets, and so some help in outlining how the theory applies to this massive subset of the crime problem is required. White collar crime is defined according to Sutherland's (1983: 7) conventional definition as 'a crime committed by a person of respectability and high social status in the course of his [or her] occupation'.

The Impact of Publicity on Corporate Offenders

It is widely concluded in the corporate crime literature that adverse publicity is a feared deterrent (e.g. Clinard and Yeager, 1980; Cullen and Dubeck, 1985; French, 1985). Similarly, individual white collar criminals are viewed as highly deterrable by adverse publicity because people in high status occupations have more to lose in social standing and respectability by having their reputations dragged through the mud; as control theorists would say, they have a more profound stake in conformity (Zimring and Hawkins, 1973: 127–8; Geerken and Gove, 1975: 509; Clinard and Meier, 1979: 248).

The Impact of Publicity on Corporate Offenders (Fisse and Braithwaite, 1983) was an attempt at systematic empirical study of how large corporations respond when exposed to concentrated adverse publicity over allegations of wrongdoing. Seventeen cases were studied (on the basis of interviews with executives and other sources) in which corporations had been through adverse publicity crises. The financial impacts of adverse publicity (on sales, earnings, stock prices, etc.) were generally found to be slight; however, non-financial impacts on the loss of repute which executives perceived their company and themselves to have suffered in the community were found to be important to them. Decline of employee morale, distraction of top management from their normal duties, and the gruelling experience of senior managers being cross-examined by Senate Committees, government prosecutors, coroners, courts and others were also perceived as important non-financial consequences of adverse publicity crises.

Moreover, it was concluded that these non-financial impacts deterred not because they had financial implications (e.g. loss of corporate repute undermining stockholder confidence), but because good repute, and employee morale associated with being proud of one's company, were valued for their own sake. As Channon suggests:

The climate of opinion, and therefore the projection of the company as a moral, useful, and likeable member of society, which creates and sustains it, becomes (as it were) a *direct* objective of management. It does not contradict the purely business objectives as they are classically understood, but it is not simply subservient or intermediate to those objectives. It exists in its own right as an operational goal of prime importance.   (Channon, 1981: 13)

This is why corporate image advertising – to promote the social value, benevolence, competence, responsibility of a corporation rather than to promote sales of specific products – has become such a major force over the past decade (Birch, 1978; Lamb *et al.*, 1980: 66–9). Business organizations are not unique in seeking repute for its own sake. Other organizations that can be venues for organizational crime – universities, sporting clubs, government agencies – are no less concerned with seeking prestige and community respectability.

Even a collectivity as diffuse as a national state is, up to a point, susceptible to shaming. After World War I, the treatment of Germany by the Allies amounted to stigmatization and national humiliation. In contrast, the post-World War II Western policy toward Germany, Japan and Italy saw a rejection of national outcasting in favor of reintegration. Even very large collectivities can be positively or negatively influenced by humiliation, and not only because they are made up of individuals who feel the shame directed at the collectivity to which they belong. Individuals who take on positions of power within the collectivity, even if they have not been personally affected by collective shaming as individuals, find that they confront role expectations to protect and enhance the repute or self-esteem of the collectivity. Many pointless battles are fought because political leaders perceive that 'the people' are demanding decisive action to save national face. To take a more mundane example, an academic might be indifferent to the reputation of his university, indeed he might do more to snipe at the incompetence of its administration than to defend it publicly. But, if he is appointed Dean, he confronts new role expectations to protect the university's reputation. He may do this diligently, not because of the views he brought to the job as an individual member of the university community, but because he knows what the job requires, and he wants to be good at his job. Thus, in organizations whose individuals are stung very little by collective shaming, shaming can have an impact if those in power are paid good salaries on the understanding that they will do what is necessary to preserve the reputation of the organization.

Thus, in shaming organizational crime, two bites may be taken from the apple. If one fails at shaming the responsible individuals, there is still the opportunity to secure compliance by shaming the collectivity. The shamed collectivity can not only pass on this shame by sanctioning guilty individuals after the event, it can also activate internal controls proactively to prevent future crimes before they occur.

Fisse and Braithwaite (1983) concluded that adverse publicity (a form of shaming as defined in the present theory) in all of their case studies played some role 'in producing some corporate reform which, although perhaps in only a small way, would reduce the probability of a recurrence of the offense or wrongdoing alleged (and often other kinds of offenses as well)' (Fisse and Braithwaite, 1983: 233). Thus the conclusion was one that I have generalized to all forms of crime in this book: 'If we are serious about controlling corporate crime, the first priority should be to create a culture in which corporate crime is not tolerated. The informal processes of shaming unwanted conduct and of praising exemplary behavior need to be emphasized' (Fisse and Braithwaite, 1983: 246).

The same conclusion applies to other forms of white collar crime. Third World nations where problems of political corruption are at their maximum are often those where shaming directed at public officials who favor corruption over administrative impartiality is less than that directed at officials who fail to show partiality toward their tribe or kin, who fail to 'return favors' to those who have helped them into power. That is, they are societies where corruption is less shameful than turning one's back on reciprocity obligations (Wraith and Simpkins, 1963; Scott, 1972), where the balance of differential shaming favors crime.

Where tax collection authorities are viewed as oppressors, tax cheating will not be shamed.

Stigmatization and Subculture Formation

At the same time, dangers of stigmatization as a result of shaming do exist with white collar crime, if less obviously than with other forms of crime. The literature frequently reports the use of techniques of neutralization (Sykes and Matza, 1957) by white collar criminals to rationalize their wrongdoing (e.g. Cressey, 1953; Geis, 1967; Benson, 1985). One of these techniques is to 'condemn the condemners'. This was the technique most frequently resorted to by Queensland car dealers in my study of used car fraud. To quote two of the dealers:

I started off honest but have been publicly trained – trained by the public to be dishonest. Most dealers start off honest but the public perverts you. We call them L.T.C.s in the trade. It's a common expression in the trade. It stands for Liars, Thieves and Cheats. You treat a customer like an L.T.C. until he's proved otherwise.

They think because you're a used car dealer you're a liar. So they treat you like one and lie to you. Can you blame the dealer for lying back?

(Braithwaite, 1978: 119)

Stigmatization of used car dealers by the general public helped sustain a criminal subculture among Queensland dealers. The criminal subculture transmitted expectations that the only way to survive in business was through dishonesty, with the alternative being to get out: 'Some of the people who leave the business are those who can't take the social stigma of the horse trader'.

Stigmatization can play a role in fostering the social solidarity of outgroups of white collar individuals who are similarly stigmatized. Criminal subcultures of a sort that can provide social support for white collar crime do develop, as Cressey has illustrated:

Among terrorists, terrorists are not intensely hated, are not considered outlaws, are not ostracized. Among those businessmen who think their government and its laws are not legitimate, white-collar criminals are not intensely hated, are not considered outlaws, are not ostracized. Accordingly, when a white-collar criminal is convicted and punished, the attitude is, 'The bastards got poor old Charlie'... a little study of medical malpractice suits found that ninety percent of the doctors reported no negative effects on their practice, and that eight percent reported that their practice improved after the suit. A radiologist whose practice improved said, 'I guess all the doctors in town felt sorry for me because new patients started coming in from doctors who had not sent me patients previously.'   (Cressey 1978:110)

While the fundamental problem in societies with rampant white collar crime is the absence of effective processes of societal shaming, there is a danger, just as with delinquent subcultures, of white collar offenders joining together with others who have been similarly rejected by agents of social control to form an oppositional subculture which rejects their rejectors. I will suggest that it is difficult to see evidence of this in Japan. In my own country, Australia, it is not a widespread problem, though one can see pockets of it in, for example, the subculture of Queensland used car dealers, discussed above, and perhaps among sections of the medical profession (for example, pathologists) who see themselves as having been stigmatized as medi-fraud specialists by a rotten government hell-bent on socializing medicine.

In the United States, however, the problem of business resisting law enforcement by forming oppositional and criminogenic business subcultures would seem to be more widespread. Bardach and Kagan (1982), for example, talk of an 'organized culture of resistance' – a subculture that facilitates the sharing of knowledge about methods of legal resistance and counterattack. To illustrate, Bardach and Kagan (1982: 114) cite the advice of one legal expert to appeal against all Occupational Safety and Health Administration citations, not just those to which companies object strongly, so that they can 'settle a case by giving up on some items in exchange for dismissal by OSHA of others. Those who leave certain things uncontested are needlessly giving up this possibility.' An organized subculture of resistance that advocates contesting all enforcement actions, that is consistently challenging and litigating the legitimacy of the government to enforce the law, is not something regulatory agencies in Japan, Australia, Britain (Hawkins, 1984; Vogel, 1986) or Sweden (Kelman, 1981) often have to contend with. This is not to suggest that regulatory agencies do not frequently encounter vigorous and effective resistance from business in these countries; it is just to say they rarely confront the organized subculture of resistance evident in many sectors of American industry. When you go with an Australian business regulatory official on company inspections, you notice that mostly what happens is that the government inspector asks that things be done, and they are done. American inspections, in contrast, tend to proceed more as a running battle between government and business; many required improvements to ensure compliance with the law are a matter of written directives which will be later contested by the company in adversarial proceedings. I would not want to overdraw a contrast between the United States and the rest of the world: the US and Japan are probably near polar extremes of a continuum of regulatory adversariness, with most countries lying somewhere in between (cf. Vogel, 1986).

Organized business subcultures of resistance develop for many reasons including deeply ingrained traditions of deferring to the legitimacy of government, or of distrusting government. One factor, however, is probably the demeanor adopted by regulatory officials themselves. This is where the stigmatization argument comes in. When regulators start out with assumptions that most business people will not comply with the law in a socially responsible way, that business will always succumb to the temptation to make an illegal fast buck, that business people are amoral calculators (Kagan and Scholz, 1984: 67), that instilling the fear of punishment is the only way to secure compliance, these assumptions run the risk of becoming self-fulfilling prophecies. A regulatory demeanor that stigmatizes business fosters an organized subculture of resistance.

When there is a willingness to do the right thing in the business community, a punitive-adversarial regulatory style is simply not the best strategy for maximizing compliance. Punishment is the best strategy when good will is wanting. We apply this common-sense psychology in educating our children, in management, and in our everyday lives. For example, if we want to get our spouse to do the washing up, and we have a spouse who basically accepts the principle of doing a fair share of the housework, we find that retaliation is more likely than compliance if we say, 'unless you do the washing up I won't do the cooking tomorrow night'. Most of us find that success is more likely if we appeal to our spouse's better nature. Punishment is something we resort to only when we confront a spouse, a student, or a colleague at work to whose better nature we cannot appeal for compliance with the goals we have in mind. If there is one thing that people who fail as spouses, teachers, or managers have in common, it is their inability to understand that you do not try to achieve goals by punishment until you have first tried appealing to peoples' better natures. Yet this is the very mistake that an American regulatory statute like the Mine Safety and Health Act makes. It imposes automatic penalties for any violation of a mandatory health and safety standard. There is no discretion for the inspector to give mine operators a second chance through a warning. Every schoolteacher knows that in some circumstances a child who would have been alienated by punishment can be given a greatly enhanced will to behave by saying, 'That's not like you, Johhny Brown', and then forgiving the transgression. This strategy is no good with students who have no flicker of will to behave; with them the giving of a second chance will only be interpreted as weakness.

Unfortunately, many critics who favor a punitive-adversarial approach to business regulation are unwilling to make these distinctions. They want uncompromising and consistent punishment of corporate wrongdoers. They want to invoke punitive social control before giving moralizing social control a try through informal expression of disapproval and reasoning about the wrongdoing. The price they must pay for such indiscriminate use of punishment is lower compliance, because by remorselessly punishing those with a genuine desire to comply, we alienate them; by rejecting opportunities to give sincerely motivated managers a second chance, we forgo the opportunity to build a commitment to try harder to ensure compliance in future. Instead, we build subcultures of regulatory resistance.

Punishment and persuasion are based on fundamentally different models of human behavior. Punishment presumes human beings to be rational actors who weigh the benefits of noncompliance against the probability and costs of punishment. Persuasion presumes human beings to be reasonable, of good faith, and motivated to heed advice. Neither model perfectly or invariably fits the situations business regulators confront in the field.

The problem with persuasion is that, based as it is on a model of human beings as basically good, it fails to recognize that there are some who are not, and thus will take advantage of being presumed to be so. The problem with the punitive model of human beings as essentially bad is that we dissipate the will of well-intentioned people to comply when we treat them as if they were ill-intentioned, we risk stigmatization and resistance.

Effective business regulators are those who have the common sense to select the right model at the right time – the art of modeling through! (apologies to Braybrooke and Lindblom, 1963). They are flexible enough to employ informal shaming and other techniques of persuasion with those who have slipped up on an otherwise strong commitment to compliance, and to use punishment coupled with adverse publicity with maximum force against the recalcitrant. When they resort to the latter, they monitor reform in the hope that a press release can be distributed touting the improvements made since the conviction: they seek opportunities for ceremonies of forgiveness and reintegration.

In business regulation, as in family life, those who are effective at social control are those who have perfected the art of strategic shaming while avoiding the pitfalls of stigmatization. In another work, I have argued in more detail for business regulators to learn the lessons of the family model of punishment (Braithwaite, 1985a). Government inspectors must punish in a way that maintains dignity and mutual respect between enforcer and offender. Where possible,

punishment should be executed without labeling people as irresponsible, untrustworthy outcasts, but instead by inviting the offender to accept the justice of the punishment:

> The competent inspector does not use command and control to achieve
> compliance unless he has to. Following Dale Carnegie's famous advice, he
> will get managers to do things by convincing them that it was their own idea
> to do so. Indeed, some of the time punishment may even be imposed with
> such finesse that the manager almost believes that the punishment was his
> own idea. To illustrate, an Australian inspector tells the story of persuading
> a manager that something which was not really required by the law ought to
> be done to make the mine safer. After writing the manager's agreement to
> make the change in the 'record book' kept for the purpose at the mine, the
> interaction finished with, 'If I come back and find it not done, we agree that
> work will be stopped until it is done'. The manager, genuinely persuaded
> that the change ought to be made, concurs. A few weeks later the inspector
> finds that, because of a strike and other production problems, the manager
> has not got around to making the change. The manager is unhappy when
> the inspector stops production, but he hardly thinks he has been unfairly
> treated.   (Braithwaite, 1985a:103)

Just as most conformity with laws prohibiting crime in the streets
does not occur out of fear of punishment, compliance with regulatory laws occurs in general because most business people believe in
being law-abiding (see Kagan and Scholz, 1984; Scholz, 1984).
Equally, however, the consciences which constitute the rightness of
obeying the law are in considerable measure nurtured by the spectacle of shame being directed at businesspeople and organizations
that are convicted for breaking the law. Persuasion is only rendered
effective as a regulatory strategy because it is underwritten by
punishment. Unfortunately, with most types of white collar crime
the moral educative functions of the law are sorely neglected by
insufficient levels of formal punishment coupled with state shaming.

First, a regulatory strategy which rejects adversariness as an
opening stance can grapple with the counterproductivity of stigmatization. Second, it reduces the risk that regulated organizations will
perceive legitimate opportunities – to make profits, grow, meet
deadlines, and achieve other organizational goals – as frustrated by
unwarranted government meddling. In a regulatory regime that sets
out to be cooperative, regulated organizations are negotiated with in
good faith on the design of controls; they often succeed in suggesting
ways of protecting the environment that will be as effective or almost
as effective as the government's suggestion, but that will make their

organizational goals easier to achieve. Even if the controls that emerge from a process of negotiated agreement are in fact as intrusive as those initially proposed, there are reduced chances of an organized subculture of resistance when the regulated organizations have been involved in and agreed to the design of the regulations. Cooperative regulatory cultures therefore have the best chance of sustaining management consciences that will punish non-compliance, and of averting perceptions that opportunities for organizational goal attainment have been blocked by an unreasonable government.

Self-regulation and the Family Model of Punishment

Just as more of the effective social control mobilized against juvenile delinquency is undertaken by families rather than by the police, self-regulation by companies is responsible for preventing more white collar crime than is enforcement by regulatory agencies. In *Corporate Crime in the Pharmaceutical Industry*, I suggested six questions to ask when deciding whether a particular company had an effective self-regulatory system for ensuring compliance with the law. One of these was: 'Can the corporation demonstrate a history of effectively sanctioning employees who violate Standard Operating Procedures designed to prevent crime?' (Braithwaite, 1984: 362). I now suspect this may not be one of the right questions to ask. This doubt arose from my subsequent study of the internal compliance systems of the companies with the best coal mine safety records in the United States (Braithwaite, 1985a). I had, in accordance with the earlier conclusion, expected that companies with outstanding records of safety compliance would be tough in disciplining employees and managers who breached corporate safety policies. There would be evidence of rule breakers being regularly dismissed, demoted, fined, or punished in some other way. However, I did not find such internal punitiveness to be a distinctive feature of the companies with exemplary safety records.

What was consistently evident across all five safety leaders in the study was clearly defined accountability for safety performance, rigorous monitoring of that safety performance, and systems for communicating to managers and workers that their safety performance was not up to standard. In general, the conclusions about what made for effective social control within companies mirrored what we know about effective socialization in families. Punitiveness is not a characteristic of the families that are most successful in producing law-abiding children. Effective parents are neither laissez-faire nor authoritarian, but authoritative (Baumrind, 1971, 1978). Similarly, companies that are effectively self-regulating seem to be neither laissez-faire nor authoritarian; what they do is to set clear standards, monitor compliance with them, communicate disappointment and issue firm reprimands when the standards are not complied with, and communicate approval when they are consistently followed. The following illustrates how, even for US Steel, the coal mining safety leader with the heaviest emphasis on punishment for non-compliance, more subtle processes of shaming were regarded as much more important to securing compliance than the crude instrument of punishment:

The accountability mechanism for general superintendents of mining districts is more interesting. The general superintendents attend a monthly meeting with the president of the mining company and other senior executives, at corporate headquarters. Each general superintendent, in turn, makes a presentation on his district's performance during the previous month – first, on safety performance (i.e., accident rates) and, second, on productive performance (tons of coal mined). After the safety presentation, the corporate chief inspector of mines has the first opportunity to ask questions. If the accident rate has worsened in comparison to previous months, or to other districts, the question invariably asked is, Why? I was told that the twenty-four or twenty-five senior people who attend these meetings exert a powerful peer-group pressure on general superintendents whose safety performance is poor. It is an extreme embarrassment for general superintendents to have to come back month after month and report safety performances falling behind those of other districts.

(Braithwaite, 1985a: 48)

As Bayley points out in his discussion of the impracticability of detailed external control of the police, and the preferability of external regulatory bodies which concentrate on catalyzing vigorous self-regulation:

the police organization has a more extensive, subtle, and discriminating set of controls over its members than do external agencies. In addition to formal disciplinary punishments involving pay, postings and promotions, it can exhort, slight, harangue, praise, embarrass and so forth. (Bayley, 1983: 154)

In short, I no longer think that effectively self-regulating companies are those that regularly dismiss or demote managers who fail to comply with the rules; rather I suspect effectively self-regulating companies are those with means of drawing everyone's attention to the failings of those who fall short of corporate social responsibility standards (shaming) while continuing to offer them advice and encouragement to improve (reintegration). Moreover, just as with social control by families, corporations and work groups characterized by communitarianism, by relationships where social approval is frequently expressed, will be more effective in securing compliance because social disapproval is more aversive when embedded within a continuum of social approval.

Communitarianism

Thus far it has been argued that low rates of white collar crime will occur where shaming is directed at offending, and especially where the shaming avoids the pitfalls of stigmatization – creating outcasts, fostering subcultures of resistance. But what of the upper part of the theory as depicted in Figure 1? Does communitarianism foster shaming? And is this communitarianism a product of interdependency?

There is very little evidence bearing on these questions with regard to white collar crime. In both my studies of internal corporate compliance systems (Braithwaite, 1984, 1985a) I concluded that a requirement for effective self-regulation is that internal compliance groups (e.g. safety department, internal auditors) have organizational clout. This means more than anything else that they have the backing of the chief executive to make their recommendations stick as to what line managers ought to do. This in a sense is another way of saying that when there is interdependency between line managers and compliance staff, chances of compliance are improved. This interdependency can take many forms; my favorite example is of the animal welfare officer from a large Australian research institution who told me that researchers had to take notice of her advice on compliance with animal welfare codes because they were dependent on her as the officer who was also responsible for the ordering and delivery of animals to be used in experiments.

It is indeed a staple of organization theory that within organizations compliance is more likely to the will of those on whom others are dependent, and between organizations, that one organization is more likely to comply with the requests of another if it is dependent on it (Perrow, 1961; Emerson, 1962; Blau, 1964; Thompson, 1967; Hickson *et al.*, 1971; Jacobs, 1974). I have argued that regulatory agencies on whom companies are dependent by virtue of the agency's control of key business contingencies have a better chance of securing compliance (Braithwaite, 1984). For example, health authorities around the world find it easier to get pharmaceutical companies to comply with their requirements than food companies. As a consequence food regulation tends to be comparatively prosecutorial and litigious (e.g. court ordered seizure of impure food), while pharmaceuticals regulation tends to be negotiated (voluntary recall of impure drugs). The Australian data clearly demonstrate this (Grabosky and Braithwaite, 1986). One reason pharmaceutical companies are relatively more compliant and less willing to embark on a litigious relationship with health authorities is that they are dependent on them for pre-marketing clearance of new drugs, approval of in-process quality controls, approval of drug testing protocols, pricing decisions on government subsidized pharmaceutical benefits programs, and other contingencies which do not apply to food manufacturers. Similarly, in Australia at least, mines are more dependent on mines departments for various approvals and assistance than are other workplaces on departments of labor. Perhaps as a consequence, one sees both more negotiated and more demanding regulation of mine safety by state mines departments in Australia, than the regulation of other workplaces by state labor departments which is both less demanding and more litigious (Braithwaite and Grabosky, 1985).

At a societal level of analysis, can we say that societies characterized by a high level of interdependency and communitarianism will have less white collar crime? While this is a prediction I have no discomfort in making from the theory, probably it is ultimately untestable because of the impossibility, given the extraordinary capacity of powerful offenders to conceal their offending, of comparing rates of white collar crime across societies.

The communitarian cultures of Japan and Switzerland are interesting cases. In both, there are outstanding examples of the communitarianism of these societies being mobilized to sustain white collar criminal subcultures of unusual coherence. Thus Japan could boast a rapacious subculture of political corruption surrounding the Tanaka faction in the Diet (Boulton, 1978), Switzerland can count on extraordinary corporate loyalty from its banking employees to sustain world leadership in the laundering of dirty money (Blum, 1984), and both countries are infamous for corporate crime in their pharmaceutical industries (Adams, 1984; Braithwaite, 1984; Hogetsu, 1986).

None of this should surprise us. After all, Japanese communitarianism is also manifested in common criminal gangs that are more highly organized, more capable of exacting total loyalty from their members to follow directions to engage in crime, than criminal gangs found in most of the rest of the world (Clifford, 1976). Communitarianism is a two-edged sword. However, the crime-preventing edge is much more important than the crime-producing edge. This is because of the fact that criminal laws, including those relating to white collar crime, enjoy such enormous consensus and community commitment (as argued in Chapter 2). If societies were equally divided between those who thought the criminal law a good thing and those who thought it a bad thing, then communitarianism would do as much harm (in securing loyalty to criminal values) as good (in better securing law observance). As it is, communitarianism does more good than harm with respect to crime.

The capacity of Japanese regulatory agencies to change business behavior in a relatively short time can be miraculous. In the late 1960s Japan decided it had a severe pollution problem, and began to deal with it by promulgating and enforcing a 'Basic Law for Environmental Pollution Control'. Notwithstanding exceptional industrial growth, within five years sulfur dioxide emissions were halved in Japan and ten years later (1977) were down further to a third of their 1967 peak (Environment Agency, 1981: 21). Similar or more striking downward trends were achieved over this period for carbon monoxide air pollution (Environment Agency, 1980: 5) and water pollution in urban rivers and streams (Environment Agency, 1980: 10–11), while there was a failure to produce improvement with coastal waters and nitrogen dioxide air pollution (Environment Agency, 1980). Japan has turned around its pollution problems more rapidly and dramatically than other countries (Vogel, 1979: 19, 73). By 1975 the Organization for Economic Cooperation and Development (OECD) found that Japanese industry was spending several times as high a proportion of its gross national product on anti-pollution investment than any other OECD member (Vogel, 1979: 73). The difference with Japan is that when a Japanese regulatory authority like the Environment Agency tells a company to do something, it does it – in circumstances when Western companies would prevaricate or litigate. When Brent Fisse and I were conducting interviews in Japanese companies and regulatory agencies (Braithwaite and Fisse, 1985) we were told a number of stories of extraordinary shame which Japanese executives had felt on receiving no more than a letter of gentle reprimand from the government for non-compliance with the law. Cases of suicide, attempted suicide, voluntary resignation, and voluntary demotion arising from shame over corporate malpractice are common in Japan. With white collar crime, as with common crime, it is shame within tightly-knit families, communities and corporate cultures that is a more profound deterrent than formal punishment.

While there are therefore reasons for predicting that communitarianism and interdependency as characteristics of societies will be associated with reduced exposure to white collar as well as common crime, some predictions at the individual level of analysis are more problematic with white collar crime. Young people and unemployed people are less locked into interdependencies than the rest of the community. They are therefore less susceptible to social control concerning white collar crime, just as they are with common crime. The more fundamental fact remains, however, that the young and unemployed are structurally excluded from opportunities to commit white collar crime. They lack the incumbency in high status legitimate occupational roles that is a necessary condition for white collar crime. Thus, at least with respect to these two individual characteristics, we must qualify the individual-level predictions from the theory. Young people and unemployed people will be more likely to engage in crimes other than those that require incumbency in high status occupational roles (white collar crime). We would still predict, however, that unmarried (controlling for age), urban, mobile, males will as individuals be more prone to white collar crime than individuals with opposite characteristics. Companies and other locations that have high concentrations of these types of individuals should also have high rates of white collar crime.

Conclusions So Far

Most white collar crime occurs in organizational contexts. The theory of reintegrative shaming leads to a similar analysis of the role of organizations in white collar crime control to that of families in delinquency control. The families and organizations that are effective at crime control will not be those that are most punitive, but those that sustain communitarian bonds, that secure compliance by expressing disapproval while maintaining ongoing relationships characterized overwhelmingly by social approval. Shame is used to internalize a commitment to the rules instead of punishment being used to tip the balance of rational calculation in favor of compliance.

Just as in developmental psychology there has been a growing consensus in favor of family socialization practices that are warm and firm rather than cold and firm or warm and permissive, a similar consensus can be seen emerging in the literature on corporate disciplinary practices. Company managements have become increasingly disenchanted with punitive approaches to discipline; the view is becoming widespread that compliance with organizational policies is best achieved by confrontation with disapproval in an attempt to internalize commitment to the rules within a nurturant corporate culture.

A worker punished with a written warning or unpaid suspension responds with resentment or apathy; absenteeism and grievances increase; communication and trust decline; 'get by' or 'get even' performance results. In fact, it is the prevalence of these very problems that has led organizations to change to a nonpunitive approach...

The first step of formal nonpunitive discipline is to issue an 'oral reminder'. The manager meets privately with the employee to discuss the problem. The manager's primary goal is to gain the employee's agreement to solve the problem. Instead of warning the employee of more serious disciplinary action to come, the manager reminds the individual that he or she has a personal responsibility to meet reasonable standards of performance and behavior. (Campbell *et al.*, 1985: 168)

Similarly, we have seen that social control based on reintegrative shaming in the family needs to be complemented by state shaming associated with formal punishment if consciences are to be nurtured concerning criminal acts beyond the immediate experience of the family. Equally, reintegrative shaming by communitarian corporate cultures will operate impotently (in a cultural vacuum with respect to the criminal law) unless the state engages in shame-based punishment of white collar crime.

It is also true that just as state punishment of common crime runs

concomitant dangers of stigmatization driving people into oppositional subcultures, so does business regulatory enforcement run risks
of creating an organized subculture of resistance. The same essential
options for minimizing this risk apply in both arenas: direct expressions of forgiveness and reconciliation to the offender, proffering a
repentant role, punishment that maintains bonds of respect between
enforcer and offender and that invites the offender to accept its
justice, eschewing outcasting sanctions such as imprisonment. In
both domains, therefore, reintegrative shaming demands routine
non-punitiveness and routine control by communitarian disapproval underwritten by occasional state shame-based punishment in
which stigmatization is minimized. With both common crime and
white collar crime, the theory predicts that, when the society exer-
cises control by shaming reintegratively in this way, the rate of
offending will be low.

Some Implications for Controlling Organizational Crime

Chapter 10 considers the implications of the theory of reintegrative
shaming for crime control policies. These general conclusions apply
to individual white collar offenders just as they do to street criminals. However, some special policy implications are best drawn here
regarding offenses committed by or on behalf of organizations by
members of the organization. These are issues of relevance only to
organizational crimes.

We have argued that most organizations – be they police departments, universities, or private corporations – are no less concerned
to protect their organizational reputation than are individuals to
protect their individual standing. Most organizations act to guarantee compliance with the law by those acting on their behalf because
organizations (or rather individuals acting in organizational roles)
believe that it would not be right for the organization to break the
law. In other words conscience (the sense of social responsibility) is
a more important safeguard against organizational crime than fear
of formal punishment. The extent to which the sense of social
responsibility is more important varies from culture to culture, being
less in business environments with an organized subculture of resistance against regulatory laws.

Beyond Economic Rationalism

Unfortunately much thinking about corporate crime, though not so much with regard to thinking about crime by public organizations, adopts an overly economically rational conception of the corporation; it excessively downplays the corporation's role as a choosing collective agent with organizational policies and values about social responsibility; it downplays the fact that the corporation is constituted of individuals with consciences. It is true that profit-seeking corporations are more guided by economic rationality and less by passion, impulse or revenge than individuals who commit crime. To this extent corporations are considerably more susceptible to deterrence than individuals, but not so much so that the desire to avoid punishment prevents more corporate crime than the desire to be law-abiding. This is inevitable because the criminal justice system is typically institutionally incapable of delivering credible deterrence against corporate offenders (Moore, 1987). As Grabosky, Fisse and I reported in a consultancy to the Victorian government:

the public must be shown that it is possible for truly dire consequences to befall those who flout the law, so that they will be deterred from offending. Yet the deterrence rationale must be kept in perspective with occupational health and safety offences. In a large workplace it will be common for hundreds of occupational health and safety offences to occur in the course of a year, more likely thousands. The inspector comes in on perhaps one day during the year; most of these offences will not be occurring on that day; many of those that are will not be noticed by the inspector or will be in parts of the workplace the inspector does not even get to. Perhaps the inspector will detect a handful of breaches. Even if the inspector decides to prosecute on the 5 most serious offences detected, a workplace with a thousand breaches in the course of a year still has 99.5% chance of offences not being prosecuted. If the inspector secured convictions and total fines of $50,000, the company will still be paying a tax of no more than $50 for each offence during the year. Depending on how much the company is saving by cutting corners on safety, even under this unusually punitive scenario it can still be economically rational for the company to ignore the law. Any enforcement policy which relies totally on fines to deter by changing the rational economic cost–benefit calculations of profit maximising companies, as American enforcement policies tend to do, is doomed to fail.

(Braithwaite *et al.*, 1986: 36)

Thus, with organizational crime as well, it is the moral education function of punishment that is more important than the deterrent function. Much more formal punishment of organizational offenders, with heavier sanctions, is needed than we see at present to serve the neglected cause of moral education for organizational crimes. However, narrow deterrence-driven policies, such as those of US agencies like the Mine Safety and Health Administration and the Occupational Safety and Health Administration, which each impose 100,000 minuscule fines on corporations each year for health and safety offenses, are misguided. Routine wrist-slapping fines fulfill no moral educative function – they are a morally neutral tax on law breaking – and they are a joke in deterring massive corporations.

The same point applies to the prescriptions of the economists who would have us wipe environmental crimes from the statute books and replace them with effluent charges (Baumol and Oates, 1971; Kneese and Schultze, 1975; Anderson *et al.*, 1977). Instead of being punished for breaking environmental laws, companies would pay a tax for each quantum of pollution they emit from their factories. They would have a right to pollute but would pay for it. The economic disincentive to pollute would ensure that pollution would be minimized, and in the most cost-efficient way. While there is scope for sensibly adapting some of the economists' ideas in some areas, to go all the way with taxes on harm as an alternative to criminalization would be a recipe for environmental anarchy (or occupational health and safety anarchy if applied in that domain).

You cannot take the moral content out of social control and expect social control to work. If there is no morality about the law, if it is just a game of rational economic trade-offs, cheating will be rife. Governments would never be able to trust the effluent figures provided by industry. An army of inspectors that no government could afford would be required to check these figures and prosecute effluent fraud. Over the past twenty years governments around the world have made quite impressive gains in reducing pollution with very modest environmental enforcement bureaucracies. These have been achieved because most companies will try to comply with an environmental law most of the time simply because it is the law, and they will do this without having an inspector looking over their shoulder. Strip pollution or consumer product safety or occupational health and safety of its moral content, make these activities a matter of discretionary rational economic calculation, confer a 'right to pollute', and the voluntary restraint of the majority is forfeited. Everyone will then have to have an inspector looking over his shoulder at everything he does. The neo-classical economists on the right and the fire and brimstone corporate deterrence advocates on the left are equally naive in the way they discount the role of conscience and a social responsibility to comply with the law as sources of majoritarian corporate compliance.

The same analysis applies to those who would replace criminal law with tort law in an area like consumer product safety or antitrust (e.g. Posner, 1977; Landes and Posner, 1984). Instead of its being an offense to sell a dangerous drug, those injured by the drug would deter such conduct by seeking damages from the company after the event. Putting aside the problems arising from the insufficiently preventive nature of this strategy (Braithwaite, 1982), its fundamental flaw is that it naively assumes that social control can work when drained of its denunciatory dimension.

What is needed is punishment for organizational crime that maximizes the sense of shame, that communicates the message that white collar crime is as abhorrent to the community as crime in the streets. Once organizational actors internalize this abhorrence, then the self-regulation of managerial consciences and organizational ethics and compliance policies will do most of the work for the government. The irony is again that the 'free market' alternative of economic incentives will ultimately require a more intrusive state apparatus to make social control work than the 'moral community' alternative.

As argued earlier, the moral educative functions of corporate criminal law are best achieved by heavy reliance on adverse publicity as a social control mechanism. Fisse and I have devoted a book to the policy options available to do this, so the specific possibilities will not be canvassed again here. Suffice it to say that the policy instruments for harnessing shame against corporate offenders include adverse publicity orders as a formal sanction (such as remedial advertisements for false advertising offenses, or requirements that reports be produced into the defects of a corporate compliance system and publicly released), the calling of press conferences following corporate convictions, encouraging consumer activism and investigative journalism by rationalizing defamation laws, liberalizing rules of standing, providing for *qui tam* suits, mandating more corporate disclosure, and using exposure through official enquiries more creatively (but more justly) (Fisse and Braithwaite, 1983).

The Struggle for Corporate Social Responsibility

As with common crime, however, the most important battles that will shape how well consciences operate to prevent organizational crime will not be fought in the justice system but in various cultural arenas. The campaign that counts most is that being fought between the corporate social responsibility movement and its opponents (Stone, 1985). The opponents of the idea of corporate social responsibility say it is wrong for corporations to pursue any goal other than profit maximization; managers who make 'socially responsible' choices in preference to the maximally profitable choice assume political powers for which they are unaccountable, undermine the integrity of the market system and fail to meet their moral obligations to stockholders (e.g. Friedman, 1962).

This position amounts to a denial that corporations, and individuals acting in corporate roles, are part of the moral community. It is a denial of communitarianism, a rationalization to insulate corporate actors from shaming by the wider community. The key to corporate crime control is for corporations to be well integrated into the community, and therefore amenable to the pressures of informal social control. An ideology which cuts corporations off from obligations to the community is as criminogenic as an ideology which contends that it is arrogant for *individuals* to act other than in self-interest because to do so assumes that they know what is best for others, to defer to others when this is not self-interested is to undermine the integrity of the systems of survival of the fittest and competitive individualism which have been the sources of evolutionary and social progress; and to fail to invest all our energies in self-advancement is to fail in the moral duty to our parents to give them the maximum return for their investment in us. The moral bankruptcy of the anti-responsibility movement is transparent when we consider that the same arguments for their position could be applied to individuals. A return to communitarianism, an assertion of the supremacy of conscience over rational calculation is needed, not a return to the jungle. Already substantial proportions of the populations of Western countries view large corporations as moral pariahs; they stigmatize executives who work for them as rapacious and exploitative. A CBS News/New York Times National Survey of 29 May to 2 June 1985 found a majority of respondents did not think 'most American corporate executives are honest' and did think that

American business engages in white collar crime 'very often' (*New York Times*, 9 June 1985, Section 3, p. 1). The labeling theory tradition sensitizes us to the dangers this creates of outcasts thereby having nothing to lose by conforming to the expectations others have of them.

Breaking Down Concerted Ignorance

The corporation must not only be reintegrated with the wider community so that informal social control from outside can penetrate the walls that isolate the executive suites, the corporation must also be more socially integrated internally. Organizational crime is often made possible by structures that enable one part of the organization to be wilfully blind to exploitative conduct in another part. Individuals and subunits build walls around their part of the operation; they take pride in how ethically they do their bit of the corporate mission, and view it as none of their business how unethically the other subunits may work. Thus, a pharmaceutical industry quality control manager can do a magnificent job in ensuring that drugs which have been fraudulently tested, and which are promoted for inappropriate uses, are produced exactly to specifications without feeling a concern for the social irresponsibility of the total process of producing the drug (Braithwaite, 1984). A pharmaceutical company researcher who discovers that a drug has a particular side-effect feels that she has responsibly done her job by reporting this side effect to her boss; the fact that subsidiary managers in many Third World countries suppress the finding is not felt to be her concern: that is the responsibility of the international marketing division. In a company which is an integrated moral community, in contrast, this researcher would be upset about the suppression of the side-effect she discovered; she would contact medical directors in those subsidiaries to attempt to shame them into acting more responsibly, complain to a corporate ethics committee, or take some other appropriate action.

Crime flourishes best in organizations that isolate people into sealed domains of social responsibility; crime is controlled in organizations where shady individuals and crooked subunits are exposed to shame by a responsible majority in the organization. Even if the majority are less than responsible, exposure gives maximum scope to such pangs of conscience as are in the offing, and increases vulnerability to control from without. Some of the companies with the best internal crime control policies explicitly set out to create an 'organization full of antennas' (for example, consider the activities of Exxon's Controller discussed by Fisse and Braithwaite (1983: 171–81)).

Worst of all, many companies have systematic policies to protect the chief executive from the taint of knowledge of illegalities. These include pharmaceutical companies having 'vice-presidents responsible for going to jail' (Braithwaite, 1984). Corporate cultures often incorporate expectations from the boss to 'get it done, but don't tell me how you do it'. 'Concerted ignorance' happens at all levels of complex organizations; 'Both superordinates and subordinates and insiders and outsiders have common interests in limiting the knowledge each obtains about the other. In what are often quite tacit ways, bargains are struck as to what each will require the other to know' (Katz, 1979: 297). There are policy solutions to these problems.

A problem in pharmaceutical companies is that recommendations of quality control managers to destroy certain batches of drugs that do not meet purity and other specifications are occasionally overruled by production managers. Typically, the middle ranking production managers who do this protect top management from the taint of knowing about such socially irresponsible, often criminal, decisions. A policy solution is to require by law all reports of the quality control director to be in writing, and all decisions to overrule a recommendation of the quality control director to be also issued in writing over the signature of the chief executive. This way the chief executive officer cannot be shielded from the shame of knowing and being punished for that which her subordinates are doing to meet her production targets.

Another policy solution is for companies to be required to have mechanisms which enable employees to blow the whistle internally on illegal practices that they have reported to their boss, but that their boss has decided to sit on. This can be done by communicating to all employees their right and obligation to report the cover-up of an offense to a corporate ombudsman or to an ethics committee of the board of directors (as many companies already do).

Exxon have a requirement that employees who spot activities that cause them to suspect illegality must report these suspicions to the Law Department. Say a financial auditor notices in the course of her work a memo that suggests an antitrust offense. In most companies, auditors would ignore such evidence because it is not their responsibility and because of the reasonable presumption that they are not expected to be experts in antitrust law. Exxon internal auditors, however, would be in hot water if they did not report their grounds for suspicion to the Law Department.

Once a violation is reported, there is an obligation on the part of the recipient of the report to send back a determination as to whether a violation has occurred, and, if it has, what remedial or disciplinary action is to be taken. Thus, the junior auditor who reports an offense and hears nothing back about it knows that the report has been blocked somewhere. She is then *required* to report the unresolved allegation direct to the audit committee of the board in New York. The key to understanding so much organizational crime, be it fraud in the safety testing of drugs or police corruption, is the way that organizational complexity can be used to protect people from their own consciences, from the shame of colleagues with stronger consciences, and from exposure to criminal liability. And the solution is clear: to liberate shame by mandating free routes to the top, instituting auditing policies that create organizations full of antennas, and to forge a communitarian corporate culture in which I feel responsible not only for my part of the operation but for the totality of the operation, and indeed in which I feel a responsibility to the community that consumes our products or services. This then is the stuff of how communitarianism and reintegrative shaming as societal traits might be an antidote to organizational as well as individual crime.

Who Audits the Auditors? From Guardianship to Trust

As ours becomes more and more an organizational society, the organizational dimensions of social control grow in importance. As Stone (1985: 13) reminds us:

The human birthrate may be on the wane, but the corporate 'birthrate' (measured by new certificates of incorporation issued) is soaring. And it is not merely in the business sector – among the 'for-profits' – that this dramatic growth is taking place. The same trend, the same proliferation of formal bureaucratic institutions, is occurring across all the governmental, charitable, and nonprofit sectors.

In this context, one does not have to buy the line that corporations are evil institutions, run by bad people, to be concerned about corporate responsibility. The fact is simply that today, when things are done, they are being done increasingly, through (and by, and to) corporations. As a consequence, when something goes wrong, whether a toxic spill or a swindle, chances are good that a corporation will be implicated. This is not to say that the law can ignore the control of ordinary persons, but that the design of social institutions, once focused almost exclusively on how to deal with individual persons acting on their own account, has to be reconsidered in the light of a society in which bureaucratic organizations have come to dominate the landscape, and when persons are accounted for if at all, not simply as individuals, but as officeholders.   (Stone 1985:13)

A criminology which remains fixed at the level of individualism is the criminology of a bygone era.

The control of organizational crime is headed for crisis. The crisis arises from the fact that the only solution we find for breaches of trust that occur in organizational contexts is to build in more guardians of trust. An internal auditor is appointed to monitor the integrity of the company accounts; an outside auditor is accredited by a licensing board; its activities are sometimes checked by a government regulatory agency; the government regulatory agency has an internal affairs unit to monitor corruption; and so on to the courts and the legislature as the ultimate guardians. Shapiro (1987) has argued that piling higher and higher orders of guardianship on relationships of trust is not always effective. New domains of trust are conferred on the new guardians which can create different problems of abuse, and organizational life becomes increasingly complex, thereby frustrating pursuit of other social goals (see also Vaughan, 1983). As Cressey has pointed out:

to argue that embezzlement and management fraud can be prevented by rigid accounting methods is to overlook the pertinent point: If strict controls were imposed on all corporation personnel, then embezzlement, management fraud, and other trust violations would be greatly reduced, but very little business would be done ... 'Weak' accounting controls are essential to modern business, just as 'weak' police controls are essential to modern democracy.   (Cressey, 1980: 125–6)

If the only solution we can find to abuses by nth order guardians is to appoint $n+1$th order guardians, then the question of who guards the guardians will be an infinite regress and organizational life will become hopelessly clogged. The solution suggested by the theory of reintegrative shaming is a communitarian culture where everyone is the guardian of everyone else when it comes to complying with the law, and no one is relied upon as the 'ultimate' guardian. In a communitarian culture, guardianship is deprofessionalized. Second, communitarian cultures create the conditions where trust is nurtured; indeed trust is a defining characteristic of the concept of communitarianism. We trust others without resort to guardianship when they have highly developed consciences and when we share with them mutual obligations and respect. Only when these conditions of communitarianism are met can we safely replace guardianship with trust.

Americans are often shocked by the lack of formal accountability mechanisms in Japanese public and private organizations. The point is that formal accountability mechanisms are inferior substitutes for trust that is nurtured by the shame, conscience and mutual obligation of a communitarian culture. Trust is cheaper too, which makes Japanese organizations leaner and more competitive.

Catalyzing Communitarian Corporate Controls

Another implication of the theory of reintegrative shaming for corporate crime control is that government regulatory agencies should look to devolve responsibility for social control to agents who are in day-to-day relationships of interdependency with those to be regulated. Thus, to follow up an earlier example, it is better to have regulation of animal welfare in a large research institution in the hands of an officer within the organization who is responsible for ordering and delivering animals for the researchers (with government inspectors auditing her) than it is to have government inspectors doing the job directly. Part of the reason for this is that trust and responsibility, which are the stuff of voluntary compliance, are better secured within close circles of interdependency. The animal welfare officer can maintain trust among a manageable group of in-house researchers with whom she has regular contact. The government inspector cannot maintain relationships of trust with these researchers and forty other such groups of researchers in other laboratories; but he might be able to secure relationships of trust with forty animal welfare officers. Similarly, effective occupational health and safety regulation involves enlisting elected employee health and safety representatives in each workplace, as well as employer safety officers, to do most of the inspection and most of the enforcement (Braithwaite *et al.*, 1986).

In short, the theory of reintegrative shaming implies shifting responsibility for monitoring illegality back into the community along with responsibility for dealing with that illegality by informal processes of social control and conscience building. The role of government then becomes increasingly one of auditing the effectiveness of these community controls, stepping in when they fail, and selecting the most egregious cases of crime for formal public punishment to fulfill the moral education functions of the criminal law and to underwrite the legitimacy of community controls by showing that the state backs them up with severe deterrence when they are snubbed.

A crime control policy based on reintegrative shaming is thus not a policy devoid of formal punishment, nor is it a policy where community controls are assumed to occur without state intervention. It is an interventionist policy for organizational crime control, but where intervention is based less on remediation and more on conscience building and underwriting institutions of interdependent monitoring within relationships of trust. While one might argue that we punish much more than necessary to achieve the moral education function of the criminal law for common offenses like assault, for most organizational crimes punishment is so rare that moral education through the criminal law is sorely deficient. Criminal laws that are almost never seen to be enforced are a shaky foundation on which to build a shame-based control strategy. As we saw in the conclusion to Chapter 6, state shaming associated with formal punishment is a crucial component of a policy of reintegrative shaming. With organizational crime, it is a crucially neglected component.

The first practical step we might take down the track of organizational crime control by reintegrative shaming might be to choose chief executives as targets for shame, because the organizational crime literature suggests that it is chief executives who have a special responsibility for setting the tone of criminogenic corporate cultures (Cressey and Moore, 1980; Clinard, 1983; Braithwaite, 1984). It is the chief executive who usually manages to get her photograph in the business magazines when record earnings are announced. Accordingly, the best way to underwrite communitarian organizational crime controls may be through regular appearances in the business magazines of pictures of chief executives convicted of corporate offenses:

What president would not give full backing to an environmental affairs director against intransigent factory managers if it will reduce the risk of a presidential mug shot in *Fortune*? Even a mug shot in the *Funeral Directors' Gazette* might be the ultimate in mortification if one's reference group is funeral directors. (Braithwaite, 1985b: 58)

Beyond underwriting the authority of environmental control directors and other agents of internal corporate compliance, mug shots in the *Funeral Directors' Gazette* are most critical for communicating the shame that builds intra-organizational consciences. More shame-based state punishment is needed, ironically, to build the consciences that will allow organizational crime control to work by interdependent monitoring within relationships of trust. Shame-based punishments therefore might sit at the tip of an enforcement pyramid wherein most regulatory activity consists of monitored self-regulation at the base of the pyramid (see further, Braithwaite, 1985a).

10

Shaming and the good society

In this chapter we draw out some of the most important policy implications that might follow if the theory of reintegrative shaming is correct. The theory, we will see, suggests a general principle of effectiveness in social control. Whether it is parents socializing children, teachers dealing with students, police with juveniles or regulatory bureaucrats with business executives, social control that is cold and punitive is not the way to go, nor is social control that is warm and permissive. Rather the strategy of first choice should be social control that is warm and firm, with shaming rather than pain-infliction providing the firmness needed in all but extreme situations.

Clearly, there are many more implications of the theory than those highlighted in this chapter. The purpose of the chapter is not to outline a systematic treatment of policy implications; that would follow more appropriately upon testing the empirical adequacy of the theory. Nor will a critique be advanced of the major alternatives to the moralizing model of criminal justice policy – the 'justice' model and other retributive models, the deterrence model of the criminal as amoral calculator, the medical model of the criminal as pathological and other rehabilitative models. Rather, my intention is to show that the theory is significant in that it puts important policy concerns in a new light and makes some interesting predictions about what crime control policies will work. A theory must not only explain the facts we know; it must also generate fresh predictions, of which policy predictions are the most useful sort; the theory must help us account for what we know and understand what we do not know.

Human Agency Revisited

A tendency for some sociologists is to see little in the way of policy implications of a theory such as this. The level of communitarianism and the nature of shaming in a society are shaped, they would contend, by grand societal forces over which policymakers have little control. Urbanization and increasing residential mobility are among these variables that might make communitarianism a lost cause, a romantic plea for a bygone age. These two structural constraints are specifically included in the theory, but others might have been posited. Cultural heterogeneity is one possibility which, although I have discounted it in Chapter 6, others might see as a central constraint. Class conflict is another. The secularization of society, the decline of religion as a force for social control, is another candidate (cf. Hammond, 1985).

While Chapter 8 proposed some historical explanations for an hypothesized rise of reintegrative shaming in the Victorian era, I have not taken up the challenge of a general theory of the rise and fall of communitarianism throughout human history. Since a century of endeavour by countless other sociologists has failed to produce such a persuasive general theory, I will not add my name to the list of failures.

In all of this, sociologists must be careful not to adopt an overly determined conception of human history that leaves insufficient space for human agency, as stressed in Chapter 1. I apply this stricture to the structural constraints which are included in the theory: while urban life does make communitarianism more difficult to attain, the Japanese have managed to attain it in the most urban of contexts (most notably Tokyo); during the Victorian era when a number of countries achieved remarkable reductions in crime rates, urbanization advanced apace in those countries.

The farm lad of a century ago who knew everyone in his local rural community, who was deeply influenced by the congregation of his local church, had some powerful interdependencies that few young people have today. Yet community lost is community regained in other ways: the modern urbanite is more densely interdependent with a collection of associates and authority figures in the workplace than was the farm lad. The local church has been replaced with a variety of groups organized around leisure and community interests (the football club, the golf club, the nursing mothers' association) of special interest to those who join them. No matter how idiosyncratic their interests, mobile modern persons find it easier than in the past to associate with others who share identical interests.

If we are right that all major groups in society share a commitment to the core values of the criminal law, then we might expect that even though special interest groups would not take the interest of the church in moralizing over non-criminal matters, they would share with the church a propensity to shame criminality among their members. This undoubtedly goes too far, however, as the church is much more geared to social control of a moralizing sort than other voluntary associations. The church is more institutionally capable of reintegratively shaming a criminal member of its flock than is a sheep breeders' association, except in relation to offenses connected with sheep breeding. The latter is an important qualification, however: the corporatization of the professions and of industry sectors through trade associations has been an important trend that has opened up new possibilities for informal social control. If one has a complaint about impropriety by one's stockbroker or dentist, one may well secure a response that the offender is more likely to heed by complaining to the stock exchange or the dental association. than by complaining to the state.

In the 1980s, more than a century of increasing centralization of government business regulation (Macdonagh, 1961) has begun to be reversed, with growing emphasis on the state levering self-regulation out of industry and professional associations and major corporations (see, e.g., Grabosky and Braithwaite, 1986). A not unrelated form of devolution of social control from the state to more proximate groups has been the accelerated privatization of policing (Shearing and Stenning, 1981, 1987). Even within state policing, community policing and neighborhood watch schemes have begun, however slightly, to reverse the centralization of state control over policing by putting more influence into the hands of local constituencies and through mobilizing the community to do their own surveillance.

Later we discuss the liberal corporatist trends in the ideologies of social democratic parties and the trends for many massive corporations to devolve responsibility to subsidiaries, divisions and workgroups for building their own communitarian corporate culture.

All this suggests that there is neither an inexorable historical march away from communitarianism nor an inexorable trend toward it. The trends are indeed mixed. A simple fact is that human organisms derive pleasure from social interaction with others as well as practical benefits from exchange relationships. Humans being the pleasure-seeking creatures they are, if some interdependencies are cut off by structural change, even in relatively individualistic cultures they will tend to seek new ones in preference to becoming hermits. If business executives see that their employees are aliented by an anomic corporate culture, they might see good business reasons for facilitating a more communitarian corporate culture.

In short, there are, as always, profound structural realities which constrain policy choices to pursue the implications of this theory. But they are structural realities which often pull in different directions. Moreover, none of the social structural constraints are so profound that they cannot be overcome by concerted human agency to mobilize collective action. I cannot conceive why anyone would have bothered to read this far if they did not also think so. None of this, of course, is to suggest that policy change is a matter of deadly simple mechanical change to the engine of society, or to deny that policy change is rarely produced without a political struggle against determined opponents.

Stanley Cohen's Dilemma

The distinction I have made between stigmatization and reintegrative shaming approximates that advanced by Stanley Cohen between exclusionary and inclusionary modes of social control (Cohen, 1985). While Cohen is attracted to inclusion – assimilation, incorporation, normalization – he despairs at terrible flaws which open up when inclusionary theory is put into practice. The theory of reintegrative shaming specifies the inclusionary ideal in a way which lays the foundations for a policy analysis that might begin to solve the problem which Cohen so eloquently put on our agenda.

First Cohen suggests that neither the 'psychological functions of scapegoating (cleansing, reminding the righteous of their purity)' nor Durkheim's social functions can be served by inclusionary control:

by not developing an alternative conception of stigma, by trying to abolish or downgrade all elements of ceremonial status degradation, and by persisting in labelling-theory's touching faith that deviants are not, after all, very different from non-deviants, inclusionary controls are ill-equipped to foster social integration. The rituals of blaming are difficult to sustain: they lose their moral edge. Exclusionary control is symbolically much richer.

                                                            (Cohen, 1985: 233)

Reintegrative shaming actually has symbolic advantages over stigmatization because ceremonies of repentance have even more integrative potential than degradation ceremonies. A social policy of reintegrative shaming would not downplay rituals of blaming as does the inclusionary practice informed by labeling theory; it would seek to foster both blaming rituals and rituals of repentance and forgiveness.

Cohen correctly points out that the symbolic emptiness of the inclusionary writings of the sixties left the field open for conservative law-and-order policies. It also did this because it was instrumentally empty; to counsel no more than tolerance and acceptance of deviants by the community is to fail to offer any solution to crime on the streets.

it [inclusion] fails to confront the moral issues of guilt, wrong-doing, punishment and responsibility and the empirical issues of harm, danger and fear raised by the problem of crime.   (Cohen, 1985: 268)

The solution, I submit, is to advocate vigorous moralizing about guilt, wrongdoing and responsibility which is informed by the theory of reintegrative shaming, in which the harm-doer is confronted with community resentment and ultimately invited to come to terms with it. The climate of moralizing must be such as to put the accused in a position where he must either attempt to persuade the community that he is innocent, to persuade them that his deviance is harmless diversity which should be tolerated, or express remorse and seek to compensate for the harm he has done. It should be a society where retreat into a world of exclusion is difficult for either the accused or his accusers to accept. Reintegrative shaming implies opposition to both a laissez faire which renounces community responsibility for caring for weaker citizens (as decarceration has sometimes been used to justify), and opposition to therapeutic professionalism which uses inclusionary slogans to justify widening the net of coerced state control over deviants. Community moralizing is the antithesis of both professional technocracy and laissez–faire. It is both symbolically and instrumentally an alternative to conservative law-and-order politics. The Japanese have the safe streets, the empty jails, and the non-retributive community values (Hamilton and Sanders,

1985) to demonstrate that forceful moralizing need not inevitably degenerate to 'moral panic' over 'folk devils' (Cohen, 1973).

Shaming and Injustice

After the fall of Singapore in World War II, my father served three years in a Japanese prison camp at Sandakan, Borneo. It was a terrible place – of 2,500 prisoners, my father was one of six who survived to see the end of the war. The Australian and British POWs who worked to build an air-strip for the Japanese were paid in Japanese occupation money for their labor: a week's wages could purchase one egg. They had nowhere to keep this money securely; each man simply kept his little pile of notes on the ledge behind his bed. Honor was maintained until one day an amount of money disappeared. Quite a bit of evidence pointed to one young man. A 'kangaroo court' was convened. The young man wept and pleaded his innocence to his comrades in a manner my father described as heart-rending. He was found guilty and sentenced to Coventry. The experience of his mates shunning conversation with him emotionally destroyed him; broken, his health deteriorated rapidly.

After about a month of this social torture compounding the physical torture of his captors, his comrades found a rat's nest in the rafters of the hut; the nest was constructed partly of the currency which had disappeared. A few months later the young man died. When my father returned to Australia, he was contacted by the family of the young man who wanted to know how their son and brother had spent his last months; my father did not tell them the terrible truth.

This book has been about the power of shaming to do good in preventing crime. The tragedy of the suffering of this young Australian soldier confirms the power of shame, but shows the need to balance the books before drawing overly strong policy inferences from this power. By increasing the capacity of societies to shame, we will increase the extent to which the power of shaming can be harnessed for both good and ill. Shaming can be used to stultify diversity which is the stuff of intellectual, political, and artistic debate and progress, or simply to oppress diversity which is harmless. Shaming can become the principal weapon of the tyranny of the majority. The tyranny of the majority might be defensible when employed to guarantee the freedom of all from something which all do not want – to be a victim of crime. When shaming is used to oppress a minority who think the standards are wrong, however, and where those standards have nothing to do with guaranteeing the freedom of all, the majority can be truly tyrannical.

Most importantly, as the story of the Australian POW illustrates, informal means of control are, because of their informality, probably more likely to convict the innocent, even when dealing with defendants who accept the rightness of the standards under which they are oppressed. If it means punishing more innocent people, do we really want to support policies that shift social control somewhat away from the formal, with its guarantees of due process, to the informal?

Much as I admire the crime control achievements of Japan, I would not want to live there because I think I would find the informal pressures to conformity oppressive. Many scholars have commented that while Japanese culture emphasizes duties (including duties to conform to the law), it de-emphasizes rights (including the right to be different within the confines of the law) (e.g. Clifford, 1976; Wilson and Herrnstein, 1985: 526–7).

There is an implied message in much of this writing that a political choice has to be made between rights and duties; we can choose Tokyo with its emphasis on duty and neglect of rights (and with its consequently low crime rate and stultification of diversity), or we can choose New York with its cultivation of rights and neglect of duty (and with its crime and artistic and intellectual ferment). Yet with this formulation there is never an explanation of why there should be a negative correlation between cultural emphases on rights and duties. It is not at all clear that there are not or cannot be societies with both a strong cultural emphasis on duties and a strong emphasis on rights. There is no reason why policies to strengthen duty will necessarily weaken rights and vice versa.

The conceptualization of some sort of hydraulic relationship between duties and rights is part of a wider tradition in criminology which has it that a high crime rate is a price we pay for a free society. Totalitarian societies are in the best position to stamp out crime, it is assumed. At one time, this seemed so self-evident to Valerie Braithwaite and me that we used scores on the Freedom House political freedom index as a control variable in a regression analysis to predict whether income inequality would be associated with high homicide rates across nations (Braithwaite and Braithwaite, 1980).

Contrary to our expectation that freedom should be controlled because of its positive correlation with homicide, the correlation was −0.7; there was a strong tendency for nations which rated well on the 100-point political freedom index to have low homicide rates. Empirically, it would seem a nonsense to suggest that we must choose between a free society and a low-crime society. Should this really surprise us? If it were the case that the successful delivery of punishment was the way to reduce crime, we would expect totalitarian states to have less crime because they can pursue punitive policies more aggressively. But we know that in fact more punishment is not the route to crime control.

Within the United States, while urbanism is associated with crime, it is also widely believed to be associated with greater tolerance. In fact, while the association between city size and crime is very strong, that between city size and tolerance (including support for civil liberties) is significant but weak and declined between 1947 and 1982 (Abrahamson and Carter, 1986). Regional effects – net of compositional variables – are stronger, with intolerance and lack of concern for civil liberties being greater in the South. Yet there is no trade-off with crime here as Southernness is associated with higher crime rates (Gastil, 1971; McCarthy *et al.*, 1975). At the interregional, just as at the international level of analysis, the evidence does not point to a trade-off between crime control and respect for civil liberties.

Public policy can and should aspire to fostering a society that is maximally free and concerned to protect rights, while citizens are at the same time maximally concerned to meet social obligations, particularly duties to comply with the law. These are tall orders, but at least they are not mutually inconsistent.

There are some obvious things a society can do to foster at the same time duties to comply with the law and rights to be different beyond that which is forbidden by law. One is to use the same mechanisms of social control that guarantee the former also to guarantee the latter. A Bill of Rights is an example – using the law to guarantee freedom, just as the law is used in other contexts to guarantee conformity. A television program that holds up to ridicule a person who persecutes young people with deviant modes of dress is an example of shaming to permit diversity outside that which is forbidden by law, just as a cops and robbers program might be an example of shaming to foster conformity with the law. There is nothing inherently contradictory about people choosing a culture that at the same time is firm in its disapproval of delinquent behavior and vigilant in its defense of diversity. This, after all, is precisely the kind of school culture that liberals tend to look for when choosing a school for their children; emphases on both rights and duties are not so incompatible that it is difficult to find such school cultures.

However, the problem most difficult to solve is the one we started with via the case of the young Australian POW: the presumed greater propensity of informal compared with formal control processes to get the facts wrong. We will not debate the possibility that the presumption is wrong – that the disadvantages of procedural sloppiness are outweighed by the advantages of more intimate familiarity with the accused, the complainant and the circumstances of the allegation under informal social control. The young man at issue was a victim of stigmatization rather than reintegrative shaming. I will argue that the best defense against the inevitable injustices of shaming is that the shaming be reintegrative rather than outcasting.

In family life, mistakes are frequently made, guilty children are falsely convicted. Because punishment by parents is made within a continuum of love, however, injustices are very often detected. Father accuses son of vandalizing the kitchen wall with his crayons, he denies the offense, father does not believe his alibi, and punishes the son by sending him to his room. Some days later when they are back on good terms, the son says, 'You know dad, I really didn't do that drawing on the wall.' The father knows the son well enough to assess that, having served his punishment, having put the conflict behind them, he would not continue to lie about his innocence now. Perhaps it was his sister after all. Father says that if he was unfair, he is sorry, and volunteers some special treat. Of course parents who cast their children out and permanently rupture the lines of communication forgo the opportunity to correct the injustices of the past.

The other point that should be made is that while formal justice may be better at getting the facts right than informal justice, it too makes mistakes. When the realization is subsequently made that the innocent have been victimized, formal justice systems perform abysmally at compensating the innocent accused. The defendant who has spent his life savings on legal fees, lost his job, broken up his family and spent months in jail on remand is simply thrown back into the community to pick up whatever pieces are left. With formal justice, the process is the punishment (Feeley, 1979) and those who are unjustly put through the process never get adequate compensation.

In keeping the failings of informal justice in perspective we should also bear in mind Christie's insight on a crucial advantage of the informal social control seen in communitarian contexts (see Chapter 6). When people have more complex experience of each other as total personalities, they are less likely to respond to anti-social behavior by labeling the person a criminal and exhibiting a knee-jerk punitive response: the crime has a better chance of becoming 'a starting point for real dialogue, and not for an equally clumsy answer in the form of a spoonful of pain' (Christie, 1981: 11).

In other words, while formal justice processes may be better at getting the facts right, when they do convict the innocent they may be more likely to do damage because of their almost automatic resort to punishment and stigma compared to communitarian justice. While one might assume that the state would have superior resources to compensate the falsely accused than do amorphous communities of shame, in practice the state rarely compensates those it wrongs through the criminal justice system. On the other hand, ordinary folk who falsely accuse a son, an employee, or a neighbor often have the wit and the goodwill to come up with some sort of peace offering by way of compensation, symbolic and material (the innocent child is taken to a movie, the neighbor falsely accused of borrowing another's mower without permission gets his own lawn mowed, the employee wrongly blamed gets an accelerated promotion). In the case of the falsely convicted Australian POW, those who felt the deepest guilt gave the greatest compensation possible for starving men – some of their food ration.

The important conclusion remains, however, that shaming is rough-and-ready justice which runs great risk of wronging the innocent, and that the most important safeguard is for shaming to be reintegrative so that communication channels remain open to learning of injustices, and social bonds remain intact to facilitate apology and recompense. Reintegrative shaming is not only more effective than stigmatization; it is also more just.

The Repentant Role

We have just seen that shaming can be more just when it occurs while bonds of respect are maintained because roles can be reversed; the wrongful accuser can adopt the repentant role instead of the accused. When the accused is guilty, of course, the theory implies an important place for the repentant role as a turning point between shame and reintegration.

The desire to end the shame, to be reintegrated with others by adopting the repentant role, can be so strong that people will even admit to crimes they did not commit:

Punishment merited by a guilty act or even undeserved punishment for an act one has not committed may be a refuge from shame. In the midst of a situation in which one is overwhelmed by shame one may confess to a crime of which one is innocent, inviting punishment in order to re-establish, even through condemnation, communication with others.   (Lynd, 1958: 66)

This suggests one of the more subtle, but more important, policy implications of the theory. Cultures which hold up models of adopting the repentant role will be cultures which succeed in shaming that is reintegrative. Such role models do exist in Christian cultures of the West, though the Prodigal Son is hardly one of our leading folk heroes. The sacrament of penance, confession, baptism as a rite during which the sinner is reborn and washed clean of past sins, and other cultural apparatus which routinize the repentant role have withered or disappeared in the West.

To the practically minded this will seem grand and vague advice: opt for a culture that promotes shaming, that ensures that shaming is reintegrative by lionizing the repentant role. Yet there are some more specific implications of this kind of advice. Rehabilitation programs can emphasize the repentant role. Trice and Roman see this as the key to the success of Alcoholics Anonymous:

Labeling theory implicitly assumes that deviant careers are relatively permanent. Little systematic effort has been devoted to consideration of delabeling and relabeling processes. Alcoholics Anonymous appears to be a unique agency for carrying out successful delabeling and relabeling of stigmatized deviants. This success appears to be accounted for largely by A.A.'s use of the repentant role available in American society, constructing a 'comeback' for 'repentant' alcoholics based on their apparently intense adherence to middle-class ideals coupled with their repudiation of the 'hedonistic underworld' to which they 'traveled' as alcoholics.

(Trice and Roman, 1970: 538)

The repentant role is manifested in Alcoholics Anonymous meetings through contrite and remorseful public expressions that amount to ceremonies to decertify deviance, to signal an upward mobility from perceived Skid-Row or near-Skid-Row situations:

> A.A. stories about 'hitting bottom' and the many degradation ceremonies that they experienced in entering this fallen state act to legitimize their claims to downward mobility. Observation and limited evidence suggests that many of these stories are exaggerated to some degree and that a large proportion of A.A. members maintained at least partially stable status-sets throughout the addiction process. However, by the emphasis on downward mobility due to drinking, the social mobility 'distance' traveled by the A.A. member is maximized in the stories. This clearly sets the stage for impressive 'comeback accomplishments'. (Trice and Roman, 1970: 543)

Unfortunately, the way we respond to deviance, particularly crime, in the West, gives free play to degradation ceremonies of both a formal and informal kind to certify deviance, while providing almost no place in the culture for ceremonies to decertify deviance. It need not be a truism that 'some of the mud always sticks'. If we can have a culture, or rehabilitative subcultures as in Alcoholics Anonymous, where those who perform remarkable feats of rehabilitation are held up as role models – the pop star who kicked the heroin habit, the football hero who repented from wanton acts of violence – where ceremonies to decertify deviance are widely understood and readily accessible (Meisenhelder, 1982), that will be a culture where intimate groups will also have more skill in the art of shaming reintegratively.

This analysis applies to the shaming of organizational offenders as well. In *The Impact of Publicity on Corporate Offenders* (1983), Fisse and I found that none of the companies which upgraded their corporate ethics and defective standard operating procedures following scandals enjoyed substantial favorable publicity as a result, and there were examples of corporate reforms which amounted to the companies concerned becoming industry leaders in certain aspects of compliance policy. For news media reflecting the priorities of a culture which thrives on scandal but is unmoved by reform, good news is no news. Regulatory agencies were similarly uninterested in publicizing the reforms of corporations whose sins they had earlier publicized. The key policy inference from the theory here is, therefore, that regulatory agencies would prevent more crime if they held more press conferences to shame corporate offenders and more press conferences to hold up as models those companies which have responded to scandal by implementing outstanding preventive reforms.

In Western culture, the consequence is that the spectacle of a corporate executive publicly adopting the repentant role is extraordinarily rare; there are no rewards for such a posture, only costs. This situation is in the starkest possible contrast with Japan, where the public is regularly plied with media coverage of repentant executives pleading public forgiveness and promising corporate rehabilitation.

The president of Japan Air Lines faced the relatives of victims of the world's worst single-plane disaster and bowed low and long.

He turned to a wall covered with wooden tablets bearing the victims' names. He bowed again. Then, in a voice that sometimes quavered, Yasumoto Takagi asked for forgiveness and accepted responsibility.

The ceremony Thursday marked the final memorial service sponsored by the airline for the 520 people who died in the Japan Air Lines crash on Aug. 12.

On Tuesday, 3,271 people attended a service in Osaka. On Thursday, about 1,400 people, 700 of them family members, 693 of them airline employees and other guests, crowded into Hibiya Public Hall...

For Mr. Takagi and his employees, the service marked the culmination of a two-month exercise in accountability. Since the night of Aug. 12, the airline has mobilized its staff, from the president on down, to offer gestures of apology and regret that Japanese require at such times...

JAL set up a scholarship fund to pay for the education of children who had lost parents in the crash. It spent $1.5 million on the two elaborate memorial services. The airline dispatched executives to every victim's funeral, although some were turned away. And Mr. Takagi has pledged to resign soon as a gesture of responsibility.

The strain of tending to grieving relatives told on some employees. In the two months since the crash, two have died. Hiroo Tominaga, 59, a maintenance engineer, killed himself on Sept. 20, and Miyoko Inoue, 54, an executive who worked with families, died of a stroke on Oct. 11.

                                        (*International Herald Tribune*, 26 Oct. 1985, p.3).

While it is a mistake to assume that Japanese cultural traditions of repentance can readily be transplanted to the West, it is also a mistake to forget that the repentant role has a place in our own culture and that our criminal justice system is one of those institutions that systematically crushes these traditions. Consider two illustrations, the first recounted by Haley (1982: 272), the second by Wagatsuma and Rosett (1986: 486). The first is of two American servicemen accused of raping a Japanese woman. On Japanese legal advice, private reconciliation with the victim was secured; a letter from the victim was tabled in the court stating that she had been fully compensated and that she absolved the Americans completely. After hearing the evidence, the judge leaned forward and asked the soldiers if they had anything to say. 'We are not guilty, your honor', they replied. Their Japanese lawyer cringed; it had not even occurred to him that they might not adopt the repentant role. They were sentenced to the maximum term of imprisonment, not suspended.

The second story is of a Japanese woman arriving in the US with a large amount of American currency which she had not accurately declared on the entry form. It was not the sort of case that would normally be prosecuted. The law is intended to catch the importation of cash which is the proceeds of illicit activities, and there was no suggestion of this. Second, there was doubt that the woman had understood the form which required the currency declaration. After the woman left the airport, she wrote to the Customs Service acknowledging her violation of the law, raising none of the excuses or explanations available to her, apologizing profusely, and seeking forgiveness. In a case that would not normally merit prosecution, the prosecution went forward *because* she had confessed and apologized; the US Justice Department felt it was obliged to proceed in the face of a bald admission of guilt.

Beyond Tolerance and Understanding

As argued in Chapter 1, the labeling perspective brought with it a more appreciative stance toward offenders, a plea for tolerance and understanding. Tolerance and understanding seem unexceptionable virtues. A conventional wisdom of modern liberal parents tends to be that, should one of their children become involved in marijuana use, they should not 'overreact' or 'blow their top'; instead they should matter-of-factly and sympathetically discuss the pros and cons of drug use with the child. Yet it might be argued that the very delinquencies toward which modern 'progressive' parents display the greatest tolerance and understanding – abuse of alcohol, marijuana and tobacco – are among the most widespread forms of delinquency in modern societies. Partly, this is because most parents have engaged or do engage in drug abuse of some sort; the evidence is that parents who are drug users are more likely to have children who are users (Pekkanen, 1973: 97–8; Akers *et al.*, 1979; Fawzy *et al*, 1983; McDermott, 1984).

Use of alcohol, tobacco and marijuana cannot be controlled in Western societies because it attracts little or no shame. Similarly, drunk driving is beyond control and does not attract the shame one would expect in proportion to the harm it does because most adults, who have themselves engaged in the offense, suffer discomfort in construing the behavior shameful.

It may be then that the liberal conventional wisdom is misguided; tolerance of drug use is the way to make the problem worse. Akers *et al.* (1979) were able to explain 68 per cent of the variance in adolescent marijuana use and 55 per cent for alcohol use with a variety of social learning theory variables such as the adolescent's perception of the approving or disapproving attitudes toward use held by adults and by other teenagers whose opinion they valued, total of all the 'admired' models (parents, friends, other adults, etc.) reported as observed using the substance, and so on (see also Akers and Cochrane, 1985). The evidence, in short, is consistent with the view that intolerance is a better way to respond to drug abuse than tolerance. The theory of reintegrative shaming implies that, rather than be tolerant and understanding, we should be intolerant and understanding. That is, we should shame what we do not presently shame, while maintaining bonds of communication, affection and respect: disappointment and dialogue rather than stigma.

At the level of the family, the theory implies that parents should strive for close attachment to their children, indeed warm loving relationships with them, but that this is not enough. Loving families which are tolerant of delinquency will raise delinquents just as will cold families which are restrictive (see, e.g., McCord *et al.*, 1959). As Maccoby (1980: 394) summarized the evidence:

A common theme in these various findings seems to be that parental warmth binds children to their parents in a positive way – it makes children responsive and more willing to accept guidance. If the parent–child relationship is close and affectionate, parents can exercise what control is needed without having to apply heavy disciplinary pressure. It is as if parents' responsiveness, affection and obvious commitment to their children's welfare have earned them the right to make demands and exercise control.

Shaming is more likely to be heeded when undertaken by a loved one whose respect and affection it would be more painful to lose. Thus, the more loving the family, the greater the possibilities for shaming to take over completely from more explicitly punitive forms of discipline. The psychological literature leaves little doubt that verbal reprimands work, especially when combined with non-verbal disapproval (e.g. a stare) (Van Houten and Doleys, 1983: 4). Once children reach an age when they can be reasoned with, the possibility of social control without resort to any sanction more harsh than verbal reprimand is a real one in loving families. There is even evidence that parental love not only increases susceptibility to parental shaming, it reduces susceptibility to influence by delinquent peers (Johnson, 1979: 101).

While shaming probably runs less risk of disrupting social relationships in the family than physical punishment, all negative sanctions increase the likelihood of the offender seeking to escape from the social situation in which the negative sanction is applied. To ensure that heavy use of shaming does not disintegrate social bonds, it is therefore important that alternatives to the shamed behaviors are made available and reinforced. The experimental literature shows that the opportunity to engage in an unpunished alternative response increases the effectiveness of punishment:

So reinforcing alternative behavior has two desirable effects: First, it helps make punishment more effective; second, it makes it less likely that the organism whose behavior is punished will escape the situation in which punishment is employed. (Van Houten, 1983: 38)

There is evidence that delinquents are more likely to have parents who never praise them for things that are well done (Chapman, 1985). Keys to the art of ensuring that shaming is reintegrative rather than stigmatizing are therefore to preserve the continuum of love even in the face of the conflict and to leaven shame with praise.

Gerald Patterson and his colleagues at the Oregon Social Learning Center have shown that parents of anti-social children lack skill in punishing. They praise and punish non-contingently upon doing the right and wrong thing; they 'natter' at their children rather than confront and follow through on transgressions:

their criterion threshold value for *confrontation* is *too low*. They threaten and scold *very* often, but they seldom follow through. As used here, confrontation means that the parent responds in such a way as to both stop the immediate deviant event *and* to reduce the likelihood of its future recurrence. Effective confrontation means both the immediate *suppression* of ongoing behavior and weakening the connection between the event and its antecedent. My hypothesis is that the problem child often wins in such an out-and-out confrontation; therefore, these parents natter, but they do not confront.

(Patterson, 1982: 227

Unfortunately, even in cultures that promote reintegrative shaming many families and other institutions will shame incompetently. They will 'natter' rather than use shame to confront and follow through on misbehavior, they will forget to temper shame with praise, they will administer shame and praise non-contingently, they will neglect to monitor behavior so that some of the worst instances of misbehavior will be ignored or tacitly approved, they will simultaneously shame and reinforce behavior ('How could you be so unkind as to take Susie's chocolate from her. Here, take this one instead.'), and they will neglect to explain the reasons for the conduct being disapproved (Parke, 1974).

Fortunately, most parents are sufficiently competent to avoid these basic errors most of the time. For those who are consistently incompetent, however, one wishes one could say that programs to train parents to follow some simple disciplinary principles would solve the problem. Regrettably, the experience of parent-training programs for parents of children with behavior problems is of only modest success not only because of difficulties in getting principles across to parents, but, more fundamentally, in motivating parents to use them (Patterson *et al.*, 1982).

Beyond Individualism

Individualism is an ideology which was useful during early capitalist development, but today we depend less and less on rugged individualists. Most economic activity occurs in bureaucratic organizations; scientific breakthoughs are increasingly the work of research teams; even contemporary artistic work is often located in public and private entertainment conglomerates, foundations, institutes. Unfortunately, many artists, scientists and entrepreneurs waste their talent because they are so wrapped up in an ideology of individualism that they cannot fit in with the bureaucracies that might use their abilities; they are incapable of being effective team players.

Obligation to the group, interdependencies with the special qualities of mutual help and trust – the defining characteristics of the ideology of communitarianism – are characteristics which have given the Japanese a contemporary advantage not only in crime control, but in making the best use of the talents of the populace in a post-industrial society. In the post-war period it is generally, though not invariably, the industrialized nations characterized by either strong 'corporatism' or 'concordance' (institutional integration of interest mediation under group auspices) which have achieved the strongest economic growth (Schmidt, 1982; Schott, 1984; Australia Reconstructed, 1987:9; Lehner, forthcoming; but see Cameron, 1984; Marks, 1986).

It is hard to argue that liberal corporatist societies like Sweden, Norway, or Austria have less political and social freedom, less ferment of ideas, than individualist societies like the United States; individuals can work cooperatively in groups to achieve common goals without having those groups constrain conduct in areas beyond certain limited foci of mutual concern. It is the same point as in the last section about strong cultural commitments to conformity within the law not precluding cultural commitments to diversity outside the restrictions set by the law. So one can be a communitarian academic – show loyalty to one's department and university, attend colleagues' seminars and contribute constructively to debate, agree to cooperate with the consensus reached at staff meetings even though one advocated a different course, feel a sense of obligation to help and trust colleagues – without compromising in the least one's freedom to be gay, to advocate an epistemology which is anathema to everyone else in the department, or to engage in political activities of which they all disapprove. Effective communitarianism in academia thus involves very delimited encroachments on freedom while opening up new possibilities for freedom (e.g. the freedom of students to choose from a balanced range of options rather than from very similar courses offered by obstinate individualists).

As far as crime control is concerned, there is a widespread view that communitarianism is a lost cause, a utopian plea for the irrecoverable virtue of a previous era. There is a justifiable consensus in the sociology of law that the power of local groups such as families, churches and residential communities to impose informal sanctions on deviance has decayed. In a brilliant monograph Bayley addresses what he sees as the 'core tradition in the sociology of law' – that 'as history marches, sanctioning on behalf of community norms becomes less dispersed and more concentrated superordinately, especially in the state' (Bayley, 1985: 117–18). This core tradition is manifest in Black's (1976) increase in 'law' (social control by the state) at the expense of informal social control as societies become more complex, Maine's (1861) movement from status to contract, Tonnies' (1887) shift from *Gemeinschaft* to *Gesellschaft*, Durkheim's (1893) organic to mechanical solidarity, and Redfield's (1947) folk to urban society.

While Bayley (1985) concedes that empirically there can be little doubt that increased social complexity has been associated with an expanding regulatory role for the state (e.g. Freeman and Winch, 1957; Adams, 1982) he argues persuasively that 'sanctioning by superior encapsulating authorities does not inevitably weaken subordinate sanctioning' (Bayley, 1985: 131). Indeed, he gives examples of new superordinate regulation actually prompting the development of subordinate or intermediate regulation. The literature on business regulation is replete with examples of industry self-regulation being introduced as a result of new government regulation (securities regulation leading to stock exchange self-regulation; government motion picture censorship resulting in voluntary rating systems, etc.). Government intervention in new areas of substance abuse (e.g. sniffing) has at times been substantially implemented by mobilizing and funding community groups to tackle the problem (e.g. funding Australian Aboriginal community groups for campaigns against petrol sniffing in the outback). Government initiatives to fund local crime prevention associations, community justice centres, village courts, and neighborhood watch associations can be seen throughout the world. In short, Bayley argues that the growth of superordinate sanctioning does not necessarily cause the decline of sanctioning by subordinate groups. Both may occur simultaneously for different reasons.

Where sanctioning occurs in social space is fundamentally a matter of political decision, according to Bayley. However, these political choices are constrained by the fact that while the state can count on peer sanctioning being effective and capable of being mobilized in communitarian societies, in individualistic societies this is not so.

Individualism habituates people to resist any group sanctioning. The individual stands alone against all sanctioning authorities. Rational calculation might convince individualists that their freedom is better assured through maintenance of countervailing centers of authority, but this political lesson is not entailed by individualist preferences. Indeed, the habit of resisting sanctioning from all auspices creates a weakness toward superordination. An individualistic society faced with debilitating amounts of crime may have nowhere to turn for control but to the maximal community. Individualism may create a sanctioning vacuum at intermediate as well as at individual levels that makes superordination the natural but desperate remedy. Leviathan is created, as Hobbes foresaw, by anarchy. I submit that anarchy is encouraged more by individualism than communitarianism.

(Bayley, 1985: 124)

And so the irony is that individualistic societies are given little choice but to rely on the state as the all-powerful agent of social control: the ideology of the minimal state produces a social reality of the maximum state. Because sanctioning by peers and intermediate groups like schools, churches, trade unions and industry associations cannot work in an individualist culture, the state responds (ineffectively) to perceived increases in crime the only way it can – by locking more people up, giving the police and business regulatory agencies more powers, trampling on the very civil liberties which are the stuff of individualist ideologies.

Bayley therefore argues that the more communitarian a society is, the more free it is to make political choices over how much of its sanctioning activity will be located at superordinate, intermediate and peer levels. This is a freedom to choose a mix which satisfices in terms of crime control and which is acceptable to the people with regard to incursions upon their liberties. The only choice of extremely individualist societies is to do nothing and learn to live with crime, or to gear up the repressive state and still learn to live with crime.

This may be too strong a conclusion, however. The United States is perhaps an extreme case of an individualist society (Bellah *et al.*, 1985), and while there is a history of failure of 'community organization' approaches to crime control, particularly from the time of President Johnson's War on Poverty, there are enough encouraging evaluations of the impact of local voluntary organizations (LVOs) (such as neighborhood watch schemes) on crime from the United States for Greenberg *et al.* to conclude from their review:

Existing research provides fairly strong evidence that LVOs can influence crime and fear of crime. Three avenues of influence receive particular support. First, participation in LVOs has been found to be positively associated with informal interaction, which in turn, has been associated

with increased bystander intervention and territorial cognitions and behaviors. Yet, there is still a lack of direct evidence to indicate that increased
informal interaction decreases the local crime rate.

(Greenberg *et al.*, 1985: 133)

Greenberg *et al.* also found that the evidence on the effect of
neighborhood informal social control (as measured by recognition of
strangers, density of local social networks, neighboring activities,
etc.) was inconclusive:

One of the major findings of this literature synthesis is that no firm conclusion can be reached on the relationship between informal social control and
neighborhood crime. The evidence suggests that informal control and a
variety of crime-related problems tend to co-vary spatially, that is, high
levels of informal control and low rates of delinquency and serious crimes
are typically found in the same neighborhoods, and the converse. As a result
– and because it makes intuitive sense – the two are often believed to be
causally related. Furthermore, their spatial co-variation may reflect a similar set of causes in which case their relationship may be spurious. In
general, the causal relationship between the two has not been established in
the existing research.   (Greenberg *et al.*, 1985: 170)

The informal control variables which were found to be most
consistently related to areal crime rates were 'the expectation that
oneself or one's neighbors would intervene in a criminal or suspi-
cious situation, sense of responsibility for and control of areas
around the house and in the neighborhood, and affective attachment
to the neighborhood. But these attitudes may well be an effect of
areal crime rates, not a cause' (Greenberg *et al.*, 1985: 102).

On the one hand, the rest of the world need not take these
somewhat discouraging findings too seriously as they are from what
is probably an extreme case of an individualist culture. On the other
hand, the evidence to date does not rule out the possibility that even
in the United States we may yet find that government programs to
foster informal social control do reduce crime. We must remain open
to the possibility that even against the tide of an anti-communitarian
culture, it is feasible for government policies effectively to foster
communitarian crime control initiatives.

This possibility comes even more to life if we consider the views of
theorists who suggest that in modern urban societies the networks of
individuals become less spatially localized, the locus of interdependency shifts from neighborhood to communities of interest
based on workplace, occupation, and leisure activities (Stein, 1960;

Keller, 1968; Webber, 1970). These alternative communities of interest might become alternative foci for communitarian crime control initiatives. Thus crime prevention associations might be set up in workplaces as in Japan; professional associations can be asked by government to set up monitoring and disciplinary committees to deal with fraud and malpractice in the profession; football associations can be asked to step in where the police have failed to solve problems of crowd hooliganism.

One advocate of communitarian crime control policies (Alderson, 1984: 213) has suggested that when juveniles appear in court a representative of a 'community forum' from the neighborhood of the offender be present. This approach could be extended to other communities of interest. Thus, a responsibility of the probation officer could be to convince representatives of a young person's school, employer, sporting clubs, and other groups that are important to the offender to attend the court and offer their opinions on what they would be able to contribute to monitoring the offender's behavior in future and to her rehabilitation. This would heighten communitarian obligations for informal social control among those present; it would also enhance shaming in the eyes of reference groups, and secure practical commitments to reintegration from those same groups.

It may be that Alderson's localism is a triumph of hope over reality for application to mass urban societies with non-communitarian cultures, yet the essential idea can still be applied. Most of us have intermediate groups beyond the family which are important to us. If I were arrested for assault, I imagine it would be maximally shameful for me to have in court a representative of my university department, of the consumer movement, perhaps of some other voluntary associations to which I belong, as well as my family and my nextdoor neighbor, and these are the groups which could give the best practical assurances to the court of keeping an eye on me in future, of guaranteeing that I will stay clear of the pub where I got into the fight and that I will comply with the conditions of a community service order. Moreover, if I did not volunteer these reference groups to the probation officer, half an hour on the telephone would readily establish them. It would be an imposition on these people to attend, but they would all have come to my funeral had I badly lost the fight, and so would surely attend the court case, especially if part of the reason for being asked to attend was to speak on my behalf by assuring the court that I was safe to be released into the community.

All in all, then, we should not overly despair about the lack of methodologically persuasive favorable evaluations of limited government initiatives to foster informal social control in the United States. Quite apart from the limited nature of both the initiatives and the evaluations, we must not discount the possibility that over time even the US will become a more communitarian culture which will better nurture such initiatives. This possibility arises from my earlier allusion that a shift to communitarianism may be in the interests of American capital. Many American business leaders have reached this conclusion and have set to work fostering more communitarian corporate cultures within their companies, some of them by sensibly adapting Japanese ideas to an American cultural heritage, others by inappropriately adopting Japanese models in an American environment. It could well be that societies that have had communitarianism swept away by the tide of urbanization over the last two hundred years could see the ideology of communitarianism slowly rebuilt in the workplaces, schools and voluntary associations of the nation.

Bridging the Discontinuity in Socialization Style Between the Family and Other Institutions

In Chapter 4 it was argued that, within the family, socialization proceeds from initial emphasis on external punishment to increasing emphasis on fostering internal controls. When the child moves out into the world of interacting with new authority figures such as teachers and police officers, this transition is sharply reversed. The child is thrown back into a world of social control by external punishment; moral development is in a sense thrust into reverse.

We might therefore consider redesigning schools and policing styles to assist rather than hinder the transition to mature internalized control. Indeed, as we saw in the last chapter, there is also scope for transforming the disciplinary practices of work organizations toward the family model and away from the punitive model.

On the policing side, the Japanese provide perhaps the best example (Bayley, 1976) with their emphasis on intimate knowledege of local communities, on involving families, schools, employers and other intimates in solving delinquency problems, in their aversion to prematurely resorting to formal punishment to solve problems of growing up, in the emphasis on guilt induction and reintegration in their policing style. For Japanese police the roles of moralist and community worker are perhaps as important as the role of law enforcer.

With respect to schooling, I can largely agree with Wilson and Herrnstein (1985: 264–88) that schools which are successful at minimizing delinquency have the same fundamental characteristics as families that succeed at controlling delinquency: they provide a 'firm but nurturant' social environment. They are neither cold and firm nor warm and permissive, but warm and firm. In reaching this conclusion Wilson and Herrnstein rely primarily on the analyses of delinquency in over 600 American schools sponsored by the National Institute of Education (Gottfredson and Gottfredson, 1985). Gottfredson and Gottfredson concluded from this massive data set on teacher and student victimization reports and student self-reports of delinquency that schools with the least delinquency problems had not only firm but also 'clear, persistent and evenhanded application of the rules. The results suggest, in short, that misconduct should not be ignored but should be responded to in ways that students can anticipate...' (Gottfredson and Gottfredson, 1985: 173).

Another important finding from this research was that 'the rotation of students through different classes taught by different teachers influences levels of teacher victimization in high schools' (Gottfredson and Gottfredson, 1985: 172). Clearly interdependency with a teacher who can establish a continuity with the socializing practices of the family has a better chance where the student has regular contact with a small range of teachers rather than with a different smorgasbord of instructors each day. Gottfredson and Gottfredson (1985: 172) recommend as a delinquency reduction policy that instruction be reorganized so that each student has much more regular contact with a particular teacher or teachers. This might mean, for example, alternating between a 'home-room' teacher and a variety of others.

The theory of reintegrative shaming suggests that a key problem with young people is a loss of social integration as they break away from total identification with the family into which they are born. The school provides one possibility for a continuity of social integration, and indeed we have seen that the evidence is strong that students who are poorly integrated with the school (who are weakly attached to it, do not like it, are failed and rejected by it) are much more prone to delinquency. The challenge for schools is to integrate all students successfully, especially those most at risk of disillusionment with the school because of low aptitude. If they wish to minimize delinquency, schools should not create outcast enclaves within the institution by ability grouping. In general all processes that marginalize weak students are potentially criminogenic. In this regard, it is hard to surpass Knight's definition of redemptive schooling:

A redemptive schooling practice would aim to integrate students into all aspects of school learning and not build fences around students through bureaucratic rituals or prior assumptions concerning student ability. A clear expectation from teachers must be that all students can be taught, and in turn, an expectation on the part of students that they can learn. A school succeeds democratically when everyone's competence is valued and is put to use in a variety of socially desirable projects. Indeed, the same may be said to hold for a good society. (Knight, 1985: 266)

In integrative schools, all students will have means of earning positive reputations: 'everyone can be someone'. In school cultures that eschew competitive individualism in favor of cooperative problem solving, ipsative competition (competition against the student's own past performance rather than against that of other students) or inter-group competition, all students can taste success as their skills improve or through useful contributions to groups which succeed as groups.

The pain of continual failure is deflected by learning through strengths, and a sense of belonging is encouraged by working within co-operative ventures. (Knight, 1985: 270)

There is a nice synergy within the implications of the theory here because this means that the way the school can help bridge the socialization discontinuity between family and adult institutions is by being integrative in a manner that would have schools laying the foundations for communitarianism in the culture – cooperative obligation to the group being elevated above competitive individualism as a value.

Other public policies might be considered to reverse the trend toward extended adolescence. After children begin the process of breaking away from dependency on the family of orientation, an extension has occurred of the period in a 'cultural no man's land'

(Silberman, 1978: 32), a cultural vacuum that has been filled by an increasingly identifiable adolescent culture incorporating distinctive tastes in clothes and music and often drug use and other forms of symbolic rebellion against adult hypocrisy.

Clearly one would not want to promote public policies to reverse this trend by pushing young people earlier into the responsibilities of interdependency with a family of procreation. However, there may be a case for intervention to reverse the receding availability of employment to young people in modern economies that have a growing preference for mature workers and an increased capacity to be choosy in rejecting young job applicants. Policies to give priority to the young in public job creation and retraining programs or to lower minimum wages for youth are not so obviously desirable as they may seem. In an economy with a finite number of jobs to go around, more jobs for the young means fewer for older workers. Unemployment may have even more severe social implications for older workers who have families to provide for, and may be a more devastating blow to their pride than for young people who have never had a job. Tackling the problem of an expanding culture of adolescent drift through aggressive youth employment policies could worsen other problems. More fundamental rethinking of the structure of capitalist economies is required.

Alternatively, the society might work at putting a more adult social construction on late-adolescent education and further extend education upwards to bridge the 'cultural no-man's land'. That might mean educational institutions run more democratically by the students, though Gottfredson and Gottfredson's (1985) study is not encouraging on the value of this. A mix of both approaches is possible: the standard career path could be for students to be thrown into the workforce for a year or two during adolescence (this being socially constructed as the transition to adulthood), at the completion of which they would complete an extended education. None of the possibilities for recreating a society in which the assumption of adult responsibilities and interdependencies will predictably occur at an early age are easy or necessarily desirable on balance.

Implications for Criminal Justice Policy

Like most sociological theories of crime, the theory of reintegrative shaming implies that solutions to the crime problem are not fundamentally to be found in the criminal justice system. Nevertheless, in so far as formal punishment by the state is important, the theory suggests that 'punishment as moral education almost certainly reduces more crime than punishment as deterrence' (Wilson and Herrnstein, 1985: 495). Wilson and Herrnstein distinguish in this way between the desire to avoid further punishment (deterrence) working to reduce crime through instrumental conditioning and the subjective sense of wrongdoing (moral education) working to reduce crime through classical conditioning:

Once established, conscience operates without external agents to enforce it, yet it arises to begin with in society's abhorrence of certain acts, encountered either in the informal disapproval that the law institutionalizes or in formal legal punishments.   (Wilson and Herrnstein, 1985: 495)

If it is the moral education rather than the deterrent qualities of punishment that contribute most toward crime control, as the theory implies, then there are lessons for the public presentation of punishment. Durkheim drew some of these lessons at the turn of the century:

Since punishment is reproaching, the best punishment is that which puts the blame – which is the essence of punishment – in the most expressive but least expensive way possible... It is not a matter of making him suffer, as if suffering involved some sort of mystical virtue, or as if the essential thing were to intimidate and terrorize. Rather it is a matter of reaffirming the obligation at the moment when it is violated, in order to strengthen the sense of duty, both for the guilty party and for those witnessing the offense – those whom the offense tends to demoralize. Every element of the penalty that does not promote this end, all severity that does not contribute to this end, is bad and should be prohibited.   (Durkheim, 1961: 181–2)

For Durkheim, to punish more cruelly than was required to achieve the moral educative functions of punishment was more than a waste of state resources, more than an immoral imposition of useless punishment on the offender; it also risked a counterproductive rupture of social integration: 'For any penalty to have an educational influence it must seem worthy of respect to the person on whom it is inflicted' (Durkheim, 1961: 197).

The theory of reintegrative shaming equally implies that punishment need be no more severe than is required to communicate the degree of community disapproval appropriate to the offense. Punishment should be visible, newsworthy, so that consciences can be moulded by the unambiguous communication of the abhorrence that society extends toward criminal acts. This is hardly a problem with crime in the streets that generates so much fodder for the journalism of disgust. Punishment with many areas of white collar crime is infrequently reported, however, because punishment is rare, the facts of the case are complex and hard to present journalistically, and fear of defamation action is greater. Thus, there is special reason for active pursuit of publicity following white collar convictions.

If we are right in concluding that even at the level of deterrence rather than moral education, informal shaming is more important than formal punishment, it follows that communications designed to secure deterrence should focus on shame. This realization has been made by the public relations experts who design publicity programs to deter shoplifting: they tend to emphasize in their campaigns the stigma of having a 'record' rather than the likely punishment (Jensen and Erikson, 1978: 120–1).

If visible shaming plus reintegration are the real stuff of crime control, then contemporary imprisonment would seem a terribly misguided institution. As Dr Johnson wrote in *The Idler* in 1759: 'In a prison the awe of publick eye is lost, and the power of the law is spent; there are few fears, there are no blushes. The lewd inflame the lewd, the audacious harden the audacious.' Prisons are warehouses for outcasts; they put problem people at a distance from those who might effectively shame them and from those who might help reintegrate them. Imprisonment is a policy both for breaking down legitimate interdependencies and for fostering participation in criminal subcultures.

If we must punish, and formal punishments are inevitable up to a point, it follows that we should do so in a way that is visible rather than hidden and that nurtures the social integration of the offender: community service orders are an example. Restitution, prominent under the Japanese emphasis on apology, shows some promise even within American culture (Schneider, 1986). Both community service orders and restitution are sanctions that undercut stigmatization by giving the offender an opportunity to be redeemed by 'paying his debt'.

There are other possibilities that at present do not exist on the sentencing landscape. A court might suspend a sentence of imprisonment until the offender had an opportunity to approach her employer with her probation officer. The proposition could be put to the employer that, instead of working a 38-hour week, the offender would work a 45-hour week for a specified period with the employer paying only half the normal hourly rate for the extra time, which would be paid to the state or the victim instead of the offender. The company would get a bit of cheap labor and be saved the cost of recruiting and training a new employee; the state would get some victim compensation money out of the offender; and the offender would stay out of jail and keep her job. Moreover, the whole social process would enhance the possibilities for employer and workmates becoming involved in both shaming and reintegration. If the package seemed sufficiently punitive and potentially rehabilitative to the probation officer, then it would be recommended to the court as an alternative to incarceration. This is but one of many possibilities for better designing punishment to comport with principles of reintegrative shaming.

It follows that, if we must resort to imprisonment, maximum effort to integrate the prison with the community – work release, study release, easy access for family visits – is recommended. Moreover, on release, maximum support is required to foster the difficult process of reintegration. There is evidence that feelings of being welcome at home and strength of interpersonal ties outside predict success at staying out of prison and other measures of post-release adjustment (Glaser, 1964; Ekland-Olson *et al.*, 1983).

Most importantly, though, a criminal justice system designed with sensitivity to the theory of reintegrative shaming would want to put shaming and reintegration up front as a common alternative to state sanctioning. We do not have to resort to romantic and potentially oppressive notions of 'people's courts' to expedite this. As suggested earlier, we can stick with the due process model while working to bring relevant audiences and representatives of support networks into the court to testify as to why the offender should be trusted in the community (or why not in the case of some victims), to shame the offender by their presence, and to offer suggestions as to how they as community or family members could take responsibility for monitoring or helping the offender were he to be released to the community. Viewed another way, the due process model can be retained for assessing guilt; the court might then throw the responsibility for responding to the problem back on to relevant communities of interest creatively assembled in the courtroom by probation professionals.

The assembly-line justice of contemporary court systems puts insufficient emphasis on reprobation in its preoccupation with efficient dispensing of formal sanctions. About 85 per cent of those who face felony court charges in California are convicted of some offense, but only about 10 per cent are tried before a judge and jury (Rosett and Cressey, 1976: 33-4). Most criminals are not confronted with the community's disdain for what they have done in the solemn ceremony of the criminal trial. Their fate is sorted out technocratically, quietly, often in deals done between prosecutors and defense lawyers. Rosett and Cressey argue that when defendants do appear in court, their appearances are almost always short, and, from the defendant's point of view, full of legal talk the import of which is not fully comprehended. Denunciation is forgotten. The offenders are on an assembly line populated by lawyers who are anything but moralizing about what the offender has done; the lawyers are matter of fact, worldly wise, keen just to do their job and move on to the next case.

For those imbued with the retributive neo-classical tradition in criminology, these policy implications will not cut much ice. If one believes that the criminal justice system should be designed to maximize the prospects of criminals getting the punishment they deserve, rather than designed to minimize crime, then these policy implications may be irrelevant.

While for utilitarian criminologists the policy implications of the theory are clearly for a shift away from punitive social control toward moralizing social control, they too must bear in mind other considerations beyond the theory. The criminal justice system must be capable of dealing with worst-case scenarios because they are the very scenarios that threaten its legitimacy. We have said that the psychopath who is beyond shame is also likely to be beyond social control by punishment. Yet imprisonment will sometimes be needed to protect the community from these psychopaths, or from terrorists for whom all the shaming that counts is from an oppositional subculture. We might not be able to shame them or deter them, but at least we might incapacitate them.

Finally, we must also remember that the levels of punishment the state provides for a particular crime themselves give a message about how shameful that offense is. When the state provides for only a $5 penalty for parking offenses it transmits the message that this kind of offense is not very shameful. It is appropriate that levels of maximum punishment should be calibrated according to how much denunciation is warranted by the offense, according to how much harm the offense inflicts upon others. In circumstances where opportunities for repentance have been persistently flouted, the denunciatory potential of these maximum penalties should be mobilized by putting them into effect. Fortunately, a shame-based criminal justice policy can deliver a lot of moral education mileage by doing this only very rarely, but with public relations flair.

To be sceptical about the deterrent value of formal punishment, moreover, is not to deny that deterrence is always theoretically possible. It is just that effective crime control by formal deterrence requires a frequency and severity of punishment that is fiscally impossible, and so destructive of civil liberties, so unjust, that it is also politically impossible. We can control crime by assigning three police officers in eight-hour shifts to look over the shoulder of each citizen as she goes about her daily life. Granted, crime can be deterred in a particular neighborhood by massive policing of it. But this policing will not change the subcultural acceptability of crime as a way of life; offenders will go elsewhere or switch to other kinds of targets that have not been hardened. And it is politically and fiscally impossible to police intensively all neighborhoods, to harden all the alternative targets. Moralizing social control, in contrast, has the virtue of being oriented to attacking the acceptability of crime as a way of life, to the goal of persuading offenders that they should not want to commit crime in any neighborhood at any time.

On Policing

Whether we are considering the work of occupational health and safety inspectors or police officers on the beat in working class neighborhoods, the theory implies that the government policing agent work hard at devolving responsibility for monitoring illegality back to the community, along with responsibility for dealing with crime by informal social control and conscience building. Thus, neighborhood watch schemes and workplace health and safety committees can be steps in the suggested direction.

The police officer on the beat should solve fewer problems by processing offenders through the criminal justice system and more by handing the matter over to the offender's family, school, workmates, football club, more by facilitating reconciliation and restitution between offender and victim. This general prescription is not to deny that there will be particular areas, notably domestic violence, where intra-family relationships are the nub of the problem, demanding community intervention into the family to protect its less powerful members. Similarly, most occupational health and safety inspectors would do better to reallocate some of their time from walking the beat to talking to elected worker health and safety representatives and company safety officers about how the latter can improve their (more frequent) walking of the beat in their own workplace.

Police officers need to be more in and of the community than they are and less seen as standing above it. Community policing has its dangers, however. A vision of community policing as police recruiting vigilantes to be their agents, or rather puppets under the control of the state, is a dangerous one, because it may amount to an extension of the power of the police state to people who are not subject to the checks and balances that democracies have imposed on those in uniform, because it is anti-democratic, increasing the control of the center over the community instead of devolving responsibility from center to periphery. Community policing is more likely to strengthen democracy rather than threaten it when it proceeds through a bottom-up rather than a top-down implementation strategy. That is, the best way to make the police effective catalysts of community crime control is for them to go into the community and ask citizens how they would like to see police priorities and practices change in their locality, to make policing policies and resource allocation more democratically accountable (Pepinsky, 1984).

A member of the most powerless minority group in a community should be in a position to complain about a police-practice by attending a meeting of a community organization which has been empowered through representation on joint police-citizen committees to get the problem on the police policy agenda. This is not to advocate replacement of the 'government of laws' with the 'government of men'; it is simply to make the policies which guide how the 'men' of the police exercise their discretion in enforcing the law more accountable to the community. The goal is not political interference in particular enforcement decisions but democratic participation in debate over the policies which shape enforcement practices. There is a healthy contemporary British debate in the aftermath of the riots of the early 1980s and the Scarman Report over different models for securing a more accountable police (Baldwin and Kinsey, 1982; Brown, 1982; Bayley, 1983; Alderson, 1984; Jefferson and Grimshaw, 1984; Kinsey *et al.*, 1985; Reiner,1985; Spencer, 1985; Downes and Ward, 1986), though different countries must find their own solutions consistent with their institutional history and traditions of democratic process.

My mission here is not to prescribe a model for democratically accountable policing; it is simply to make the point that there is a synergy rather than a tension between the goals of better accountability to the community and greater effectiveness of policing. This is because the police, according to the theory, will be most effective when they are of the community, catalyzing, devolving social control responsibilities to the citizenry, creatively fostering apology, compensation and forgiveness. When police are of the community, it need no longer be true that 'police often arrest simply for lack of an alternative' (Pepinsky, 1984: 263). Yet this will fail, may even produce a backlash, if the police attempt to do it by imposing themselves on the community. If, in contrast, the police approach the community through allowing citizens to impose themselves more on the police, then the community may want the police to become of them rather than above them. The police more than anyone must learn that they can best become effective agents of crime control by putting themselves in relationships of *inter*dependency with the community instead of persisting with what they perceive as a dependency of the community on them – a perception not shared by many of those who are supposed to be dependent. When police–community interdependency is attained, we may all benefit from a cheaper, more effective, more humane criminal justice system that moves away from repressive social control in favor of moralizing social control.

Conclusion: Reintegrative Shaming and the Good Society

We have seen that shaming is a powerful weapon of social control that can be used for good or ill. I have argued that the most important characteristic of cultural patterns of shaming that determine whether it will be used more to guarantee freedom than to trample upon it is whether the shaming is reintegrative. Communities which maintain bonds of respect throughout the shaming process are those most likely to tolerate with affection the 'village idiot', the 'wag', the transvestite. They will also be more just in detecting and remedying cases when the innocent are shamed.

My main mission in writing this chapter is to contend that, in deciding what policy sense to make of the theory of reintegrative shaming, we should avoid the trap of assuming that we must make a choice between a society of consensus and a society with conflict, between a culture oriented to duties and one oriented to rights, between crime and freedom.

The good society is one in which there is consensus over certain core values, including the criminal law, but that has institutions to encourage conflict outside those areas of near-universal agreement. Among the core values on which the good society must have consensus are freedom, the promotion of diversity and constructive conflict. If there is not consensus over the value of institutions which simultaneously protect freedom and foster conflict – like courts of law and free trade unions – then there will be less freedom and conflict in the society.

The good society is intolerant of deviance from the core consensus values, and tolerant, nay encouraging, of diversity beyond the limitations set by those core values. Among the core values that the good society will not tolerate being undermined are the criminal law, and freedom and diversity outside the criminal law. The good society, in short, is both strong on duties and strong on rights, and especially strong on duties that protect rights.

The mix of rights and duties is a matter for political choice and conflict. We must all do battle for our vision of the good society, but in doing so we do not need to put up with the slings and arrows of those who see rights and duties as locked into a simplistic hydraulic relationship. The serious policy debates will be about what kind of mix of rights and duties, trust and accountability, we should struggle for politically.

For my part, I am most keen to do battle with those on the right who want a criminal law which is overly inclusive of individual conduct the reprehensibility of which is subject to doubtful consensus (e.g. drug use, prostitution), and insufficiently inclusive of organizational conduct which is seen in the community as reprehensible beyond doubt (e.g. health and safety, pollution offenses). I am also keen to do battle with those on the left who still believe that 'The task is to create a society in which the facts of human diversity, whether personal, organic or social, are not subject to the power to criminalize' (Taylor *et al.*, 1973: 282). While I obviously would not subscribe to Dahrendorf's cynicism about communitarianism, who can challenge his conclusion that the ideology of contesting any power to criminalize is one which would create a society begging domination by the authoritarian right?

The absence of a credible state, lawlessness, the resulting mix of chaos and rebellion describe not totalitarianism, but the condition which gives rise to it. Some of its ingredients were clearly present in Weimar Germany, though in retrospect the 1920s look much less anomic than its contemporaries thought. Whether there were elements of anomy in the Soviet Union which Stalin inherited when he took over, or what other conditions enabled him to set up his murderous tyranny, is a question which I must leave open at this point. In any case, we have seen that Anomia cannot last. It is not just chaos, but also a vacuum which attracts the most brutal forces and powers. We have also seen traces of such crude power and its arrogance in the contemporary world. Suffice it to say that my worry is that the road to Anomia will awaken Behemoth as well as Leviathan, and that a new wave of totalitarianism will sweep the world.   (Dahrendorf, 1985: 158–9)

We must reject a crass functionalism, a crudely Durkheimian view of social solidarity, which would have it that a communitarian society will inevitably use its power to shame both rapists and homosexuals. Equally, it can use its capacities to shame rapists and police who harass homosexuals. Good societies can and do use shame against encroachments on the freedom of people to deviate. This is the realm of political choice, of conflict, of human agency. There is no functional imperative that determines which breaches of duty will be shamed and which freedoms will be protected. What is certain, however, is that societies that lack the capacity to exert community control over breaches of duty, and to exert community control to protect freedoms, will lose their freedom. This is so first because freedom can never be protected if encroachments on freedom cannot be sanctioned. Second, if citizens' persons and property cannot be secured by moralizing against criminals, then political demands for the repressive state will prevail. To the extent that moralizing social control collapses, a vacuum is created that will attract the most brutal, repressive and intrusive of police states.

References

Abrahamson, M. and Carter, V.J. (1986) 'Tolerance, Urbanism and Region', *American Sociological Review*, **51**, 287–94.

Adams, R. N. (1982) 'The Emergence of the Regulatory Society', in J. P. Gibbs (ed.), *Social Control*, Beverly Hills: Sage.

Adams, S. (1984) *Roche Versus Adams*, London: Jonathan Cape.

Adler, F. (1975) *Sisters in Crime: The Rise of the New Female Criminal*, New York: McGraw-Hill.

Adler, F. (1983) *Nations Not Obsessed With Crime*, Littleton, Colo.: F.B. Rothman.

Ageton, S.A. (1983) 'The Dynamics of Female Delinquency, 1976-1980', *Criminology*, **21**, 555–84.

Ageton, S. A., and Elliott, D.S. (1974) 'The Effects of Legal Processing on Self-Concept', *Social Problems*, **22**, 87–100.

Agnew, R. (1985) 'A Revised Strain Theory of Delinquency', *Social Forces*, **64**, 151–67.

Agnew, R., and Peters, A. A. R. (1986) 'The Techniques of Neutralization: An Analysis of Predisposing and Situational Factors', *Criminal Justice and Behavior*, **13**, 81–97.

Akers, R. L., and Cochrane, J. K. I. (1985) 'Adolescent Marijuana Use: A Test of Three Theories of Deviant Behaviour', *Deviant Behaviour*, **6**, 323–46.

Akers, R. L., Krohn, M.D., Lanza-Kaduce, L., and Radosevich, M. (1979) 'Social Learning and Deviant Behavior: A Specific Test of a General Theory', *American Sociological Review*, **83**, 114–53.

Alderson, J. (1984) *Law and Disorder*, London: Hamish Hamilton.

Ames, W.L. (1981) *Police and Community in Japan*, Berkeley: University of California Press.

Andenaes, J. (1974) *Punishment and Deterrence*, Ann Arbor: University of Michigan Press.

Anderson, F. R., Kneese, A. V., Reed P. D., Stevenson, R. B. and Taylor, S. (1977) *Environmental Improvement Through Economic Incentives*, Baltimore: Johns Hopkins University Press.

Anderson, L.S., Chiricos, T.G., and Waldo, G.P. (1977) 'Formal and Informal Sanctions: A Comparison of Deterrent Effects', *Social Problems*, **25**, 103–14.

Archer, D. and Gartner, R. (1984) *Violence and Crime in Cross-National Perspective*, New Haven: Yale University Press.

Aultman, M.G. (1979) 'Delinquency Causation: A Typological Comparison of Path Models', *Journal of Criminal Law and Criminology*, **70**, 152–63.

Austin, R.L. (1977) 'Commitment, Neutralization and Delinquency', in T.N. Ferdinand (ed.), *Juvenile Delinquency*, London: Sage.

Austin, W.T. (1984) 'Crow Indian Justice: Strategies of Informal Social Control', *Deviant Behavior*, **5**, 31–46.

Australia Reconstructed (1987) Canberra: Australian Government Publishing Service.

Australian Law Reform Commission (1980) *Sentencing of Federal Offenders: Interim Report No. 15*, Sydney: Australian Law Reform Commission.

Bailey, W.C. (1984) 'Poverty, Inequality and City Homicide Rates: Some Not So Unexpected Findings', *Criminology*, **22**, 531–50.

Bailey, W. C., and Lott, R.P. (1976) 'Crime, Punishment and Personality: An Examination of the Deterrence Question', *Journal of Criminal Law and Criminology*, **67**, 99–109.

Baldwin, R. and Kinsey, R. (1982) *Police Powers and Politics*, London: Quartet.

Ball, R.A. (1983) 'Development of Basic Norm Violation: Neutralization and Self-Concept Within a Male Cohort', *Criminology*, **21**, 75–94.

Banks, C. (1965) 'Boys in Detention Centres', in C. Broadhurst and P.L. Broadhurst (eds.), *Studies in Psychology*, London: London University Press.

Bardach, E. and Kagan, R.A. (1982) *Going By the Book: The Problem of Regulatory Unreasonableness*, Philadelphia: Temple University Press.

Bartrip, P.W.J. and Fenn, J.T. (1980) 'The Administration of Safety: The Enforcement Policy of the Early Factory Inspectorate 1844-1864', *Public Administration*, **58**, 87–102.

Baumol, W. J. and Oates, W. E. (1971) 'The Use of Standards and Prices for Protection of the Environment', in P. Bohm and A. V. Kneese (eds.) *The Economics of Environment*, London: Macmillan.

Baumrind, D. (1971) 'Current Patterns of Parental Authority', *Developmental Psychology Monograph*, **4**, 1 Pt. 2.

Baumrind, D. (1978) 'Parental Disciplinary Patterns and Social Competence in Children', *Youth and Society*, **9**, 239–76.

Bayley, D. H. (1976) *Forces of Order: Police Behavior in Japan and the United States*, Berkeley: University of California Press.

Bayley, D. H. (1983) 'Accountability and Control of the Police: Some Lessons for Britain', in T. Bennet (ed.), *The Future of Policing*, Cambridge: Institute of Criminology.

Bayley, D. H. (1985) *Social Control and Political Change*, Research Monograph No. 49, Woodrow Wilson School of Public and International Affairs, Princeton University.

Bazemore, G. (1985) 'Delinquent Reform and the Labeling Perspective', *Criminal Justice and Behavior*, **12**, 131–69.

Becker, H.S. (1963) *Outsiders: Studies in the Sociology of Deviance*, New York: Free Press.

Bellah, R.N., Madsen, R., Sullivan, W.M., Swindler, A. and Tipton, S.M. (1985) *Habits of the Heart: Individualism and Commitment in American Life*, Berkeley: University of California Press.

Benedict, R. (1934) *Patterns of Culture*, New York: Mentor.

Benedict, R. (1946) *The Chrysanthemum and the Sword: Patterns of Japanese Culture*, Boston: Houghton Mifflin.

Benson, M.L. (1985) 'Denying the Guilty Mind: Accounting for Involvement in a White-Collar Crime', *Criminology*, **23**, 583–607.

Berkowitz, L. (1973) 'Control of Aggression', in B.M. Caldwell and R. Riecute (eds.), *Review of Child Development Research*, Chicago: University of Chicago Press.

Birch, R. (1978) 'Corporate Advertising: Why, How and When', *Advertising Quarterly*, **57**, 5–9.

Bishop, D. M. (1984) 'Legal and Extralegal Barriers to Delinquency: A Panel Analysis', *Criminology*, **22**, 403–20.

Black, D. J. (1976) *The Behavior of Law*, New York: Academic Press.

Blau, P.M. (1964) *Exchange and Power in Social Life*, New York: Wiley.

Block, A.A., and Scarpitti, F.R. (1985) *Poisoning for Profit*, New York: William Morrow.

Blum, R. H. (1984) *Offshore Haven Banks, Trusts and Companies*, New York: Praeger.

Bott, E. (1971) *Family and Social Network: Roles, Norms and External Relationships in Ordinary Urban Families*, 2nd edition, New York: Free Press.

Boulton, D. (1978) *The Grease Machine*, New York: Harper and Row.

Bourne, J.M. (1986) *Patronage and Society in Nineteenth-Century England*, London: Edward Arnold.

Bowker, L.H. and Klein, M.W. (1983) 'The Etiology of Female Juvenile Delinquency and Gang Membership: A Test of Psychological and Social Structural Explanations', *Adolescence*, **18**, 739–51.

Boyer, P. (1978) *Urban Masses and Moral Order in America, 1820-1920*, Cambridge: Harvard University Press.

Box, S. (1981) *Deviance, Reality and Society*, London: Holt, Rinehart and Winston.

Box, S., and Hale, C. (1983) 'Liberation and Female Criminality in England and Wales',*British Journal of Criminology*, **23**, 35–49.

Braithwaite, J. (1977) 'Australian Delinquency: Research and Practical Considerations', in P.R. Wilson (ed.), *Delinquency in Australia: A Critical Appraisal*, Brisbane: University of Queensland Press.

Braithwaite, J. (1978) 'An Exploratory Study of Used Car Fraud', in P.R.Wilson and J.B. Braithwaite (eds.), *Two Faces of Deviance: Crimes of the Powerless and Powerful*, Brisbane: University of Queensland Press.

Braithwaite, J. (1979) *Inequality, Crime and Public Policy*, London: Routledge and Kegan Paul.

Braithwaite, J. (1980) 'The Political Economy of Punishment', in E.L. Wheelwright and K. Buckley (eds.), *Essays in the Political Economy of Australian Capitalism*, Volume IV, Sydney: ANZ Books.

Braithwaite, J. (1981) ' "The Myth of Social Class and Criminality" Reconsidered', *American Sociological Review*, **46**, 36–57.

Braithwaite, J. (1982) 'The Limits of Economism in Controlling Harmful Corporate Conduct', *Law and Society Review*, **16**, 481–506.

Braithwaite, J. (1984) *Corporate Crime in the Pharmaceutical Industry*, London: Routledge and Kegan Paul.

Braithwaite, J. (1985a) *To Punish or Persuade: Enforcement of Coal Mine Safety*, Albany: State University of New York Press.

Braithwaite, J. (1985b) 'Taking Responsibility Seriously: Corporate Compliance Systems', in B. Fisse and P.A. French (eds.), *Corrigible Corporations and Unruly Law*, San Antonio: Trinity University Press.

Braithwaite, J., and Biles, D. (1980a) 'Overview of Findings from the First Australian National Crime Victims Survey', *Australian and New Zealand Journal of Criminology*, **13**, 41–51.

Braithwaite, J., and Biles, D. (1980b) 'Crime Victimisation Rates in Australian Cities', *Australian and New Zealand Journal of Sociology*, **16**, 79–85.

Braithwaite, J., and Braithwaite, V. (1980) 'The Effect of Income Inequality and Social Democracy on Homicide', *British Journal of Criminology*, **20**, 45–53.

Braithwaite, J., and Braithwaite, V. (1981) 'Delinquency and the Question of Values', *International Journal of Offender Therapy and Comparative Criminology*, **25**, 273–89.

Braithwaite, J., and Fisse, B. (1985) 'Varieties of Responsibility and Organizational Crime', *Law and Policy*, **7**, 315–43.

Braithwaite, J., and Geis, G. (1982) 'On Theory and Action for Corporate Crime Control', *Crime and Delinquency*, **April**, 292–314.

Braithwaite, J., and Grabosky, P. (1985) *Occupational Health and Safety Enforcement in Australia*, Canberra: Australian Institute of Criminology.

Braithwaite, J., Grabosky, P., and Fisse, B. (1986) *Discussion Paper: Occupational Health and Safety Enforcement Guidelines*, Melbourne: Department of Labour.

Braybrooke, D. and Lindblom, C.E. (1963) *A Strategy of Decision*, New York: Free Press.

Brennan, T. and Huizinga, D. (1975) *Theory Validation and Aggregate National Data*, Integration Report of the Office of Youth Opportunity Research FY 1975, Boulder, Colo.: Behavioral Research Institute.

Broadhurst, R., Indermauer, D., and Maller, R. (1981) 'Crime Seriousness Ratings: The Relationship of Information Accuracy and General Attitudes in Western Australia', University of Western Australia: mimeographed.

Brown, J. (1982) *Policing by Multi-Racial Consent*, London: Bedford Square Press.

Bruce, N. (1970) 'Delinquent and Non-Delinquent Reactions to Parental Deprivation', *British Journal of Criminology*, **10**, 270–6.

Buckle, A. and Farrington, D.P. (1984) 'An Observational Study of Shoplifting', *British Journal of Criminology*, **24**, 63–73.

Burgess, R. and Akers, R. (1966) 'A Differential Association-Reinforcement Theory of Criminal Behavior', *Social Problems*, **14**, 128–47.

Burkett, S.R. and Jensen, E.L. (1975) 'Conventional Ties, Peer Influence and the Fear of Apprehension: A Study of Adolescent Marijuana Use', *Sociological Quarterly*, **16**, 522–33.

Burns, J.L. (1971) 'Delinquents Failed by the System',*Special Education*, **60**, 13–16.

Calahan, M. (1979) 'Trends in Incarceration in the United States since 1880', *Crime and Delinquency*, **25**, 9–41.

Cameron, D.R. (1984) 'Social Democracy, Corporatism, Labour Quiescence and the Representation of Economic Interest in Advanced Capitalist Society', in J.R. Goldthorpe (ed.) *Order and Conflict in Contemporary Capitalism*, Oxford: Clarendon Press.

Campbell, D.N., Fleming, R.L. and Grote, R.C. (1985) 'Discipline Without Punishment At Last', *Harvard Business Review*, **July-August**, 162–78.

Campbell, D.T. (1979) ' "Degrees of Freedom" and the Case Study', in T.D. Cook and C.S. Reichardt (eds.), *Qualitative and Quantitative Methods in Evaluation Research*, Beverly Hills: Sage.

Campbell, J. (1964) *Honour, Family and Patronage*, Oxford: Clarendon Press.

Canter, R.J. (1982) 'Family Correlates of Male and Female Delinquency', *Criminology*, **20**, 149–67.

Carr-Saunders, A.M. (1942) *Young Offenders*, Cambridge: Cambridge University Press.

Carroll, R.M. and Jackson, P.I. (1983) 'Inequality, Opportunity and Crime Rates in Central Cities', *Criminology*, **21**, 178–94.

Carroll, R.M., Pine, S.P., Cline, S.J. and Kleinhans, B.R. (1974) 'Judged Seriousness of Watergate-Related Crimes', *Journal of Psychology*, **86**, 235–9.

Carson, W.G. (1975) 'Symbolic and Instrumental Dimensions of Early Factory Legislation: A Case Study in the Social Origins of Criminal Law', in R. Hood (ed.), *Crime, Criminology and Public Policy*, Glencoe, Ill.: Free Press.

Cernkovich, S.A. (1978) 'Value Orientations and Delinquency Involvement' *Criminology*, **15**, 443–58.

Challinger, D. (1982) 'Crime, Females and Statistics', *Australian and New Zealand Journal of Criminology*, **15**, 123–8.

Channon, C. (1981) 'Corporations and the Politics of Perception', *Advertising Quarterly*, **60**, 12–15.

Chapman, W.R. (1985) 'Parental Attachment to the Child and Delinquent

Behavior', Paper to American Society of Criminology Meeting, San Diego.

Chetley, A. (1979) *The Baby Killer Scandal*, London: War on Want.

Chilton, R. and DeAmicis, J. (1975) 'Overcriminalization and the Measurement of Consensus', *Sociology and Social Research*, **15**, 318–29.

Chilton, R., and Markle, G.E. (1972) 'Family Deprivation, Delinquent Conduct and the Effect of Subclassification', *American Sociological Review*, **37**, 93–9.

Chiricos, T.G. (1987) 'Rates of Crime and Unemployment: An Analysis of Aggregate Research Evidence', *Social Problems*, **34**, 187–212.

Chodorow, N. (1971) 'Being and Doing: A Cross-Cultural Examination of the Socialization of Males and Females', in V. Gornick, and B.K. Moran (eds.), *Women in Sexist Society*, New York: Basic Books.

Christie, N. (1981) *Limits to Pain*, Oslo: Universitetsforlaget.

Clifford, W. (1976) *Crime Control in Japan*, Lexington, Mass.: Lexington Books.

Clinard, M.B. (1964) 'The Relation of Urbanization and Urbanism to Criminal Behaviour', in E.W. Burgess and D. Bogue (eds.), *Contributions to Urban Sociology*, Chicago: University of Chicago Press.

Clinard, M.B. (1978) *Cities With Little Crime*, Cambridge: Cambridge University Press.

Clinard, M.B. (1983) *Corporate Ethics and Crime: The Role of Middle Management*, Beverly Hills: Sage.

Clinard, M.B., and Abbott, D.J. (1973) *Crime in Developing Countries: A Comparative Perspective*, New York: Wiley.

Clinard, M.B., and Meier, R. F. (1979) *Sociology of Deviant Behaviour*, 5th ed., New York: Holt Rinehart and Winston.

Clinard, M.B., and Yeager, P.C. (1980) Corporate Crime, New York: Free Press.

Cloward, R.A. and Ohlin, L.E. (1960) *Delinquency and Opportunity: A Theory of Delinquent Gangs*, Glencoe, Ill.: Free Press.

Cohen, A.K. (1955) *Delinquent Boys: The Culture of the Gang*, Glencoe, Ill.: Free Press.

Cohen, B. and Fishman, G. (1985) 'Homicide and Suicide Rates: A Macrosocial Analysis', Paper to American Society of Criminology Meeting, San Diego.

Cohen, L. (1978) 'Sanction Threats and Violation Behavior: An Inquiry Into Perceptual Variation', in C.F. Wellford (ed.), *Quantitative Studies in Criminology*, Beverly Hills: Sage.

Cohen, S. (1973) *Folk Devils and Moral Panics*, St Albans: Paladin.

Cohen, S. (1985) *Visions of Social Control: Crime, Punishment and Classification*, Cambridge: Polity Press.

Cole, S. (1975) 'The Growth of Scientific Knowledge: Theories of Deviance as a Case Study', in L. Coser (ed.), *The Idea of Social Structure: Papers in Honor of Robert K. Merton*, New York: Harcourt Brace Jovanovich.

Coleman, J.S. (1986) 'Social Theory, Social Research and a Theory of Action', *American Journal of Sociology*, **91**, 1309–35.

Conger, R.D. (1976) 'Social Control and Social Learning Models of Delinquent Behavior: A Synthesis', *Criminology*, **14**, 17–40.

Conklin, J.E. (1977) *Illegal But Not Criminal*, Englewood Cliffs, N.J.: Prentice Hall.

Cressey, D.R. (1953) *Other Peoples' Money: The Social Psychology of Embezzlement*, New York: Free Press.

Cressey, D.R. (1960) 'Epidemiology and Individual Conduct: A Case from Criminology', *Pacific Sociological Review*, **3**, 47–58.

Cressey, D.R. (1976) 'Restraint of Trade, Recidivism, and Delinquent Neighbourhoods', in J.F. Short, Jr. (ed.), *Delinquency, Crime and Society*, Chicago: University of Chicago Press.

Cressey, D.R. (1978) Testimony to Subcommittee on Crime of the Committee on the Judiciary, House of Representatives, 95th Congress, Serial No. 69, *White-Collar Crime*, Washington: US Government Printing Office.

Cressey, D.R. (1980) 'Management Fraud Controls and Criminological Theory', in R. K. Elliott and J. J. Willingham, *Management Fraud: Detection and Deterrence*, New York: Petrocelli Books.

Cressey, D.R., and Moore, C.A. (1980) *Corporation Codes of Ethical Conduct*, New York: Peat, Marwick and Mitchell Foundation.

Crutchfield, R.D., Geerken, M.R. and Gove, W.R. (1982) 'Crime Rate and Social Integration: The Impact of Metropolitan Mobility', *Criminology*, **20**, 467–78.

Cullen, F.T., Clark, G.A., Mathers, R.A., and Cullen, J.B. (1983) 'Public Support for Punishing White-Collar Crime: Blaming the Victim Revisited?' *Journal of Criminal Justice*, **11**, 481–93.

Cullen, F.T., and Dubeck, P.J. (1985) 'The Myth of Corporate Inmmunity to Deterrence: Ideology and the Creation of the Invincible Criminal', *Federal Probation*, **September**, 3–9.

Cullen, F.T., Link, B.G., and Polanzi, C.W. (1982) 'The Seriousness of Crime Revisited: Have Attitudes Toward White-Collar Crime Changed?' *Criminology*, **20**, 83–102.

Cullen, F.T., Link, B.G., Travis, L.F., and Wonziak, J.F. (1985) 'Consensus on Crime Seriousness: Empirical Reality or Methodological Artifact?' *Criminology*, **23**, 99–118.

Dahrendorf, R. (1985) *Law and Order: The Hamlyn Lectures*, London: Stevens and Sons.

Datesman, S., and Scarpitti, F. (1975) 'Female Delinquency and Broken Homes', *Criminology*, **13**, 35–56.

Datesman, S., Scarpitti, F.R., and Stephenson, R.M. (1975) 'Female Delinquency: An Application of Self and Opportunity Theories', *Journal of Research in Crime and Delinquency*, **12**, 107–23.

Dienstbier, R.A., Hillman, D., Lehnkoff, J., Hillman, J., and Valkenaar, M.F. (1975) 'An Emotion-Attribution Approach to Moral Behavior:

Dienstbier, R.A., Hillman, D., Lehnkoff, J., Hillman, J., and Valkenaar, M.F. (1975) 'An Emotion-Attribution Approach to Moral Behavior: Interfacing Cognitive and Avoidance Theories of Moral Development', *Psychological Review*, **82**, 1299–315.

Douglas, J.W.B., Ross, J.M. and Simpson, R.R. (1968) *All Our Future*, London: Peter Davies.

Downes, D. (1966) *The Delinquent Solution*, London: Routledge and Kegan Paul, 236–9.

Downes, D., and Ward, T. (1986) *Democratic Policing*, London: Labour Campaign for Criminal Justice.

Durkheim, E. (1893) *The Division of Labor in Society*, New York: Free Press.

Durkheim, E. (1951) *Suicide*, trans. J.A. Spaulding and G. Simpson, New York: Free Press.

Durkheim, E. (1961) *Moral Education: A Study in the Theory and Application of the Sociology of Education*, trans. E.K. Wilson and H. Schnurer, New York: Free Press.

Eaton, J.W. and Polk, K. (1961) *Measuring Delinquency: A Study of Probation Department Referrals*, Pittsburgh: University of Pittsburgh Press.

Edelman, J.M. (1964) *The Symbolic Uses of Politics*, Urbana: University of Illinois Press.

Ekland-Olson, S., Supancic, M., Campbell, J. and Lenihan, K. J. (1983) 'Post-Release Depression and the Importance of Familial Support', *Criminology*, **21**: 253–75.

Elliott, D.S. (1961) 'Delinquency, Opportunity and Patterns of Orientations', PhD dissertation, University of Washington.

Elliott, D.S. (1962) 'Delinquency and Perceived Opportunity', *Sociological Inquiry*, **XXXII**, 216–22.

Elliott, D.S., Ageton, S.S., and Canter, R.J. (1979) 'An Integrated Theoretical Perspective on Delinquent Behavior', *Journal of Research in Crime and Delinquency*, **16**, 3–27.

Elliott, D.S., Huizinga, D. and Ageton, S.S. (1985) *Explaining Delinquency and Drug Use*, Beverly Hills: Sage.

Elliott, D.S., Knowles, B. A. and Canter, R. J. (1981) *The Epidemioloy of Delinquent Behavior and Drug Use Among American Adolescents*, Boulder: Behavioral Research Institute.

Elliott, D.S., and Voss, H.L. (1974) *Delinquency and Dropout*, Lexington, Mass.: Lexington Books.

Ellis, L. (1985) 'Religiosity and Criminality: Evidence and Explanations of Complex Relationships', *Sociological Perspectives*, 28:501–20.

Emerson, R. (1962) 'Power Dependence Relations', *American Sociological Review*, **27**, 31–40.

Empey, L.T. and Lubeck, S.G. (1971) *The Silverlake Experiment: Testing Delinquency Theory and Community Intervention*, Chicago: Aldine.

Empey, L.T. and Lubeck, S.G. with Laporte, R.L. (1971) *Explaining Delinquency: Construction, Test, and Reformulation of a Sociological Theory*, Lexington: Heath Lexington Books.

Environment Agency [of Japan] (1980) *Quality of the Environment in Japan*, Tokyo: Environment Agency.

Environment Agency [of Japan] (1981) *Introduction to the Environment Agency of Japan*, Tokyo: Environment Agency.

Erickson, M. and Empey, C.T. (1965) 'Class Position, Peers and Delinquency', *Sociology and Social Research*, **49**, 268–82.

Erickson, R.V. (1977) 'Social Distance and Reaction to Criminality', *British Journal of Criminology*, **17**, 16–29.

Erikson, K.T. (1962) 'Notes on the Sociology of Deviance', *Social Problems*, **9**, 307–14.

Eron, L.D., Walder, L.O., Huesmann, L.R., and Leftkowitz, M.M. (1974) 'The Convergence of Laboratory and Field Studies of the Development of Aggression', in J. DeWit and W.W. Hartup (eds.), *Determinants and Origins of Aggressive Behavior*, The Hague, Paris: Mouton.

Eron, L.D., and Lefkowitz, M.M. (1971) *Learning of Aggression in Children*, Boston: Little Brown.

Eysenck, H.J. (1973) *Crime and Personality*, St Albans: Paladin.

Farnworth, M. (1984) 'Family Structure, Family Attributes, and Delinquency in a Sample of Low-Income, Minority Males and Females', *Journal of Youth and Adolescence*, **13**, 349–64.

Farrington, D.P. (1973) 'Self-Reports of Deviant Behaviour: Predictive and Stable?', *Journal of Criminal Law and Criminology*, **64**, 99–100.

Farrington, D.P. (1977) 'The Effects of Public Labeling', *British Journal of Criminology*, **17**, 112–25.

Farrington, D.P., Osborn, S.G. and West, D.J. (1978) 'The Persistence of Labeling Effects' *British Journal of Criminology*, **18**, 277–84.

Fataba, I. (1984) 'Crime, Confession and Control in Contemporary Japan', *Law in Context*, **2**, 1–30.

Fawzy, F. I., Coombs, R. H. and Gerber, B. (1983) 'Generational Continuity in the Use of Substances: The Impact of Parental Substance Use on Adolescent Substance Use', *Addictive Behaviors*, **8**, 109–14.

Federal Bureau of Investigation (FBI) (1981) *Crime in the United States, 1980*, Washington, D.C.: US Department of Justice.

Federal Bureau of Investigation (FBI) (1985) *Crime in the United States, 1984*, Washington, D.C.: US Department of Justice.

Feeley, M.M. (1979) *The Process is the Punishment: Handling Cases in Lower Criminal Court*, New York: Russel Sage.

Feinberg, J. (1970) *Doing and Deserving*, Princeton: Princeton University Press.

Fenwick, C.R. (1983) 'Law Enforcement, Public Participation and Crime Control in Japan: Implications for American Policing', *American Journal of Police*, **3**, 83–109.

Fenwick, C.R. (1985) 'Culture, Philosophy and Crime: The Japanese Experience', *International Journal of Comparative and Applied Criminal Justice*, **9**:67–81.

Ferdinand, T.N. (1967) 'The Criminal Patterns of Boston Since 1849', *American Journal of Sociology*, **73**:688–98.

Ferguson, T. (1952) *The Young Delinquent in His Social Setting*, London: Oxford University Press.

Feshbach, S. (1970) 'Aggression', in P.H. Mussen (ed.), *Carmichael's Manual of Child Psychology*, Vol. 2, New York: Wiley.

Figlio, R.M. (1975) 'The Seriousness of Offenses: An Evaluation of Offenders and Non-Offenders', *Journal of Criminal Law and Criminology*, **66**, 189–200.

Figueira-McDonough, J. (1984) 'Feminism and Delinquency', *British Journal of Criminology*, **24**, 325–42.

Fisher, G.A. and Erickson, M.L. (1973) 'On Assessing the Effects of Official Reaction to Juvenile Delinquency', *Journal of Research in Crime and Delinquency*, **10**, 177–94.

Fisher, S. (1970) 'Borstal Recall Delinquency and the Cloward-Ohlin Theory of Criminal Subcultures', *British Journal of Criminology*, **10**, 52–63.

Fisher, S. (1972) 'Stigma and Deviant Careers in Schools', *Social Problems*, **20**, 78–83.

Fisse, B. and Braithwaite, J. (1983) *The Impact of Publicity on Corporate Offenders*, Albany: State University of New York Press.

Foster, J.D., Dinitz, S. and Reckless, W.C. (1972) 'Perceptions of Stigma Following Public Intervention for Delinquent Behavior', *Social Problems*, **20**, 202–8.

Foucault, M. (1977) *Discipline and Punish: The Birth of the Prison*, London: Allen Lane.

Francis, R.D. (1981) *Migrant Crime in Australia*, Brisbane: University of Queensland Press.

Frank, J., Cullen, F.T., and Travis, L.F. (1984) 'Sanctioning Corporate Crime: Public Support for Civil and Criminal Intervention', Paper to Annual Meeting of Mid-West Criminal Justice Association.

Frank, N. (1985) *Crimes Against Health and Safety*, New York: Harrow and Heston.

Frease, D.E. (1973) 'Delinquency, Social Class and the Schools', *Sociology and Social Research*, **57**, 443–59.

Fredericks, M.A. and Molnar, M. (1969) 'Relative Occupational Anticipations of Delinquents and Non-Delinquents', *Journal of Research in Crime and Delinquency*, **6**, 1–7.

Freeman, L. C. and Winch, R. F. (1957) 'Societal Complexity: an Empirical Test of a Typology of Societies', *American Journal of Sociology*, **62**, 461–6.

Freidson, E. and Rhea, B. (1972) 'Processes of Control in a Company of Equals', in E. Freidson and J. Lorber (eds.), *Medical Men and Their Work*, Chicago: Aldine-Atherton.

French, P. A. (1985) 'Publicity and the Control of Corporate Conduct: Hester Prynne's New Image', in B. Fisse and P. A. French (eds.), *Corrigible Corporations and Unruly Law*, San Antonio: Trinity University Press.

Friedman, M. (1962) *Capitalism and Freedom*, Chicago: University of Chicago Press.

Garland, D. (1985) *Punishment and Welfare: A History of Penal Strategies*, Aldershot: Gower.

Gastil, R.D. (1971) 'Homicide and a Regional Culture of Violence', *American Sociological Review*, **36**, 412–27.

Gatrell, V.A.C. (1980) 'The Decline of Theft and Violence in Victorian and Edwardian England', in V.A.C. Gatrell, B.P. Lenman and G. Parker (eds.), *Crime and the Law Since 1850*, London: Europa.

Gatrell, V.A.C. and Hadden, T.B. (1972) 'Criminal Statistics and Their Interpretation', in E.A. Wrigley (ed.), *Nineteenth Century Society*, Cambridge: Cambridge University Press.

Geerken, M. R. and Gove, W. R. (1975) 'Deterrence: Some Theoretical Consideration', *Law and Society Review*, **9**, 497–513.

Geis, G. (1967) 'The Heavy Electrical Equipment Antitrust Cases of 1961', in M. Clinard and R. Quinney (eds.), *Criminal Behavior Systems*, New York: Holt, Rinehart and Winston.

George, B.J. (1984) 'Discretionary Authority of Public Prosecutors in Japan', *Law in Japan*, **17**, 42–72.

Gibbons, D. (1969) 'Crime and Punishment: A Study of Social Attitudes', *Social Forces*, **47**: 391–5.

Giddens, A. (1984) *The Constitution of Society*, Berkeley: University of California Press.

Glaser, D. (1964) *The Effectiveness of a Prison and Parole System*. Indianapolis: Bobbs-Merrill.

Glaser, D. (1978) *Crime in Our Changing Society*, New York: Holt, Rinehart and Winston.

Gluckman, M. (1963) 'Gossip and Scandal', *Current Anthropology*, **4**, 307–15.

Glueck, S. and Glueck, E. (1950) *Unravelling Juvenile Delinquency*, Nw York: The Commonwealth Fund.

Goffman, E. (1968) *Stigma: Notes on the Management of Spoiled Identity*, Hammondsworth: Pelican.

Goffman, E. (1971) *Relations in Public*, New York: Basic Books.

Gold, M. (1963) *Status Forces in Delinquent Boys*, Ann Arbor: University of Michigan, Institute for Social Research.

Gold, M. (1970) *Delinquent Behavior in an American City*, Belmont, California: Brooks-Cole.

Gold, M., and Williams, J.R. (1969) 'The Effect of Getting Caught: Apprehension of the Juvenile Offender as a Cause of Subsequent Delinquencies', *Prospectus*, **3**, 1–12.

Gold, M., and Mann, D. (1973) 'Delinquency as Defense', *American Journal of Orthopsychiatry*, **42**, 463–79.

Gottfredson, G. D. and Gottfredson, D. C. (1985) *Victimization in Schools*, New York: Plenum Press.

Gove, W. R. (1980) *The Labelling of Deviance: Evaluating a Perspective*, 2nd edition, Beverly Hills :Sage.

Gove, W.R., and Crutchfield, R.D. (1982) 'The Family and Juvenile Delinquency', *The Sociological Quarterly*, **23**, 301–19.

Grabosky, P.N. (1977) *Sydney in Ferment: Crime, Dissent and Official Reaction 1788 to 1973*, Canberra: ANU Press.

Grabosky, P.N, (1984) 'The Variability of Punishment', in D. Black (ed.), *Toward A General Theory of Social Control*, Vol. 1, New York: Academic Press.

Grabosky, P.N., and Braithwaite, J. (1986) *Of Manners Gentle: Enforcement Strategies of Australian Business Regulatory Agencies*, Melbourne: Oxford University Press.

Grabosky, P.N., Braithwaite, J. and Wilson, P.R. (1987) 'The Myth of Community Tolerance of White-Collar Crime', *Australian and New Zealand Journal of Criminology*, **20**, 33–44.

Grabosky, P.N., Persson, C. and Sperlings, S. (1977) 'Stockholm: The Politics of Crime and Conflict, 1750 to the 1970s', in T.R. Gurr, P.N. Grabosky and R.C. Hula, *The Politics of Crime and Conflict*, Beverly Hills: Sage.

Graham, F.P. (1969) 'A Contemporary History of American Crime', in H.D. Graham and T.R. Gurr (eds.), *Violence in America: Historical and Comparative-Perspectives: A Report to the National Commission on the Causes and Prevention of Violence*, New York: Praeger.

Grasmick, H.G. and Green, D.E. (1980) 'Legal Punishment, Social Disapproval and Internalization of Illegal Behavior', *Journal of Criminal Law and Criminology*, **71**, 325–35.

Greenberg, D.F. (1977) 'Delinquency and the Age Structure of Society', *Contemporary Crises*, **1**, 189–223.

Greenberg, D.F. (1985) 'Age, Crime and Social Explanation', *American Journal of Sociology*, **91**, 1–21.

Greenberg, S.W., Rohe, W.R. and Williams, J.R. (1985) *Informal Citizen Action and Crime Prevention at the Neighborhood Level: Synthesis and Assessment of the Research*, Washington, D. C.: National Institute of Justice.

Griffiths, J. (1970) 'Ideology in Criminal Procedure or A Third "Model" of the Criminal Process', *Yale Law Journal*, **79**: 359–417.

Gurr, T.R. (1977a) 'Contemporary Crime in Historical Perspective: A Comparative Study of London, Stockholm, and Sydney', *Annals of the American Academy*, **434**, 114–36.

Gurr, T.R. (1977b) 'Crime Trends in Modern Democracies since 1945', *International Annals of Criminology*, **6**, 41–85.

Gurr, T.R. (1981) 'Historical Trends in Violent Crime: A Critical Review of the Evidence', in M. Tovey and N. Morris (eds.), *Crime and Justice: An Annual Review of Research*, Vol. 3, Chicago: University of Chicago Press.

Gurr, T.R., Grabosky, P. N. and Hula, R. C. (1977) *The Politics of Crime and Conflict: A Comparative History of Four Cities*, Beverly Hills: Sage.

Gusfield, J. (1967) *Symbolic Crusade*, Urbana: University of Illinois Press.

Hagan, J., Simpson, J.H., and Gillis, A.R. (1979) 'The Sexual Stratification of Social Control', *British Journal of Sociology*, **30**, 25–38.

Haley, J.O. (1982) 'Sheathing the Sword of Justice in Japan: An Essay on Law Without Sanctions', *Journal of Japanese Studies*, **8**, 265-81.

Haley, J.O. (1986) 'Comment: The Implications of Apology', *Law and Society Review*, **20**, 499–507.

Hamilton, V.L. and Rytina, S. (1980) 'Social Consensus on Norms of Justice: Should the Punishment Fit the Crime?' *American Journal of Sociology*, **85**, 1117–44.

Hamilton, V.L., and Sanders, J. (1985) 'Accountability, Punishment and the Self in Japan and the U.S.', Paper to Law and Society Association, San Diego.

Hammond, P.E. (ed.) (1985) *The Sacred in a Secular Age*, Berkeley: University of California Press.

Hamparian, D. M., Schuster, R., Dinitz, S., and Conrad, J. P. (1978) *The Violent Few*, Lexington: Lexington Books.

Hampton, J. (1984) 'The Moral Education Theory of Punishment', *Philosophy and Public Affairs*, **13**, 208–30.

Hancock, L. (1980) 'The Myth that Females are Treated More Leniently than Males in the Juvenile Justice System', *Australian and New Zealand Journal of Sociology*, **16**, 4–14.

Hannerz, V. (1967) 'Gossip, Networks and Culture in a Black American Ghetto', *Ethnos*, **32**, 35–60.

Hardt, R. H. and Peterson, S. J. (1968) 'Arrests of Self and Friends as Indicators of Delinquency Involvement', *Journal of Research in Crime and Delinquency*, **5**, 44–51.

Harry, J. and Minor, W.W. (1986) 'Intelligence and Delinquency Reconsidered: A Comment on Menard and Morse', *American Journal of Sociology*, **91**, 962–8.

Hartstone, E. and Hansen, K.V. (1984) 'The Violent Juvenile Offender: An Empirical Portrait', in R.A. Mathias, P. De Muro, and R.S. Allinson (eds.), *Violent Juvenile Offenders: An Anthology*, San Francisco: National Council on Crime and Delinquency.

Haskell, M.R. and Yablonsky, L. (1982) *Juvenile Delinquency*, 3rd ed., Boston: Houghton Miffin.

Hassall, P. (1974) *Schools and-Delinquency: A Self-Report Study of Delinquency in Christchurch, New Zealand*, Paper to Sociological Association of Australia and New Zealand Conference, University of New England.

Hawkins, K. (1984) *Environment and Enforcement: Regulation and the Social Definition of Pollution*, Oxford: Clarendon Press.

Hepburn, J. R. (1977a) 'Testing Alternative Models of Delinquency Causation' *Journal of Criminal Law and Criminology*, **67**, 450–60.

Hepburn, J. R. (1977b) 'The Impact of Police Intervention upon Juvenile Delinquents', *Criminology*, **15**, 235–62.

Hewitt, J.D. and Hoover, D.W. (1982) 'Local Modernization and Crime: The Effects of Modernization on Crime in Middletown, 1845-1910', *Law and Human Behavior*, **6**, 313–25.

Hickson, D.J., Hinings, C.R., Lee, C.A., Schneck, R.E. and Pennings, J.M. (1971) 'A Strategic Contingencies Theory of Intraorganizational Power', *Administrative Science Quarterly*, **16**, 216-29.

Hindelang, M.J. (1970) 'The Commitment of Delinquents to their Misdeeds: Do Delinquents Drift?' *Social Problems*, **17**, 502–9.

Hindelang, M.J. (1973) 'Causes of Delinquency: A Partial Replication and Extension', *Social Problems*, **20**, 471–87.

Hindelang, M.J. (1974) 'Moral Evaluations of Illegal Behavior', *Social Problems*, **21**, 370–85.

Hindelang, M.J. (1979) 'Sex Differences in Criminal Activity', *Social Problems*, **27**, 143–56.

Hindelang, M.J., Gottfredson, M.R. and Garofalo, J. (1978) *Victims of Personal Crime: An Empirical Foundation for a Theory of Personal Victimization*, Cambridge, Mass.; Ballinger.

Hindus, M.S. (1980) *Prison and Plantation: Crime, Justice and Authority in Massachusetts and South Carolina, 1767-1878*, Chapel Hill: University of North Carolina Press.

Hirschi, T. (1969) *Causes of Delinquency*, Berkeley: University of California Press.

Hirschi, T. (1983) 'Crime and the Family', in J.Q. Wilson (ed.), *Crime and Public Policy*, San Francisco: Institute for Contemporary Studies.

Hirschi, T., and Gottfredson, M. (1983) 'Age and the Explanation of Crime', *American Journal of Sociology*, **89**, 552–84.

Hirschi, T., and Gottfredson, M. (1985) 'Age and Crime, Logic and Scholarship: Comment on Greenberg', *American Journal of Sociology* **91**, 22–7.

Hirschi, T., and Hindelang, M.J. (1977) 'Intelligence and Delinquency: A Revisionist Review', *American Sociological Review*, **42**, 571–87.

Hoffman, M. L. (1970) 'Moral Development', in P.H. Mussen (ed.), *Carmichael's Manual of Child Psychology*, Volume 2, New York: Wiley.

Hoffman, M.L., and Saltzstein, H.D. (1967) 'Parent Discipline and the Child's Moral Development', *Journal of Personality and Social Psychology*, **5**, 45–7.

Hogetsu, M. (ed.) (1986), *A Sociology of Pharmaceutical Damages*, Kyoto, Japan: Sekai Shiso Sha.

Hopkins, A. and Parnell, N. (1984) 'Why Coal Mine Safety Regulations in Australia are not Enforced', *International Journal of the Sociology of Law*, **12**, 179–84.

Huba, G., and Bentler, P. (1983) 'Test of a Drug Use Causal Model Using Asymptotically Distribution Free Methods', *Journal of Drug Education*, **13**, 3–14.

Hula, R.C. (1977) 'Calcutta: The Politics of Crime and Conflict 1800 to the 1970's', in T.R. Gurr, P.N. Grabosky and R.C. Hula, *The Politics of Crime and Conflict*, Beverly Hills: Sage.

Jacobs, D. (1974) 'Dependency and Vulnerability: An Exchange Approach to the Control of Organizations', *Administrative Science Quarterly*, **10**, 45–59.

Jefferson, T. and Grimshaw, R. (1984) *Controlling the Constable: Police Accountability in England and Wales*, London: Fredrick Muller.

Jensen, G.F. (1972a) 'Delinquency and Adolescent Self-Conceptions: A Study of the Personal Relevance of Infraction', *Social Problems*, **20**, 590–603.

Jensen, G.F. (1972b) 'Parents Peers and Delinquent Action: A Test of the Differential Association Perspective', *American Journal of Sociology*, **78**, 562–75.

Jensen, G.F., and Erickson, M. (1978) 'The Social Meaning of Sanctions', in M. Krohn and R. Akers (eds.), *Crime, Law and Sanctions: Theoretical Perspectives*, Beverly Hills: Sage.

Jensen, G.F., and Eve, R. (1976) 'Sex Differences in Delinquency: An Examination of Popular Sociological Explanations', *Criminology*, **13**, 427–48.

Jensen, G.F., and Rojek, D.G.(1980) *Delinquency*, Lexington, Mass.: D.C. Heath.

Jessor, R., Graves, T., Hanson, R. and Jessor, S. (1968), *Society, Personality, and Deviant Behavior*, New York: Holt, Rinehart and Winston.

Johnson, P.E. (1978) *A Shopkeeper's Millennium: Societies and Revivals in Rochester, New York, 1815-1837*, New York: Hill and Wang.

Johnson, R.E. (1979) *Juvenile Delinquency and Its Origin*, Cambridge: Cambridge University Press.

Joint Commission on Correctional Manpower and Training (1968) *The Public Looks at Crime and Corrections*, Washington D.C.

Jones, S. and Levi, M. (1983) 'Police-Public Relationships', Unpublished Research Report, University College, Cardiff.

Junger, J. and Junger, M. (1905) *Juvenile Delinquency II: The Impact of Judicial Intervention*, The Hague: Research and Documentation Centre, Ministry of Justice.

Kagan, R. A. and Scholz, J. T. (1984) 'The "Criminology of the Corporation" and Regulatory Enforcement Strategies', in K., Hawkins and J. M. Thomas, *Enforcing Regulation*, Boston: Kluwer-Nijhoff.

Kandel, D. B. (1973) 'Adolescent Marijuana Use: Role of Parents and Peers', *Science*, **181**, 1067–70.

Kandel, D.B., Kessler, R. C. and Margulies, R. Z. (1978) 'Antecedents of Adolescent Initiation into Stages of Drug Use: A Developmental Analysis', in D. B. Kandel (ed.), *Longitudinal Research on Drug Use*, New York: Wiley.

Kaplan, H. B. and Robbins, C. (1983) 'Testing a General Theory of Deviant Behavior in Longitudinal Perspective', in K. T. Van Dusen and S. A. Mednick (eds.), *Prospective Studies of Crime Delinquency*, Boston: Kluwer-Nijhoff.

Katz, J. (1979) 'Concerted Ignorance: The Social Construction of Cover-up', *Urban Life*, **8**, 295–316.

Keller, S. (1968) *The Urban Neighborhood: A Sociological Perspective*, New York: Random House.

Kelly, D.H. (1971) 'School Failure, Academic Self-Evaluation, and School Avoidance and Deviant Behaviour', *Youth and Society*, **2**, 489–503.

Kelly, D.H., and Balch, R.W. (1971) 'Social Origins and School Failure: A Reexamination of Cohen's Theory of Working-Class Delinquency', *Pacific Sociological Review*, **14**, 413–30.

Kelman, S. (1981) *Regulating America, Regulating Sweden: A Comparative Study of Occupational Safety and Health Policy*, Cambridge: MIT Press.

Kett, J.F. (1977) *Rites of Passage: Adolescence in America, 1790 to the Present*, New York: Basic Books.

Kinsey, R., Lea, J. and Young, J. (1985) *Losing the Fight Against Crime*, Oxford: Basil Blackwell.

Kitsuse, J. (1962) 'Social Reaction to Deviant Behavior', *Social Problems*, **9**, 253.

Klein, M. W. (1986) 'Labeling Theory and Delinquency Policy: An Experimental Test', *Criminal Justice and Behavior*, **13**, 47–79.

Klemke, L. W. (1978) 'Does Apprehension for Shoplifting Amplify or Terminate Shoplifting Activity ?', *Law and Society Review*, *12*, 391–403.

Kluckhohn, C. (1967) *Navaho Witchcraft*, Boston: Beacon Press.

Kneese, A. V. and Schultze, C. L. (1975) *Pollution, Prices and Public Policy*, Washington, D. C.: Brookings.

Knight, T. (1985) 'Schools and Delinquency', in A. Borowski and J. M. Murray (eds.), *Juvenile Delinquency in Australia*, Melbourne: Methuen.

Kornhauser, R.R. (1978) *Social Sources of Delinquency: An Appraisal of Analytic Models*, Chicago: University of Chicago Press.

Kraut, R. (1976) 'Deterrent and Definitional Influences on Shoplifting', *Social Problems*, **23**, 358–68.

Krohn, M. (1974) 'An Investigation of the Effect of Parental and Peer Associations on Marijuana, Use: An Empirical Test of Differential Association Theory, in M. Riedel and T. P. Thornberry (eds.), *Crime and Delinquency: Dimensions of Deviance*. New York: Praeger.

Krohn, M., Curry, J.P. and Nelson-Kilger, S. (1983) 'Is Chivalry Dead?' *Criminology*, **21**, 417–37.

Kutchinsky, B. (1973) 'The Legal Consequences: A Survey of Research on Knowledge and Opinion About Law', in A. Podgorecki, W. Kaupen, J. Vanhoutte, P. Vinke, and B. Kutchinsky (eds.), *Knowledge and Opinion About Law*, London: Martin Robertson

Kvaraceus, W.C. (1945) *Juvenile Delinquency and the School*, New York: World Book Co.

Kwasniewski, J. (1984) *Society and Deviance in Communist Poland: Attitudes Towards Social Control*, trans. M. Wilson, Leamington Spa, Warwickshire: Berg Publishers.

Lamb, R., Armstrong, W. G. and Morigi, K. R. (1980) *Business, Media and the Law*, New York: New York University Press.

Landau, S.F. (1984) 'Trends in Violence and Aggression: A Cross-Cultural Analysis', *International Journal of Comparative Sociology*, **25**, 133–58.

Landes, W. M. and Posner, R. A. (1984) 'Tort Law as a Regulatory Regime for Catastrophic Personal Injuries', *Journal of Legal Studies*, **13**, 417–34.

Landis, J.R. (1962) 'Social Class Differentials in Self, Value and Opportunity Structure as Related to Delinquency Potential', PhD dissertation, Ohio State University (Landis study reported in W.C. Reckless (1961) *The Crime Problem*, 3rd edn., New York: Appleton-Century-Crofts, 452–3).

Landis, J.R., and Scarpitti, F.R. (1965) 'Perceptions Regarding Value Orientation and Legitimate Opportunity: Delinquents and Non-Delinquents', *Social Forces*, **44**, 83–91.

Lane, R. (1967) *Policing the City: Boston, 1822-1885*, Cambridge: Harvard University Press.

Lane, R. (1969) 'Urbanization and Criminal Violence in the 19th Century: Massachusetts as a Test Cast', in H.D. Graham and T.R. Gurr (eds.), *Violence in America: Historical and Comparative Perspectives: A Report to the National Commission on the Causes and Prevention of Violence*, New York: Praeger.

Lane, R. (1979) *Violent Death in the City: Suicide, Accident and Murder in 19th Century Philadelphia*, Cambridge: Harvard University Press.

Lane, R. (1980) 'Urban Police and Crime in Nineteenth-Century America', in N. Morris and M. Tonry (eds.), *Crime and Justice: An Annual Review of Research*, Vol. 2, Chicago: University of Chicago Press.

Lane, R.E. (1953) 'Why Businessmen Violate the Law?', *Journal of Criminal Law, Criminology and Police Science*, **44**, 151–65.

Lanphier, C.M. and Faulkner, J.E. (1970),'Deviance in a Middle-Class Community', *International Journal of Comparative Sociology*, **11**, 146–56.

Laqueur, T.W. (1976) *Religion and Respectability: Sunday Schools and Working Class Culture, 1780-1850*, New Haven: Yale University Press.

Latham, B.B. and Shimura, M. (1967) 'Folktales Commonly Told by American and Japanese Children: Ethical Themes of Omission and Comission', *Journal of American Folklore*, **Jan.-Mar.**, 33–48.

Laub, J. H. (1983) 'Urbanism, Race and Crime', *Journal of Research in Crime and Delinquency*, **20**, 183–98.

Lehner, F. (forthcoming) 'The Political Economy of Distributive Conflict in the Welfare State', in F. Castles, F. Lehner and M. Schmidt (eds.), *Managing Mixed Economics*, De Gruyter.

Lemert, E.M. (1967) *Human Deviance, Social Problems and Social Control*, New York: Prentice-Hall.

Lerman, P. (1968) 'Individual Values, Peer Values, and Subcultural Delinquency', *American Sociological Review*, **33**, 760–73.

Liebow, E. (1967) *Tally's Corner*, Boston: Little, Brown.

Lintott, A.W. (1968) *Violence in Republican Rome*, Oxford: Clarendon Press.

Lipton, D., Martinson, R. and Wilks, J. (1975) *The Effectiveness of Correctional Treatment: A Survey of Evaluation Studies*, New York: Praeger.

Liska, A.E. (1971) 'Aspirations, Expectations and Delinquency: Stress and Additive Models', *Sociological Quarterly*, **12**, 99–107.

Liska, A.E., and Reed, M.D. (1985) 'Ties to Conventional Institutions and Delinquency: Estimating Reciprocal Effects', *American Sociological Review*, **50**, 547–60.

Longmoor, E.S. and Young, E.F. (1936) 'Ecological Interrelationships of Juvenile Delinquency, Dependency, and Population Movements: A Cartographic Analysis of Data from Long Beach, California', *American Journal of Sociology*, **41**, 598–610.

Luchterhand, E. and Weller, L. (1966) 'Delinquency Theory and the Middle-Size City: A Study of Problem and Promising Youth', *Sociological Quarterly*, **7**, 413–23.

Lunden, W.A. (1964) *Statistics on Delinquents and Delinquency*, Springfield, Ill.: Charles C. Thomas.

Lynd, H. M. (1958) *On Shame and the Search for Identity*, London: Routledge and Kegan Paul.

McCandless, B.R., Persons, W.S. and Roberts, A. (1972) 'Perceived Opportunity, Delinquency, Race, and Body Build Among Delinquent Youth', *Journal of Consulting and Clinical Psychology*, **38**, 281–7.

McCarthy, J.D., Galle, O.R. and Zimmern, W. (1975) 'Population Density, Social Structure and Interpersonal Violence', *American Behavioral Scientist*, **18**, 771–89.

McCarthy, J.D., and Hoge, D.R. (1984) 'The Dynamics of Self-Esteem and Delinquency', *American Journal of Sociology*, **90**, 396–410.

Macaulay, S. (1986) Lecture, Australian National University Law School.

Maccoby, E.E. (1980) *Social Development: Psychological Growth and the Parent-Child Relationship*, New York: Harcourt Brace Jovanovich.

McCord, J. (1978) 'A Thirty-Year Follow-Up of Treatment Effects', *American Psychologist*, **33**, 284–9.

McCord, W., McCord, J. and Zola, I. (1959) *Origins of Crime*, Montclair, N.J.: Patterson Smith.

McDermott, D. (1984) 'The Relationship of Parental Drug Use and Parent's Attitude Concerning Adolescent Drug Use to Adolescent Drug Use', *Adolescence*, **19**, 89–97.

Macdonagh, O. (1961) *A Pattern of Government Growth: The Passenger Acts and Their Enforcement*, London: Macgibbon and Kee.

McEachern, A.W. (1968) 'The Juvenile Probation System', *American Behavioral Scientist*, **11**, 27–38.

McGarrell, E.F. and Flanagan, T.J. (1985) *Sourcebook of Criminal Justice Statistics – 1984*, Washington, D.C.: US Department of Justice.

MacIntyre, A. (1984) 'The Virtues, the Unity of a Human Life and the Concept of a Tradition', in M. Sandel (eds.), *Liberalism and Its Critics*, Oxford: Basil Blackwell.

Maine, H. S. (1861) *Ancient Law: Its Connection with the Early History of Society and Its Relation to Modern Ideas*, Boston: Beacon Press.

Marks, G. (1986) 'Neocorporatism and Incomes Policy in Western Europe and North America', *Comparative Politics*, **18**, 253–78.

Martin, J., Rook, M.K., and Filton, P. (1979) *Trends in Prison Population in Victoria*, Melbourne: Department of Community and Welfare Services.

Matsueda, R.L. (1982) 'Testing Control Theory and Differential Association', *American Sociological Review*, **47**, 489–504.

Matza, D. (1964) *Delinquency and Drift*, New York: Wiley.

Matza, D., and Sykes,G.M. (1961) 'Delinquency and Subterranean Values', *American Sociological Review*, **26**, 712–19.

Mead, G.H. (1934) *Mind, Self and Society*, Chicago: University of Chicago Press.

Mednick, S. and Christiansen, K.O. (1977) *Biosocial Bases of Criminal Behavior*, New York: Gardner Press.

Meier, R.F. (1982) 'Jurisdictional Differences in Deterring Marijuana Use', *Journal of Drug Issues*, **12**, 61–71.

Meier, R.F., and Johnson, W. (1977) 'Deterrence as Social Control: The Legal and Extra-Legal Production of Conformity', *American Sociological Review*, **42**, 292–304.

Meisenhelder, T. (1982) 'Becoming Normal: Certification as a Stage of Exiting from Crime', *Deviant Behavior*, **3**, 137–53.

Menard, S. and Morse, B.J. (1984) 'A Structuralist Critique of the IQ–Delinquency Hypothesis: Theory and Evidence', *American Journal of Sociology*, **89**, 1347–78.

Menard, S. and Morse, B.J. (1986) 'IQ and Delinquency: A Response to Harry and Minor', *Americal Journal of Sociology*, **91**, 1962–8.

Merry, S.E. (1984) 'Rethinking Gossip and Scandal', in D. Black (ed.), *Toward a General Theory of Social Control*, Volume 1, Orlando, Florida: Academic Press.

Merton, R.K. (1957) *Social Theory and Social Structure*, Glencoe, Ill.: Free Press.

Messner, S.F. (1982) 'Poverty, Inequality and the Urban Homicide Rate: Some Unexpected Findings', *Criminology*, **20**, 103–14.

Miethe, T.D. (1982) 'Public Consensus on Crime Seriousness: Normative Structure or Methodological Artifact?', *Criminology*, **20**, 515–26.

Miethe, T.D. (1984) 'Types of Consensus in Public Evaluations of Crime: An Illustration of Strategies for Measuring "Consensus"', *Journal of Criminal Law and Criminology*, **75**, 459–73.

Miller, W.B. (1958) 'Lower-Class Culture as a Generating Mileu of Gang Delinquency', *Journal of Social Issues*, **XIV**, 5–9.

Minor, W.W. (1977) 'A Deterrence-Control Theory of Crime', in R. Meier (ed.), *Theory in Criminology: Contemporary Views*, Beverly Hills: Sage.

Minor, W.W. (1980) 'The Neutralization of Criminal Offences', *Criminology*, **18**, 103–20.

Monahan, T.P. (1957) 'Family Status and the Delinquent Child: A Reappraisal and Some New Findings', *Social Forces*, **35**, 257.

Monkkonen, E.H. (1981a) 'A Disorderly People? Urban Order in the Nineteenth and Twentieth Centuries', *Journal of American History*, **68**, 536–59.

Monkkonen, E.H. (1981b) *Police in Urban America, 1860-1920*, New York: Cambridge University Press.

Monkkonen, E.H. (1982) 'From Cop History to Social History: The Significance of the Police in American History', *Journal of Social History*, **15**, 573–91.

Moore, C.A. (1987) 'Taming the Giant Corporations: Some Cautionary Remarks on the Deterrability of Corporate Crime', *Crime and Deliquency*, **33**, 379–403.

Morash, M. (1986) 'Gender, Peer Group Experiences and Seriousness of Delinquency', *Journal of Research in Crime and Delinquency*, **23**, 43–67.

Mugishima, F. and Matsumoto, Y. (1973) 'An Analysis of Delinquent Differentiation Related to Boys' Social Origin and Educational Attainment', *Report of the Japanese Research Institute of Police Science*, **14**.

Mukherjee, S.K. (1981) *Crime Trends in Twentieth-Century Australia*, Sydney: Allen and Unwin.

Mukherjee, S.K. (1985) 'Book Review: Nations Not Obsessed With Crime', *Australian and New Zealand Journal of Criminology*, **18**, 190–1.

Mukherjee, S.K., and Fitzgerald, R.W. (1981) 'The Myth of Rising Female Crime', in S.K. Mukherjee and J.A. Scutt (eds.), *Women and Crime*, Sydney: Allen and Unwin.

Najman, J.M. (1980) 'Victims of Homicide: An Epidemiologic Approach to Social Policy', *Australian and New Zealand Journal of Criminology* **13** 272–80.

Newman, D.J. (1957) 'Public Attitudes to a Form of White-Collar Crime', *Social Problems*, **4**, 228–32.

Newman, G. (1976) *Comparative Deviance: Perception and Law in Six Cultures*, New York: Elsevier.

New South Wales Bureau of Crime Statistics and Research (1974) *Crime, Correction and the Public*, Statistical Report 17, Sydney.

Nisbet, R. (1979) *Twilight of Authority*, London: Heinemann.

Nye, I.F. (1958) *Family Relationships and Delinquent Behavior*, New York: Wiley.

Offord, D.R., Poushinsky, M.F. and Sullivan, K. (1978) 'School Performance, IQ and Delinquency', *British Journal of Criminology*, **18**, 110–27.

O'Malley, P. (1980) 'Theories of Structural Versus Causal Determination : Accounting for Legislative Change in Capitalist Societies', in R. Tomasic (ed.), *Legislation and Society in Australia*, Sydney: Allen and Unwin.

Ouston, J. (1984) 'Delinquency, Family Background and Educational Attainment', *British Journal of Criminology*, **24**, 2–26.

Page, R.M. (1984) *Stigma*, London: Routledge and Kegan Paul.

Palmara, F., Cullen, F.T. and Gersten, J.C. (1986) 'The Effect of Police and Mental Health Intervention on Juvenile Deviance: Specifying Contingencies in the Impact of Formal Reaction', *Journal of Health and Social Behavior*, **27**, 90–105.

Parisi, N., Gottfredson, M.R., Hindelang, M.J. and Flanagan,T.J. (eds.) (1979) *Sourcebook of Criminal Justice Statistics 1978*, Washington, D.C.: US Government Printing Office.

Parke, R. D. (1974) 'Rules, Roles and Resistance to Deviation: Recent Advances in Punishment, Discipline and Self-control', in A. D. Pick (ed.), *Minnesota Symposium on Child Psychology*, Vol. 8, Minneapolis: University of Minnesota Press.

Paternoster, R., and Iovanni, L. (1986) 'The Deterrent Threat of Perceived Severity: A Reexamination', *Social Forces*, **64**, 751–77.

Paternoster, R., Saltzman, L., Chiricos, T., and Waldo, G. (1983a) 'Estimating Perceptual Stability and Deterrent Effects: The Role of Perceived Legal Punishment in the Inhibition of Criminal Involvement', *Journal of Criminal Law and Criminology*, **74**, 270–97.

Paternoster, R., Saltzman, L., Chiricos, T., and Waldo, G. (1983b) 'Perceived Risk and Social Control: Do Sanctions Really Deter?' *Law and Society Review*, **17**, 457–79.

Patterson, G.R. (1982) *Coercive Family Process*, Eugene, Oregon: Castalia Publishing Co..

Patterson, G.R., Chamberlain, P. and Reid, J. (1982) 'A Comparative Evaluation of a Parent-Training Program', *Behavior Therapy*, **13**, 638–50.

Patterson, G.R., and Dishion, T.J. (1985) 'Contribution of Families and Peers to Delinquency', *Criminology*, **23**, 63–79.

Paulus, I. (1978) 'Strict Liability: Its Place in Public Welfare Offences', *Criminal Law Quarterly*, **20**, 445–67.

Peirce, D., Grabosky, P.N. and Gurr, T.R. (1977) 'London: The Politics of Crime and Conflict, 1800 to the 1970s', in J.R. Gurr, P.N. Grabosky and R.C. Hula, *The Politics of Crime and Conflict*, Beverly Hills: Sage.

Pekkanen, J. (1973) *The American Connection*, Chicago: Follett.

Pepinsky, H.E. (1984) 'Better Living through Police Discretion', *Law and Contemporary Problems*, **47**, 249–67.

Perrow, C. (1961) 'The Analysis of Goals in Complex Organizations', *American Sociological Review*, **26**, 854–65.

Phillips, J.C. (1974) 'The Creation of Deviant Behavior in High Schools: An Examination of Cohen's General Theory of Subcultures', PhD dissertation, University of Oregon.

Phillips, J.C., and Kelly, D.H. (1979) 'School Failure and Delinquency: Which Causes Which?' *Criminology*, **17**, 194–207.

Picou, J.S., Cosley, A.J., Lemke, A.W. and Azuma, H.T. (1974) 'Occupational Choice and Perception of Attainment Blockage: A Study of Lower Class Delinquent and Non-Delinquent Black Males', *Adolescence*, **9**, 289–98.

Pike, L. O. (1876) *A History of Crime in England*, Vol.II, London: Smith Elder and Co.

Piliavin, I., Gartner, R., Thornton, C. and Matsueda, R.C. (1986) 'Crime, Deterrence and Rational Choice', *American Sociological Review*, **51**, 101–19.

Polk, K. (1965a) 'An Exploration of Rural Delinquency', in L. Burchinal (ed.), *Youth in Crisis: Facts, Myths and Social Change*, Washington, D.C.: US Government Printing Office, 221–32.

Polk, K. (1965b) *Those Who Fail*, Eugene, Oregon: Lane County Youth Project.

Polk, K., and Halferty, D.S. (1966) 'Adolescence, Commitment and Delinquency', *Journal of Research in Crime and Delinquency*, **3**, 82–96.

Pontell, H.N., Keenan, C., Granite, D. and Geis, G. (1983) 'White-Collar Crime Seriousness: Assessments by Police Chiefs and Regulatory Agency Investigators', *American Journal of Police*, **3**, 1–16.

Poole, E.D. and Regoli, R.M. (1979) 'Parental Support, Delinquent Friends, and Delinquency: A Test of Interaction Effects', *Journal of Criminal Law and Criminology*, **70**, 188–93.

Porterfield, A.L. (1948) 'A Dread of Serious Crime in the United States: Some Trends and Hypotheses', *American Sociological Review*, **13**, 44–54.

Posner, R.A. (1977) *Economic Analysis of Law*, 2nd ed., Boston: Little, Brown.

Radcliffe-Brown, A.R. (1933) 'Social Sanctions', in *Encyclopedia of the Social Sciences*, Vol.13, pp.531–34, New York: Macmillan.

Ramsay, M. (1982) 'Two Centuries of Imprisonment', *Research Bulletin: Home Office Research and Planning Unit*, **14**, 45–7.

Ramsay, M. (1984) 'Women and Crime: A Changing Pattern of Convictions?' *Research Bulletin: Home Office Research and Planning Unit*, **17**, 39–41.

Rankin, J.H. (1977) 'Investigating the Interrelations Among Social Control Variables and Conformity', *Journal of Criminal Law and Criminology*, **67**, 470–80.

Ray, M.C. and Downs, W.R. (1986) 'An Empirical Test of Labeling Theory Using Longitudinal Data', *Journal of Research in Crime and Delinquency*, **23**, 269–94.

Reasons, C.E., Ross, L.L. and Paterson, C. (1981) *Assault on the Worker: Occupational Health and Safety in Canada*, Scarborough, Ontario: Butterworths.

Reckless, W.C. (1967) *The Crime Problem*, 4th ed., New York: Appleton-Century-Crofts.

Redfield, R. (1947) 'The Folk Society', *American Journal of Sociology*, **52**, 293–308.

Reed, J.P. and Reed, R.S. (1975) 'Doctor, Lawyer, Indian Chief: Old Rhymes and New on White-Collar Crime', *International Journal of Criminology and Penology*, **3**, 279–93.

Reiman, J. (1979) *The Rich Get Richer and the Poor Get Prison*, New York: Wiley.

Reiner, R. (1985) *The Politics of the Police*, London: Wheatsheaf.

Reiss, A.J. (1951) 'Delinquency and the Failure of Personal and Social Controls', *American Sociological Review*, **16**, 196–207.

Reiss, A.J. (1980) 'Understanding Changes in Crime Rates', in S.E. Feinberg and A.J. Reiss (eds.), *Indicators of Crime and Criminal Justice: Quantitative Studies*, Washington, D.C.: US Government Printing Office.

Reiss, A.J., and Rhodes, A. L. (1964) 'An Empirical Test of Differential Association Theory', *Journal of Research in Crime and Delinquency*, **1**, 13–17.

Rettig, S. and Pasamanick, B. (1959) 'Changes in Moral Values Over Three Decades, 1929-1958', *Social Problems*, **6**, 320–8.

Rhodes, A.L. and Reiss, A.J. (1969) 'Apathy, Truancy and Delinquency as Adaptations in School', *Social Forces*, **48**, 12–22.

Richardson, J.F. (1970) *The New York Police, Colonial Times to 1901*, New York: Oxford University Press.

Riedel, M. (1975) 'Perceived Circumstances, Inferences of Intent and Judgments of Offense Seriousness', *Journal of Criminal Law and Criminology*, 66, 201–8.

Riley, D. (1986) 'Sex Differences in Teenage Crime: The Role of Lifestyle', *Research Bulletin, Home Office Research and Planning Unit*, **20**, 34–8.

Riley, D., and Shaw, M. (1985) *Parental Supervision and Juvenile Delinquency*, Home Office Research Study No. 83, London: HMSO.

Rose, A.M. and Prell, A.E. (1955) 'Does the Punishment Fit the Crime? A Study in Social Validation', *American Journal of Sociology*, **61**, 247–59.

Rosen, L. and Neilson, K. (1978) 'The Broken Home and Delinquency', in L.D. Savitz and N. Johnston (eds.), *Crime in Society*, New York: Wiley.

Rosenberg, B. and Silverstein, H. (1969) *The Varieties of Delinquent Experience*, Waltham, Mass.: Blaisdell.

Rosett, A. and Cressey, D.R. (1976) *Justice by Consent*, Philadelphia: Lippincott.

Rossi, P. H., Simpson, J. E. and Miller, J. L. (1985) 'Beyond Crime Seriousness: Fitting the Punishment to the Crime', *Journal of Quantitative Criminology*, **1**, 59–90.

Rossi, P.H., Waite, E., Bose, C.E. and Berk, R.E. (1974) 'The Seriousness of Crimes: Normative Structure and Individual Differences', *American Sociological Review*, **39**, 224–37.

Rowe, A.R. and Tittle, C.R. (1977) 'Life Cycle Changes and Criminal Propensity', *Sociological Quarterly*, **18**, 223–36.

Rusche, G. and Kirchheimer, O. (1939) *Punishment and Social Structure*, New York: Columbia University Press.

Sagarin, E. and Montanio, F. (1976) 'Anthologies and Readers in Deviance', *Contemporary Sociology*, **5**, 259–67.

Salas, L., Solano, S.N., and Vilchez, A.I.G. (1982) 'Comparative Study of White Collar Crime in Latin America With Special Emphasis on Costa Rica', *Revue Internationale de Droit Penale*, **53**, 505–21.

Sampson, R.J. (1985) 'Structural Sources of Variation in Race-Age-Specific Rates of Offending Across Major U.S. Cities', *Criminology*, **23**, 647–60.

Sampson, R.J., Castellano, T.C. and Laub, J.H. (1981) *Juvenile Criminal Behavior and Its Relation to Neighborhood Characteristics*, Washington, D.C.: Office of Juvenile Justice and Delinquency Prevention.

Schafer, W.E. and Polk, K. (1967) 'Delinquency and the Schools', in The President's Commission on Law Enforcement and Administration of Justice, *Task Force Report: Juvenile Delinquency and Youth Crime*, Washington, D.C.: US Government Printing Office, 222–7.

Schmidt, M. G. (1982) 'The Role of the Parties in Shaping Macroeconomic Policy', in F. G. Castles (ed.), *The Impact of Parties*, Beverly Hills: Sage.

Schneider, A.L. (1986) 'Restitution and Recidivism Rates of Juvenile Offenders: Results from Four Experimental Studies', *Criminology*, **24**, 533–52.

Scholz, J. T. (1984) 'Cooperation, Deterrence and the Ecology of Regulatory Enforcement', *Law and Society Review*, **18**, 179–224.

Schott, K. E. (1984) *Policy, Power and Order: The Persistence of Economic Problems in the Capitalist State*, New Haven: Yale University Press.

Schrager, L.S. and Short, J.F. (1980) 'How Serious a Crime? Perceptions of Organizational and Common Crimes', in G. Geis and E. Stotland, *White-Collar Crime: Theory and Research*, Beverly Hills: Sage.

Schulman, H.M. (1949) 'The Family and Juvenile Delinquency', *Annals of the American Academy of Political and Social Science*, **261**, 21–31.

Schur, E.M. (1973) *Radical Non-Intervention*, Englewood Cliffs: Prentice Hall.

Schwartz, R.D. and Orleans, S. (1967) 'On Legal Sanctions', *University of Chicago Law Review*, **34**: 274–300.

Schwendinger, H. and Schwendinger, J. (1967) 'Delinquent Stereotypes of Probable Victims', in M.W. Klein (ed.), *Juvenile Gangs in Context: Theory, Research, and Action*. Englewood Cliffs: Prentice Hall.

Scott, J. C. (1972) *Comparative Political Corruption*, London: Routledge and Kegan Paul.

Scott, J. C. and Al-Thakeb, F. (1977) 'The Public's Perceptions of Crime: A Comparative Analysis of Scandinavia, Western Europe, the Middle East and the United States', in C. Huff (ed.), *Contemporary Corrections*, Beverly Hills: Sage.

Scutt, J.A. (1979) 'The Myth of the "Chivalry Factor" in Female Crime', *Australian Journal of Social Issues*, **14**, 3–20.

Sebba, L. (1983) 'Attitudes of New Immigrants Toward White-Collar Crime: A Cross-Cultural Exploration', *Human Relations*, **36**, 1091–110.

Segrave, J.O. and Hastad, D.N. (1985) 'Evaluating Three Models of Delinquency Causation for Males and Females: Strain Theory, Subculture Theory, and Control Theory', *Sociological Focus*, **18**, 1–17.

Sellin, T. and Wolfgang, M. (1964) *The Measurement of Delinquency*, New York: Wiley.

Shapiro, S. P. (1987) 'The Social Control of Impersonal Trust', *American Journal of Sociology*, **93**, 623-58.

Shaw, C.R. and McKay, H.D. (1969) *Juvenile Delinquency and Urban Areas*, Chicago: University of Chicago Press.

Shearing, C.D. and Stenning, P.C. (1981) 'Modern Private Security: Its Growth and Its Implications', in M. Tonry and N. Morris (eds.), *Crime and Justice: An Annual Review*, Chicago: University of Chicago Press.

Shearing, C.D. and Stenning, P.C. (1984) 'From the Panopticon to Disney World: The Development of Discipline', in A.N. Doob and E.L. Greenspoon (eds.), *Perspectives in Criminal Law: Essays in Honour of John L.J. Edwards*, Aurora, Ontario: Canada Law Book Inc. (eds.)

Shearing, C.D. and Stenning, P.C. (1987) *Private Policing*, Beverly Hills: Sage.

Shoemaker, D.J. (1984) *Theories of Delinquency*, New York: Oxford.

Shoham, S. (1970) *The Mark of Cain*, Jerusalem: Israel Universities Press.

Short, J.F. (1957) 'Differential Association and Delinquency', *Social Problems*, **4**, 233–9.

Short, J.F. (1964) 'Gang Delinquency and Anomie', in M.B. Clinard (ed.), *Anomie and Deviant Behavior*, New York: Free Press.

Short, J.F., and Strodtbeck, F.L. (1965) *Group Process and Gang Delinquency*, Chicago: University of Chicago Press.

Short, J.F., Rivera, R., and Tennyson, R. A. (1965) 'Perceived Opportunities, Gang Membership and Delinquency', *American Sociological Review*, **30**, 56–67.

Shott, S. (1979) 'Emotion and Social Life: A Symbolic Interactionists Analysis', *American Journal of Sociology*, **84**, 1317–34.

Shover, N., Norland, S., James, J. and Thornton, W.E. (1979) 'Gender Roles and Delinquency', *Social Forces*, **58**, 162–75.

Siegel, L.J., Rathus, S.A. and Ruppert, C.A. (1973) 'Values and Delinquent Youth: An Empirical Re-Examination of Theories of Delinquency', *British Journal of Criminology*, **13**, 237–44.

Silberman, C.E. (1976) 'Toward a Theory of Criminal Deterrence', *American Sociological Review*, **41**, 442–61.

Silberman, C.E. (1978) *Criminal Violence, Criminal Justice*, New York: Random House.

Simon, R.J. and Sharma, N. (1979) 'Women and Crime: Does the American Experience Generalize?', in F. Adler and R.J. Simon (eds.), *Criminology of Deviant Women*, Boston: Houghton Mifflin.

Skogan, W.G. (1975) *Chicago Since 1840: A Time-Series Data Handbook*, Urbana: Institute of Government and Public Affairs, University of Illinois.

Slocum, W.L. and Stone, C. (1963) 'Family Culture and Patterns of Delinquent Type Behaviour', *Marriage and Family Living*, **25**, 202–8.

Smart, C. (1976) *Women, Crime and Criminology*, London: Routledge and Kegan Paul.

Smith, D.A. (1979) 'Sex and Deviance: An Assessment of Major Sociological Variables', *The Sociological Quarterly*, **20**, 183–95.

Smith, D.A., and Visher, C.A. (1980) 'Sex and Involvement in Deviance/ Crime: A Quantitative Review of the Empirical Literature', *American Sociological Review*, **45**, 691–701.

South Australian Office of Crime Statistics (1980) *Statistics from Courts of Summary Jurisdiction*, Series II, No. 4, Adelaide: Attorney-General's Department.

Spencer, S. (1985) *Called to Account*, London: National Council for Civil Liberties.

Spergel, I. (1961) 'An Exploratory Research in Delinquent Subcultures', *Social Service Review*, **35**, 33–47.

Spergel, I. (1967) 'Deviant Patterns and Opportunities of Pre-Adolescent Negro Boys in Three Chicago Neighborhoods', in M.W. Klein (ed.), *Juvenile Gangs in Context: Theory, Research and Action*, Englewood Cliffs: Prentice Hall.

Staples, W.G. (1984) 'Toward a Structural Perspective on Gender Bias in the Juvenile Court', *Sociological Perspectives*, **27**, 349–67.

Stedman Jones, G. (1984) *Outcast London: A Study in the Relationships Between Classes in Victorian Society*, Harmondsworth: Pelican.

Steffensmeier, D.J. (1978) 'Crime and the Contemporary Woman: An Analysis of Changing Levels of Female Property Crime, 1960-75', *Social Forces*, **57**, 566–84.

Steffensmeier, D.J., and Steffensmeier, R. H. (1980) 'Trends in Female Delinquency', *Criminology*, **18**, 62–85.

Stein, M. A. (1960) *The Eclipse of Community: An Interpretation of American Studies*. Princeton: Princeton University Press.

Stephen, J.F. (1883) *A History of Criminal Law in England*, London: Macmillan.

Stinchcombe, A.L. (1964) *Rebellion in a High School*, Chicago: Quadrangle Books.

Stone, C. D. (1985) 'Corporate Regulation: The Place of Social Responsibility', in B. Fisse and P. A. French (eds.), *Corrigible Corporations and Unruly Law*, San Antonio: Trinity University Press.

Sullenger, T.E. (1936) *Social Determinants in Juvenile Delinquency*, New York: Wiley.

Sunley, R. (1955) 'Early Nineteenth-Century American Literature on Child Rearing', in M. Mead and J. Wolfenstein (eds.), *Childhood in Contemporary Cultures*, Chicago: University of Chicago Press.

Sutherland, E.H. (1983) *White Collar Crime*, New Heaven: Yale Press.

Sutherland, E.H., and Cressey, D.R. (1978) *Criminology*, 10th edition, New York: Lippincott.

Suttles, G.D. (1968) *The Social Order of the Slum*, Chicago: University of Chicago Press.

Sykes, G. and Matza, D. (1957) 'Techniques of Neutralization: A Theory of Delinquency', *American Sociological Review*, **22**, 664–70.

Tannenbaum, F. (1938) *Crime and the Community*, New York: Columbia University Press.

Taylor, I., Walton, P. and Young, J. (1973) *The New Criminology: For a Social Theory of Deviance*, London: Routledge and Kegan Paul.

Teevan, J. (1976a) 'Deterrent Effects of Punishment: Subjective Measures Continued', *Canadian Journal of Corrections*, **18**, 152–60.

Teevan, J. (1976b) 'Subjective Perceptions of Deterrence', *Journal of Research in Crime and Delinquency*, **13**, 155–64.

Teevan, J. (1976c) 'Deterrent Effects of Punishment for Breaking and Entering and Theft', in Law Reform Commission of Canada, *Fear of Punishment*, Ottawa: Law Reform Commission.

Thomas, C.W. and Bishop, D.M. (1984) 'The Effect of Formal and Informal Sanctions on Delinquency: A Longitudinal Comparison of Labeling and Deterrence Theories', *Journal of Criminal Law and Criminology*, **75**, 1222–45.

Thomas, C.W., Cage, R. and Foster, S. (1976) 'Public Opinion on Criminal Law and Legal Sanctions: An Examination of Two Conceptual Models', *Journal of Criminal Law and Criminology*, **67**, 110–16.

Thomas, C.W., and Hyman, J.M. (1978) 'Compliance Theory, Control Theory and Juvenile Delinquency', in M.D. Krohn and R.L. Akers (eds.), *Crime, Law and Sanctions*, London: Sage.

Thomas, C.W., Kreps, G.A. and Cage, R.J. (1977) 'An Application of Compliance Theory to the Study of Juvenile Delinquency', *Sociology and Social Research*, **61**, 156–75.

Thomas, W.I. (1951) *Social Behavior and Personality* (ed. E.H. Volkhart), Chicago: University of Chicago Press.

Thompson, F.M.L. (1986) 'Review of *Patronage and Society in Nineteenth-Century England*, by J.M. Bourne', *Times Higher Education Supplement*, 29 August, p.14.

Thompson, J.D. (1967) *Organizations in Action*, New York: McGraw-Hill.

Thompson, W.E., Mitchell, J. and Dodder, R.A. (1984) 'An Empirical Test of Hirschi's Control Theory of Delinquency', *Deviant Behavior*, **5**, 11–22.

Thornton, W.E. (1982) 'Gender Traits and Delinquency Involvement of Boys and Girls', *Adolescence*, **17**, 749–68.

Thurman, Q.C. (1984) 'Deviance and the Neutralization of Moral Commitment: An Empirical Analysis', *Deviant Behavior*, **5**, 291–304.

Time Magazine (1969) 'Changing Morality: The Two Americas; A Time Louis Harris Poll', 26 June, p. 93.

Tittle, C. R. (1980a) 'Labelling and Crime: An Empirical Evaluation', in W.R. Gove (ed.), *The Labelling of Deviance: Evaluating a Perspective*, Beverly Hills: Sage.

Tittle, C. R. (1980b) *Sanctions and Social Deviance*, New York: Praeger.

Tittle, C.R., Villemez, W.J. and Smith, D.A. (1978) 'The Myth of Social Class and Criminality: An Empirical Assessment of the Empirical Evidence', *American Sociological Review*, **43**, 643–56.

Tittle, C.R., and Welch, M.R. (1983) 'Religiosity and Deviance: Toward a Contingency Theory of Constraining Effects', *Social Forces*, **61**, 653–82.

Tobias, J.J. (1979) *Crime and Police in England, 1700-1900*, London: Gill and Macmillan.

Toby, J. (1957) 'The Differential Impact of Family Disorganization', *American Sociological Review*, **22**, 505–12.

Toby, J. (1964) 'Is Punishment Necessary?' *Journal of Criminal Law, Criminology and Political Science*, **55**, 332–7.

Toby, J., and Toby, M.L. (1957), *Low School Status as a Predisposing Factor in Subcultural Delinquency*, Washington: US Office of Education and Rutgers University.

Tonnies, F. (1887) *Community and Society*, New York: Harper and Row.

Trasler, G. (1972) 'The Context of Social Learning', in J.B. Mays (ed.), *Juvenile Delinquency, the Family and the Social Group*, Longman.

Trice, H. M. and Roman, P. M. (1970) 'Delabeling, Relabeling and Alcoholics Anonymous', *Social Problems*, **17**, 538–46.

Udry, J.R. (1974) *The Social Context of Marriage*, New York: Lippincott.

Van Houten, R. (1983) 'Punishment: From the Animal Laboratory to the Applied Setting', in S. Axelrod and J. Apsche (eds.), *The Effects of Punishment on Human Behavior*, New York: Academic Press.

Van Houten, R., and Doleys, D.M. (1983) 'Are Social Reprimands Effective?', in S. Axelrod and J. Apsche (eds.), *The Effects of Punishment on Human Behavior*, New York: Academic Press.

Vaughan, D. (1983) *Controlling Unlawful Organizational Behavior: Social Structure and Corporate Misconduct*, Chicago: University of Chicago Press.

Vogel, D. (1986) *National Styles of Regulation: Environmental Policy in Great Britain and the United States*, Ithaca: Cornell University Press.

Vogel, E. F. (1979) *Japan as No. 1*, Cambridge: Harvard University Press.

von Hippel, R. (1925) *Deutsches Strafrecht*, Berlin.

Voss, H. L. (1964) 'Differential Association and Reported Delinquent Behavior: A Replication', *Social Problems*, **12**, 78–85.

Wadsworth, M. E. J. (1979) *Roots of Delinquency*, New York: Harper and Row.

Wagatsuma, H. and Rosett, A. (1986) 'The Implications of Apology: Law and Culture in Japan and the United States', *Law and Society Review*, **20**, 461–98.

Waldo, G.P. and Chiricos, T. G. (1972) 'Perceived Penal Sanction and Self-Reported Criminality: A Neglected Approach to Deterrence Research', *Social Problems*, **19**, 522–40.

Walker, J. and Biles, D. (1985) *Australian Prisoners 1984: Results of the National Prisons Census – June 1984*, Canberra: Australian Institute of Criminology.

Warner, C. (1982) 'A Study of Self-Reported Crime of a Group of Male and Female High School Students', *Australian and New Zealand Journal of Criminology*, **15**, 255–72.

Warner, S.B. (1934) *Crime and Criminal Statistics in Boston*, Cambridge: Harvard University Press.

Webber, M. M. (1970) 'Order in Diversity: Community Without Propinquity', in R. Gutman and D. Popenoe (eds.), *Neighborhood, City and Metropolis: An Integrated Reader in Urban Sociology*, New York: Random House.

Weeks, H.A. and Smith, M.G. (1939) 'Juvenile Delinquency and Broken Homes in Spokane, Washington', *Social Forces*, **18**, 48–59.

Wellford, C.F. and Wiatrowski, M.D. (1975) 'On the Measurement of Delinquency', *Journal of Criminal Law and Criminology*, **66**, 175-88.

Welsh, R.S. (1976) 'Severe Parental Punishment and Delinquency: A Developmental Theory', *Journal of Clinical Child Psychology*, **5**, 17–21.

West, D.J. (1967) *The Young Offender*, London: Duckworth.

West, D.J. (1973) *Who Becomes Delinquent?*, London: Heinemann.

West, D.J. (1982) *Delinquency: Its Roots, Careers and Prospects*, London: Heinemann.

West, D.J., and Farrington, D.P. (1977) *The Delinquent Way of Life*, London: Heinemann.

Wiatrowski, M.D., Griswald, D.B., and Roberts, M.R. (1981) 'Social Control Theory and Delinquency', *American Sociological Review*, **46**, 525–41.

Wilcox, L.D. (1969) 'Social Class, Anomie and Delinquency', PhD dissertation, Colorado State University.

Wilkins, L. (1964) *Social Deviance*, London: Tavistock.

Wilkinson, K. (1974) 'The Broken Family and Juvenile Delinquency: Scientific Explanation or Ideology?', *Social Problems*, **21**, 726–39.

Williams, F.P., III (1985) 'Deterrence and Social Control: Rethinking the Relationship', *Journal of Criminal Justice*, **13**, 141–54.

Wilson, J.Q. and Herrnstein, R. (1985) *Crime and Human Nature*, New York: Simon and Schuster.

Wilson, P.R. and Brown, J.W. (1973) *Crime and the Community*, Brisbane: University of Queensland Press.

Wolfe, N.T., Cullen, F.T., and Cullen, J.B. (1984) 'Describing the Female Offender: A Note on the Demographics of Arrests', *Journal of Criminal Justice*, **12**, 483–92.

Wolfenstein, M. (1955) 'Fun Morality: An Analysis of Recent American Child-Training Literature', in M. Mead and M. Wolfenstein (eds.), *Childhood in Contemporary Cultures*, Chicago: University of Chicago Press.

Wolfgang, M. E. (1980) 'National Survey of Crime Severity Final National Level Geometric Means and Ratio Scores', unpublished paper, Philadelphia: University of Pennsylvania.

Wolfgang, M. E., and Ferracuti, F. (1967) *The Subculture of Violence: Towards an Integrated Theory in Criminology*, London: Tavistock.

Wolfgang, M E., Figlio, R.M. and Sellin, T. (1972) *Delinquency in a Birth Cohort*, Chicago: University of Chicago Press.

Wolpin, K.I. (1978) 'Capital Punishment and Homicide: The English Experience', unpublished paper, Yale University.

Wood, A.L. (1961) 'A Socio-Structural Analysis: Murder, Suicide and Economics', *American Sociological Review*, **26**, 744–52.

Wraith, R. and Simpkins, E. (1963) *Corruption in Developing Countries*, London: Allen and Unwin.

Wright, D. and Cox, E. (1967a) 'Religious Belief and Co-education in a Sample of 6th Form Boys and Girls', *British Journal of Social and Clinical Psychology*, **9**, 23–31.

Wright, D. and Cox, E. (1967b) 'A Study of the Relationship Between Moral Judgment and Religious Belief in a Sample of English Adolescents', *Journal of Social Psychology*, **72**, 135–44.

Young, J. (1975) 'Working-Class Criminology', in I. Taylor, P. Walton and J. Young (eds.), *Critical Criminology*, London: Routledge and Kegan Paul.

Young, M. and Wilmott, P. (1957) *Family and Kinship in East London*, Harmondsworth: Penguin.

Zehr, H.G. (1976) *Crime and the Development of Modern Society*, London: Croom Helm.

Zimring, F.E. (1981) 'Kids, Groups and Crime: Some Implications of a Well-Known Secret', *Journal of Criminal Law and Criminology*, **72**, 867–85.

Zimring, F.E., and Hawkins, G.J. (1973) *Deterrence: The Legal Threat in Crime Control*, Chicago: University of Chicago Press.

Zingraff, M. and Thompson, R. (1984) 'Differential Sentencing of Women and Men in the U.S.A.', *International Journal of the Sociology of Law*, **12**, 401–13.

Znaniecki, F. (1971) *Nauki o Kulturze*, Warsaw: PWN.

Index